Sue Leamy Kies' memoir is a must read for anyone who has stepped inside a high school, whether as a student, a parent, or a faculty member. Kies writes with humor, honesty, compassion, and self-reflection about both personal and universal experiences as a teacher of teenagers she obviously cared deeply about and upon whose lives she must certainly have made an impact. I found Kies' book to be both enlightening and entertaining.
~Peggy Joque Williams, author of **Courting the Sun: A Novel of Versailles**

Why teach? In Wisconsin—and nationally—interest in participating in this labor-intensive and life-changing profession has decreased dramatically. If you have ever wondered why anyone would feel called to teach, read this memoir by Sue Kies, who gives us a close look at the reality and rewards of a profession that has changed its methods but not its mission.
~Catherine Stover, educator and author of **Three Ways to Write Memoir**

In **My Homecoming Dance**, Sue Kies offers a lovely reflection on her noteworthy career as an educator, combined with a fascinating glimpse into the timeline of education in Wisconsin. Readers will finish with an understanding of teaching in a small town and what it means to be an educator over the past few decades.
~Christy Wopat, educator, and author of **After All**

My Homecoming Dance

Reflections on Teaching in Wisconsin

Books by WWA Press

Gravedigger's Daughter: Growing Up Rural
Memoir
Debra Raye King

Memoir, *Gravedigger's Daughter* is a collection of short stories and essays based on actual events in the 1950-1970s in northern west-central Wisconsin. Little Elk Creek is a tightly knit community of Norwegian immigrant farm families who assist one another at harvest time and share their skills so all could succeed.

Red Road Redemption:
Country Tales from the Heart of Wisconsin
Short Story Collection
Pamela JA Fullerton

Short Story Collection, *Red Road Redemption* is an unforgettable collection of short stories filled with haunting characters, both human and animal, overflowing with thought-provoking drama, humor, and nostalgia. Take an unquiet walk in the woods, peer through a poignant lens at disappearing family farms, and cheer for the dog pack struggling to bring home the best gifts ever.

Coming October 25, 2024
Fire Conditions
Fiction
Tom Malin

A tale of adventure, tragedy, trust, and young love... In the summer of 1958, two brothers are sent to Grandma's while their parents work on their marriage.

Coming Spring 2025
Milking for Barn Cats
Memoir
PJA Fullerton

My Homecoming Dance

Reflections on Teaching in Wisconsin

Sue Leamy Kies

WWA PRESS
Noble Literary Art

My Homecoming Dance: Reflections on Teaching in
Wisconsin
Copyright ©2024 by Susan Leamy Kies
All Rights Reserved
First Edition, June 11, 2024
Memoir

Cover design by Paul Ruane
Interior artwork by Susan Leamy Kies
Author photo by Ric Genthe

Library of Congress Cataloging-in-Publication Data
Names: Kies, Susan Leamy, My Homecoming Dance: Reflections
on Teaching in Wisconsin
Library of Congress Control Number; 2024930781
ISBN 979-8-9863365-4-1 (pbk. book)|ISBN 979-8-9863365-6-5
(hardback)| ISBN 979-8-9863365-5-8 (epub)
Subjects: Biography/Autobiography/Personal Memoirs |
Biography/Autobiography/Educators | Education/essays
More info available at https://lccn.loc.gov

Published by
Wisconsin Writers Association Press
www.WiWrite.org
10490 Fox Ridge Drive
Hillsboro, Wisconsin 54634

Table of Contents

Foreword

To be a teacher is to find the joy in the human struggles faced by every student and family. To be a teacher is to celebrate the range of successes from a major academic achievement for one student to another who found accomplishment in just showing up. It is to live a life of sacrifice for other people's children in a society that rewards a "me first" approach to life. It is to plant seeds in a slow-growing garden and to water saplings that will only bear fruit beyond your years.

To be a teacher is to sacrifice a weekend grading papers or exams, planning lessons or setting up lab experiments, making bulletin boards, supervising ball games or concerts, or any of a myriad of other possibilities. The sacrifices are real. Other sacrifices are emotional, a lesson diligently planned that went awry. Or it might be a student who is simply not ready to hear the lesson of the day or whose spot on their journey makes you the target of their frustration or confusion with the challenges of growing up. To be a teacher is to laugh at life's realities and to weep at its disappointments—realities and disappointments that are your own or those of the students in whom you invest your heart.

For fifteen years, I had the joy of sharing this journey with Susan Leamy Kies as she fought the battle in the great enterprise that is public education in America. Her memoir is one personal story that is shared by thousands of teachers across the country. Like so many others, Sue brought her entire being to her teaching and shared her heart and soul with her students, peers and even administrators like me. It is this level of giving that makes teaching a risky profession. But it is also this level of giving that makes teaching such a rewarding profession. Mrs. Kies shares her risks and rewards in this memoir to let you laugh and cry along with a teacher, but also to share the immense struggle it is to nurture young ambitions, to shape young thinkers, and to watch as the world evolves around you. Being a teacher is to have sleepless nights wondering how to reach a student. And it is to sleep well knowing you have fought the good fight.

Sue, what fun it is to share in your journey in person and in this memoir. Sleep well.

Dr. Jeffrey D. Jacobson
Monona, Wisconsin
January, 2024

Introduction

In the Beginning...

While we teach, we learn.
Seneca, Roman philosopher

One Saturday afternoon in the spring of 1967, my family and I inspected the footprint of the new high school going up on the east side of town. Curious, we wandered through the maze of poured concrete footings for the walls.

"It's too bad you won't be attending the *real* PHS," my brother said.

He was referring to the building four blocks west on Madison Street where he had been a Hillmen nine years earlier. Henry Hillmen was still the PHS mascot. Decked out in red and white lederhosen and toting a pickaxe, he graced the wall of our gymnasium. It wasn't until becoming a teacher at PHS that I learned Henry's history. In 1920 Wilfred Hill became a science teacher at PHS. He coached track, basketball, and football, accumulating far more wins than losses. Originally called the Cardinals because of the red color of their uniforms, the PHS sports teams soon became known as "Hill's Men." In 1945 it was shortened to Hillmen.

My brother loved to embellish his exploits in the old building whenever we drove by on his visits home. Like *accidentally* knocking his books off the second story window ledge in order to escape class to retrieve them—or forging passes so he could roam the halls with his friends. That Gothic structure, complete with gargoyle adornments, a grand entrance, and a labyrinth of echoing halls, was soon to be demoted to Platteville Middle School. Accordingly, Jasper, my brother's dog, christened the dirt in several corners of what would become the *new* Platteville High School.

In our city of about ten thousand people, this construction represented an architectural rebellion reflective of the budding counterculture of the 1960s. Bricks laid out in simple rectangular formations rose from the pasture on the hill like huge stacks of earth-toned building blocks. As it took shape, the building garnered either the approval or disdain of area residents. To some, the modern style represented a welcome shift into the future, and to others it resembled a factory; a hideous one at that.

One might think that these architects would know better than to construct a building in the Midwest and top it with a flat roof. After only a couple of winters, the mounds of snow, with no other escape route, melted in the spring, seeping through the ceilings and into rooms and hallways. Many times, as a student, and years later as a teacher, I dodged the strategically placed waste baskets that caught the resulting drips. When the brown, stained ceiling tiles threatened mold, yearly replacement costs became the bane of administrators and school boards.

The IMC (Instructional Materials Center), or library, was intended to be the uniter of all disciplines and sat smack in the center with all areas of study branching out from it. Science, math, and business classrooms lined the curved hallways to the north of the library, while English, social studies, and foreign language fanned out to the south. The commons area, serving as a cafeteria at lunch time, and the gymnasium, provided large open spaces on the west side. East of the library, the auditorium, music, vocational, and art rooms sprawled into a web of active learning spaces.

Small, angled classrooms circled the two big lecture halls, one each on the north and the south side of the IMC. We students met twice a week for lectures in the Large Group Room on the south side, then divided into smaller groups in the surrounding rooms for discussions and activities on the other three days. Throughout my years as a teacher, I witnessed many educational trends similar to this come and go as fast as late Wisconsin spring snowfalls. After the large/small group room fad went the way of the Edsel, some of the tinier rooms became graveyards for outdated technology and other discarded stuff because the space could not accommodate an average-sized class of twenty-five students.

In 2000 the district proposed and passed a referendum for additions to update the original design. A second gym, a new art room, a hallway of bigger English and social studies rooms, a new choral area, and more space for technology education were added on the north and east sides of the school. The district anticipated a larger student body in the coming years, but, instead, enrollment declined. My graduating class of 1972 boasted 205 students, the largest in PHS history. According to the statistics tallied by guidance office secretary Sue Musara and yearbook editor Maizie Lyght, the graduating class of 1987 was

165, and after that it fell every year until reaching the all-time low of 87 students in 2007. Since then it has risen to reach a count of 135 seniors in 2023.

This trend of sagging enrollment plagues every rural small school throughout the Midwest. Agricultural technology allowed farms to become larger with fewer landowners and laborers. When I was a student, small family farmsteads with small milking herds of twenty to forty cows dotted the countryside and supplied milk for cheese and provided school districts with as many as sixteen children per household.

In Southwest Wisconsin, many workers migrated closer to larger cities like Madison for better employment.

Also, homeschooling did not exist to the extent it does now, nor did we then have the burgeoning population of self-educating Amish farm families in the area. According to the Wisconsin Department of Instruction, homeschooled children can attend public schools as part-time students and take two classes without paying any extra fees beyond their taxes to the district. However, the state only counts full-time students in a district when dispersing state funding.

Until 1991 private and parochial schools were not funded with public money (National Education Policy Center, Jan Resseger, 12/1/2021). If families wanted to send their children to a private school, they had to pay their child's tuition. Voucher schools and private schools, who do not have to abide by all public school regulations, get students who come to them with stipends paid for with taxpayer money. According to Phoebe Petrovic in an article for Wisconsin Watch, May 5, 2023, students with disabilities or those who identify as part of the LGBTQ community, are not protected by law in these private schools.

These policy changes are a detriment to the funding of public schools, and with less funding, it becomes more difficult to maintain desired standards.

Public schools in rural areas struggled, and continue to struggle, to survive. To save money, some of them resorted to consolidation, especially in sports programs. Platteville and other area schools began charging fees for taking part in extracurricular activities and relying on booster clubs to raise money. Inadequate funding also results in teachers in these smaller rural districts earning much less than in urban areas, some having as many as five or six different class preparations, and many coaching or advising two or more activities to boot.

"Wisconsin school districts are increasingly dependent on referendums, report says," is the headline in an article by Abbey Machtig for the November 14, 2023 *Wisconsin State Journal.* We in Platteville can relate. In 2022, our community passed a referendum to make needed updates to the elementary, middle, and high schools. The good thing is that, for the first time ever, the Hillmen have their own performance field and athletic complex behind the school. In my day, football games were played at Legion Field, a community field on the north side of Platteville. Then in 1972, the year I graduated, UW Platteville built a new stadium, allowing the Hillmen to pay a rental fee to play there. Now, because of a school district budget shortfall for operating expenses in the coming year, another referendum will be coming our way soon (*Platteville Journal*, November 15, 2023).

When I pulled open the heavy metal door of PHS in the fall of 1968, I remember being both nervous about being a lowly freshman and thrilled about becoming a Platteville Hillmen. In freshman World History class I easily memorized dates and names of ancient wars and battles. But history books lacked human interest, the background information about common everyday people who were affected by those noted wars and battles—particularly women. Every week Mr. McKichan gave a test on the material, and the student who got the highest score was honored as "Historian of the Week." One week I got a 97 percent, the best in the class, but Mr. McKichan mistakenly gave it to a male classmate who'd gotten a 96 percent. I didn't say anything, and I've been disgusted with myself ever since. That's how women became overlooked in history—by not speaking up.

The classes I remembered most from high school were the ones where I actively created something. A group of us made an audio recording of *War of the Worlds* for Miss Rassman's sophomore English class. Dianne, Patti, Vicki, and I planned and performed the script. In my basement that weekend, we banged wildly on pans and emitted screams of terror, simulating the sounds of what we imagined would occur if the Earth were invaded by Martians. In Senior English, Mr. Trickel assigned demonstration speeches. I brought my fire baton to school to perform and explain the rudiments of lighting and then twirling it. My speech was a hit, but I have come to appreciate how lucky I was that the can of gasoline I inanely stored in my locker all day didn't explode.

Though my high school experiences were mostly positive and I respected most of my teachers, at the time I had no dreams of coming back after graduation to spend more time under that leak-prone roof dealing with moody teens like me on a daily basis. My calling as an English teacher came much later in life.

"You know you didn't always get A's in English," my mother pointed out when I returned to college at the age of thirty-one and declared English as my major.

Though Mom read to me almost every day as a child, in grade school and high school I often found it difficult to sit still long enough to read or study lengthy passages of text. I had a short attention span when I was little. My aunt called me Little Lulu after the spunky girl in the comic strip who thrived on being the ringleader of the action. In retrospect, that's an apt explanation why I chose to return to teach classes of rambunctious teenagers in high school. It was a good fit.

Dear Mom,

Remember those afternoons when I was little and you sat with me on the old brown couch and read me *The Little Mailman of Bayberry Lane, Ping, Curious George,* or *The Little Majorette?* I do too.

Thank you!

Love,

Your English Teacher Daughter

The teens I taught could have been me twenty years earlier, bopping down the halls of PHS with friends, chatting about homework and checking out their reflections in the long panels of library windows. Like me, their high school years would launch them into adulthood: driver's licenses, proms, homecomings, popular songs, first kisses, acne. And let's not forget lunch time in the cafeteria, which determined the cliques and friendships that would be forged or forsaken in the pique of drama.

As their teacher, Mrs. Kies (pronounced Kize), I encouraged active learning, thinking, and questioning. As you'll see, my hands-on strategies sometimes got me into a few precarious situations. But, if my students didn't think and ask questions, how would they ever know what could be possible? Some of my best classroom lessons evolved from listening to my students. It was an exchange of sorts: they kept me up to date with their culture and times, which I then used to design my lessons on classic and contemporary literature, writing strategies, and projects to educate them.

When my students discovered that I graduated from the hallowed halls of PHS, they showed no mercy. "You went here—and you came back? Are you crazy? What were you thinking?"

I took their criticism in stride. When I was their age, I too thought my future would commence only when I *left* high school...and Platteville. Teaching English helped me learn that tenses build on each other. We learn from the past to shape our present. And the future unfolds because of what happens in the present. In managing my classroom, and my life, I reminded myself of that sequence on more than one occasion.

PART I – THAT ROSY GLOW

Chapter 1 – Riding the School Cycle

*Life is a journey up a spiral staircase; as we grow older we cover
the ground we have covered before, only higher up; as we look
down the winding stair below us we measure our progress by the
number of places where we were but no longer are.*
William Butler Yeats

On Monday, August 26, 2019, I ambled onto the deck of our
home, still in my robe. Coffee cup in hand, I watched yellow leaves
spiral through the morning air. One landed in my hair, and others
coated in dew stuck to the soles of my slippers.

For twenty-seven years the walnut trees in our backyard had
been my work calendar—leaves off, go to school—leaves on, go
to the pool. I hoisted my mug toward the trees: "Sláinte! Here's to
my next life!" I said, a toast I learned on a visit to Ireland. The
birds scattered from the feeder, and I took a swig of coffee to
celebrate.

I retired in June at the end of the school year, and this day
was the first official day of my retirement. It was the first
inservice day for teachers and staff for the 2019-2020 school
year. I watched first Janis's car go by, then Maureen's a few
minutes later. They both lived in my neighborhood and taught in
business and physical education, respectively. In the coming year
the pandemic and George Floyd's murder would cause our
country and world much grief and turmoil, but, for now, we
remained innocently unaware.

If still on the payroll, I would be arriving at school by 7:35
a.m. and heading down the beige halls to an inservice session at
8:00. In previous years the agenda included such workshops in

designing *active lessons*, where we listened to the presenter lecture for two hours.

I also remember a presentation on the new concept called *flipped classrooms.* Flipped classrooms promoted instructional video lessons for homework, allowing teachers to build on those taped clips and answer questions the next day in class. "But what if the students don't watch the video the night before?" a teacher in the audience asked, anticipating the obvious problem.

By mid-morning, all Platteville School District teachers and staff would meet in the PHS auditorium. It was here in this space that I had played my clarinet in concerts, attended class meetings, tried out for majorette, and watched my classmates' productions of *Brigadoon*, *The Sound of Music*, *Carnival,* and *Fiddler on the Roof.* It seemed bigger then. However, the prickly brick walls still scraped bare elbows and drew blood if you inadvertently ran into them, and the red upholstered seats folded up and smacked you in the rear when you got up.

As a student, I viewed my teachers as older, mature adults. Role models. When I got to know the teachers I'd had as peers, I hesitated to address them by their first names. How could I call my algebra teacher Jerry? Or the French teacher Marie? As time passed and I worked with them day to day, I became more comfortable. Teachers were merely human, older versions of the students they taught.

At the inservice gatherings, I joined the high school staff members clumped together in their usual spots according to sex and department in the back corner of the auditorium as if there were a seating chart. I usually sat by Cheryl, a former English teaching peer, who was now our librarian. I remember one time at this all-district gathering when the middle school teachers paraded into the rows in front of us high school teachers. Their matching bright blue T-shirts brandished an inspirational logo: "PMS Hearts (the symbol, not the word) Kids and Education."

They even had a group cheer. I rolled my eyes and shook my head at their prepubescent conformity and clueless use of acronyms.

In front of them, the elementary teachers bellied up to the stage, a few even having the audacity to raise their hands and ask questions. We grumbled at their lack of consideration for those of us who just wanted to get this meeting over and proceed to our rooms to prepare for the first day.

I wondered if teachers' inherent personalities attracted them to teach a particular grade level or if the transformation into acting like their students happened over time. Maybe this is a good topic for a master's thesis?

The superintendent delivered his yearly monologue about the state of the district. Halfway through, a sound like a tire leaking air caught our attention. A muffled popping noise followed. After some covert head-turning, we traced the racket to Jane, a special education teacher. She had dozed off somewhere during the third slide of data. We didn't bother to wake her. Her sputtering and occasional gasps provided us with welcome comic relief and fodder for future ridicule. It brought to mind the time a student fell asleep in my class. He didn't wake up until ten minutes into the next class with a sweaty red mark across his face where his head had become stuck to his arm.

During my first years of teaching at PHS in the early 1990s, the veterans grumbled incessantly about inservice: "It's the same every year. Why can't we have more time in our rooms? My plate is already full—why are they giving me more stuff to do? Who's got the time to do this? What does this have to do with teaching the kids?" *Blah-blah-blah!*

Oh, quit complaining already! I wanted to tell them. For two and a half years I worked as a substitute, teacher's aide, and part time teacher. All paid diddly squat. I was just happy to have a full time job and benefits.

Then, after enduring umpteen inservice trainings, I, too, got tired of administrators introducing us to *new and improved* ideas that were merely recycled methods disguised with pseudonyms. Every few years a *new and improved* software program replaced the old one for rewriting curriculum, or a *new and improved* way to design a lesson or discipline students became the fad.

"If I have to sit through another one of these sessions, my head is going to explode," I complained at lunch time, a certified curmudgeon just like my predecessors.

Dear Administrators:

I know you have a lot of responsibility, but please recall what it was like to be a teacher. When planning in-service training, take into consideration teachers' varied levels of experience, number of class preparations and subject areas. Better yet, ask them what they need to teach their students. Like our students, we become rebellious and whiny when assigned *busy work.*

Signed,

Me...and Every High School Teacher Ever

Laced with buzzwords like *Common Core* and *College and Career Readiness Standards,* the educational rhetoric in these inservice meetings was supported by a litany of alphabet goulash, like RTI, IEP, SIP, PBIS, SLO, and PPG. I remember taking a deep breath during my last year and thinking: *OMG, TMI! Please—just let me teach the kids!*

On the second day of inservice three years before I retired, our superintendent delivered the specifics about the Educator Effectiveness Plan our district would be implementing. Her brown hair flipped with each pivot as she paced back and forth in the area in front of the stage in the auditorium.

"Many of you in the pilot group have expressed how fearful you are of this evaluative process coming down the pike from the state level, and that's understandable," she said with a strained smile. "It may seem foreboding, and there is a lot to prepare for. But, district administrators who've used the Teachscape software have said that it makes evaluations much more objective. And, teachers like it because it is more inclusive and a fair assessment of their teaching."

Her positivity about the cesspool into which we would be jumping reeked of euphemism. *But, it's still crap!* I wanted to inject. I've talked to teachers in other districts who hate this system. It complicates and lengthens the process for both administrators and staff. Couldn't we just keep it simple? How much does this program cost? How could this money better serve the students? Hire another teacher, maybe? Raises for the existing ones so they might choose to remain in the profession?

But, as I routinely instructed my students, there are certain things one may think but should not say. Especially when it's a done deal and could come back to bite a person in the butt. In this case, for me, during my Teachscape evaluation. Instead, my mind escaped to other places. On my notepad, I scribbled down an analogy that came to mind concerning a recent nightmare where my doctor pronounced, "Guess what? You're pregnant!" NOOOO! *I already have five kids. I've reproduced more than my share! More than some people think I should! Tell me it isn't so!*

My notes from that meeting read as follows:

Nine-month school year = Human gestation period.

First trimester = Initial shock until boundless energy kicks in with lofty dreams of wonderful possibilities to come. Feeling invigorated, enjoying excessive planning and preparation.

Second trimester = Days begin to feel long. Feet are tired. Work begins to pile up. Determined to push through the days. Making progress. Main thing is to stay healthy. Hold on to the positive. It will be worth it in the end.

Last trimester = Becoming sluggish and moody. Feeling

overwhelmed. Put feet up whenever possible. Take a mental health day. End can't come soon enough. Last week arrives. Whew! Time to get the kids outta here! Intense elation accompanied by extreme exhaustion on the final day.

Post-event adjustment period = Can't imagine repeating this cycle. Then regenerative hormone kicks in and memory fades. Get feeling rested again. Hope resurfaces. Begin to accept that the process is worth repeating.

The end of the school year is distinctive in the school year cycle. Yes, during the summer break teachers continued to think of lessons, update curriculum, improve classroom management, and build technology skills for the future, and students continued to learn. Many teachers teach summer school. But the next year kicks off a fresh start for all involved.

"No matter if it has been a good year or a tough one, come May or early June, there is a definitive end to that year," my colleague said at lunch one day. He had worked a desk job for several years before becoming a math teacher. "I like that teaching has a new beginning, a fresh start, every year."

An acquaintance once told me how lucky I was to only work nine months of the year. I had to stifle my laughter...and my frustration.

"Teachers accomplish in nine months what most people do in a year," I told him. It was cocky of me, I know. By then I'd heard plenty about this frequent *lucky* description of the teacher's work calendar. I might have said, *If the schedule is that wonderful, why don't you become a teacher?*

Most people who have never been a teacher don't stop to think that the preparation and act of teaching in a public school is only a fraction of the job from day to day. I explained to this person the related tasks of social work, record keeping, continued training, communication with other teachers and with parents, and satisfying the administrators who were trying to satisfy DPI (Department of Public Instruction) requirements. Not to mention the hours upon hours I spent correcting papers, tests, quizzes, and assignments outside the school day.

"Teachers aren't the only ones to bring work home, you know," he said.

It became clear there would be no meeting of the minds that day. I would have liked to explain that because I taught six class periods (110 to 140 students per day depending on the year), I often had to strategize to make time for eating, drinking, and peeing. But it sounded defensive, so I refrained.

To accumulate some solid evidence, I began logging the hours I worked. No one could dispute cold, hard data. Right? At the end of the year, I averaged twelve hours per day, five days per week. This figured out to be a sixty-hour work week during the school year. Receiving a solid gold statuette or a pricey commemorative ring at the end of a good year would be cool, yes, but most teachers would settle for some genuine validation of their work to educate students. As in any other profession, there are a few teachers who skate by, doing the minimum. By and large, though, people who enter the teaching profession work hard and do not expect to achieve excessive fame or fortune. As the saying goes, they teach to "make a difference."

Given some free time in my room, I worked at arranging my bulletin board near the classroom door. Along with the fire escape route, tornado drill instructions, the daily schedule, and the lunch menu, I tacked up comic strips I'd collected. One *Foxtrot* cartoon showed the Fox kids at the beach trying to cram everything fun into their last day of freedom before school started: swimming, building sand castles, basking in the sun, flying kites, reading comic books, etc. I could relate. The day before inservice, I'd gone shopping in the morning, lunched with a friend, and spent the afternoon in the hammock reading.

On my planning calendar for September, I sat at my desk and plugged in the holidays and specially scheduled days, like early release or state teachers' convention. I penciled in my lessons for each day of my three classes: Junior English, Advanced Placement Language and Composition, and Creative Writing. The next job was to clean and pitch stuff I hadn't used in the past year—well, maybe two or three years. I'm not as bad as the collectors on TV's *American Pickers*, but I do tend to hold on to things. You never know if you might need them. And, of course, as soon as you throw something out, you need it. Never fails.

When we farmed, my husband explained to me, a town girl, the process of culling the cows: "If they're good milkers or show promise to be a good milker, they stay," he said. "If not, they're sold or sent to the packing plant." Culling amounts to keeping what works and getting rid of what doesn't.

I found that the beginning of the school year was a good time to do this at home and at school: clothes, belongings, emails, lessons, etc. Once the year got under way, time for culling would become scarce because of all the daily duties and decisions concerning my one hundred-plus students.

Over the course of a day, all these decisions could get tedious and often overwhelming. According to an *Education Week* (12/6/21) article by Alyson Klein, teachers make at least fifteen hundred decisions per day. Multiply that times 180 days per year, and that's a whopping 270,000 decisions per year. If teachers are tired by the end of the day, imagine how tired they are by the end of the year. It takes about two to three weeks after that last day of school to get my brain to decompress from the stress of the school year cycle.

I remember peeling potatoes for Thanksgiving dinner one year and listening to the featured guest on a Wisconsin Public Radio program. She was discussing a malady called "decision-making fatigue." Apparently, having to make too many decisions causes people to shut down when they simply tire of weighing the choices they have to make. The guest said that many people often overeat toward the end of the day because of feeling besieged by the day's decisions. They find it easier to eat what is handy rather than making yet another decision about what foods might be healthiest.

This theory applied to my teaching life too. After a day of deciding if so and so could go to the bathroom or borrow a pencil or work in the library or use this word or that word in their paper, I was spent. Aha! That's why my eighth period classes got away with more off-task shenanigans and became more chaotic than my morning classes. That, and they were tired of sitting and listening all day.

Dear Teachers,
Give yourselves a break. No one, absolutely no one,
can be Super Teacher every second of the day.
Remind yourself to take care of you. Don't skip lunch,
make sure to hydrate, and don't put off peeing all day like I
did. Make it a point to find ways to organize your workday
so that you have time for your needs, too. Your students,
your family, and your body will appreciate it.
Best regards,
Been There, Done That, and Know Better Now

I always began my year by making seating charts. Alphabetizing them by first names made the names easier to remember. Over the years, by far "J" was the most popular initial letter for names: Jason, Jeremy, Jeremiah, Jaron, Jarred, Jenny, Jacob, Jeb, Jenna, John, Jeff, Jackie, Jaxin, Josh, Jordan, Jamie, Jace, Jocylyn, Jackie, Jesse, Jessica, Joe, Janna, etc. It was no wonder I stuttered at times. During the first week, okay, throughout the year, I mistakenly called students by their brother or sister's name, especially if it began with the same letter. Students resented this. I get it. Who wants to be mistaken for a sibling?

"I'm sorry," I told them. "Just so you know, I mistake names a lot. At home I call my dogs by my kids' names and my kids by my dogs' names." This helped smooth things over a little.

Over the summer many of my posters fell down, resisting poster putty, masking tape, and even duct tape. One of them was a life-sized image of Mark Twain in a white suit that I bought years ago at a National Council of Teachers of English Convention. Students have mistaken him for Albert Einstein and even Colonel Sanders. "This is an English room, not a science lab or fast food joint. Duh!" I scolded them.

The poster flopped down across the middle, making it look like the author was taking a bow. This is so much like Twain that I was tempted to leave him like that. Double-stick foam tape was the only thing I found to hold up posters for an entire year. I attached him to the wall where they entered so he could greet them. I cut a hole out of his side to fit around the light switch plate and imagined the chorus of groans and giggles when, after watching a video in the dark, I'd say to the student in the front desk: "Hey, will you please go turn Mark Twain on for me?"

Chapter 2 – The Yips

Your dreams are the children of an idle
brain begot of nothing but vain fantasy.
Mercutio to Romeo (Shakespeare's *Romeo and Juliet*)

The term "the yips" is used in the context of sports to describe the situation when performance anxiety affects actual physical performance. When a batter in baseball chokes or a golfer's wrist movement fails after having mastered the moves, they are said to have "the yips." Apparently, Scottish-American professional golfer Tommy Armour first used the term in the 1920s when he lost the ability to drive or putt the ball for reasons no one could explain.

More recently, in the 2021 international olympic games in Tokyo, sportscasters used the term in reference to gold medalist Simone Biles. Biles said she had the "twisties" and was struggling with her mind and body connection when performing her routines. Afraid of injury and hindering her team, she dropped out of the team competition.

Teachers also experience a form of the yips. Every year in mid to late August as the first day approached, the yips came to me in the form of dreams. I have yet to find a teacher who is immune to this phenomenon. The mounting anxiety of the impending first day and coming year plays with our minds in subliminal ways.

In my most prevalent dream, I walk down the familiar halls—inspirational photos on one side, empty blue lockers on the other. Room 15 is missing. It is gone. Vanished. I look into Room 16 and 14 and 17. My peers are preparing for the first day, hanging posters, writing on the board, and arranging desks. I retrace my steps, my heart back-flipping, my mind in a tizzy. *Where's my room? Where did it go? I need to find it! What is going on?*

Embarrassed, I decide to confront my long-time social studies neighbor. He was prone to practical jokes, some of which were pretty elaborate, like once helping a colleague place another colleague's desk in the men's bathroom. "Have you seen my room? What did you do with it? Look at me! Where did my room go?" He doesn't answer, doesn't even turn around. The one thing that can freak out a teacher more than not being able to find her room? Being ignored and unheard.

In another nighttime scenario we teachers arrive for our first day of inservice to find that the superintendent did some remodeling over the summer. In his ongoing crusade to view students as our customers, he's connected a mini shopping mall to the science wing and erected an amusement park on the practice football field. A bevy of fast food restaurants fill the cafeteria. Sure, these additions will get them to come to school, but how will we get them to go to class?

A number of years ago, I experienced a spine-tingling chiller. I am running down the hall and I duck into the custodial closet. I hear screams, followed by the pop of gunshots. This triggers a flight response in me. I am disappointed, as I'd always thought of myself as more of a fighter. I remove a vent and climb into a duct and belly-crawl to an opening that leads to the roof. I am shaking and have no idea where I acquired the gun I am packing or where my students are. Like Stephen King stories, this dream establishes just enough roots in reality to induce sheer fright.

It didn't help that over the summer my book club read *The Hour I First Believed* by Wally Lamb. The novel tells the story of a school nurse who experiences, but survives, the Columbine shootings by hiding in a storage cupboard. Memories of the year we evacuated the school three times for bomb threats may have provided fodder for this dream as well.

The protocol for a bomb threat at PHS required teachers to gather their students and walk five blocks to the city's Armory. This was a large brick building where the local National Guard met and other city activities like voting and community sports took place. During the first bomb threat incident students laughed and joked around, elated about scoring a two-hour respite from school, a paid vacation. The second time was more tedious and a bit frustrating, and the third... Well...

I was handing out the rubrics for their persuasive papers when Dr. Jacobson's serious principal voice rained down from the ceiling mounted speaker: "Excuse me, everyone. We are evacuating the school and you are to walk to the Armory with your teacher. You may not go to your lockers. After you get to the Armory, teachers will take attendance and further instructions will follow."

"Aw, not again! Do we have to?" By now, they knew the drill. "Why do we have to leave? We all know it's a fake." "Yeah. I don't want to walk to the Armory again. Can't we take our cars?" "I texted my mom, and she said she can give me a ride. Okay?"

I grabbed my coat from the closet in my room and slid the clipboard with the roster into my bag. "All right, let's go."

"Why do you get to take your coat and we don't?" Jeremy asked as we exited.

Because I'm the teacher, Jeremy, I wanted to say. *Go to college and become a teacher and then you can keep your coat in the room and wear it to evacuate for bomb threats, too.* Like them, I was frustrated and had to remind myself that more than likely only one student caused this inconvenience. Correction. Now the count was up to *three* inconveniences. It was early spring, and the weather was cold and damp. I was going to wear my damned coat, damn it! Maybe students might be compelled to rat on the culprit and put an end to this bomb threat baloney if they became uncomfortable enough. Someone knew something. They had to. Why would anyone do this—three times—and not brag about it to others?

In a spotty drizzle, newly sprouted leaves on the row of maple trees flapped their applause as our parade of 450 students began at about 10 a.m. Chatter was sparse, and those who spoke hugged their bodies and mumbled words of displeasure.

At the Armory I checked off names while students sprawled in clusters on the floor and in the corners of the gymnasium, texting and talking to friends and parents. Light filtered through the row of glass block windows high on the walls above the basketball hoops, making sure we hostages had no view of the outside. As the noon hour approached, stomachs became vocal.

Finally, Mr. Kennedy, a tall math teacher they could see over the crowd, yelled: "Attention, everyone! Just want to let you all know I talked to Dr. Jacobson, and apparently, some words mentioning a bomb were found on the wall of the boys' bathroom near the math area. Police are leading a mandatory search of the building. When they call and say it is safe, we can return."

"How long?" someone called out.

"Probably about a half hour."

A couple of teachers manned the front door of the Armory to assure concerned parents that their kids were fine. Dr. Jacobson said that if parents chose to take their children with them, they could. A few did, even though we would be returning to school shortly. Any one of the students allowed to leave could have been the culprit who wrote the threat. It seemed to me that barring all exits until someone fessed up might be the best plan of action. Good thing I wasn't the principal.

On the trek back to school shortly after lunchtime, students clipped up the hill like cattle to the trough. Until they didn't. And the procession slowed to a crawl. I found out why when I came upon two girls. Arm in arm, one girl leaned on her shorter friend as students made their way around them. I looked down and saw the tall girl walking barefoot, her heels bloody.

"Are you okay?" I asked. A stupid question, I know, but someone needed to ask. I'd seen her around school but didn't know her name.

"My new shoes aren't broken in, yet," she said, attempting a smile.

"Stop in the office and get some bandages when we get back, okay?"

She nodded and continued to hobble up the hill.

What kind of individual gets his kicks from causing this kind of disruption? I thought as we neared the school. Unfortunately, several suspects came to mind.

Because someone cried wolf—*three times*—many of us at PHS became cynical. Would we take it the least bit seriously if there were a next time? The crime took weeks to investigate, but eventually the culprit was found. I was surprised by the revelation. This young man had not been a second thought on my mental list of suspects. He was involved in school activities and a pretty good student to boot. I'm not sure why he did it, but it proves that we never really know what is going on in the minds of others.

In 2000, the year after Columbine, we teachers at PHS, and most high schools across the country, practiced "shooter drills," known to us as a "Code Black." During these drills, we rehearsed what to do in case an intruder with a weapon gained entrance to our school. We locked the doors to our rooms, turned out the lights, and gathered all the students in the back corner away from any windows. We were told to stay there quietly and not answer the door until the school authorities or police told us we could leave.

This seemed sensible. But, upon further imagining the reality of a situation like this, I surmised intruders would likely be aware of this plan. During my preparation time that week, I experimented with removing the screens from my windows in order to get students and me out fast. We could then make a break for the parking lot to hide among the cars. In my mind, we stood more of a chance as running rabbits than sitting ducks. But, a shooter may expect this too, and another shooter could be stationed outside in that event.

"If it happened for real, we should stack all the desks and furniture up against the locked door to slow down entry," a colleague said during one of these drills. He was right. We all agreed that we would do that. However, there was no plan that would work in all circumstances.

When I became a teacher in 1992, I never anticipated these kinds of discussions with my students. I contemplated the job of Secret Service agents who had to anticipate every possible scenario and work out endless logistics when guarding our presidents and other public officials on a day-to-day basis. That was their full-time job, though. Mine was supposed to be teaching.

As a result of school shootings throughout the country, Platteville High School not only looked like a prison, as some of the townspeople once suggested, it felt like one. Instead of an open door to encourage visitors to visit our place of learning, security cameras and a buzzer entry system became the first to greet them.

After the Sandy Hook Elementary school shooting in 2012, local officials thought it important that teachers and staff in the Platteville School District receive emergency training in the treatment of bullet wounds. Just in case. Emergency Medical Technicians (EMTs), the district nurse, and local police personnel showed us a related video and taught us how to react if someone were to be shot. We were instructed how to evaluate, treat, and bandage wounds while waiting for help to arrive. Then we were divided into groups and given tourniquets to practice what we'd learned upon our peers.

All this stress could give Wonder Woman a case of the yips. (But, unlike her, at least I only work nine months out of the year.)

We teachers did not take the possibility of violence lightly. We knew that tragedy could occur at any school in any part of the country—including ours. This reality was not only unsettling for teachers but students and their parents. The *Sandy Hook Promise* website reported the following *Washington Post* statistics: "Since Columbine in 1999, more than 338,000 students in the United States have experienced gun violence at school," and "In 2022, 34 students and adults died while more than 43,000 children were exposed to gunfire at school" ("17 Facts About Gun Violence and School Shootings").

This should give everyone a case of the yips.

According to the site, gun violence is best prevented by knowing the warning signs indicated by a potential shooter. I would think schools should be training staff and students about this. When I was in school we had one drill, the fire drill. Except when I was in third grade, and we were instructed to get on the floor under our desks in case of a Cuban missile attack.

CNN reporter Annette Choi says that children and teens are more likely to die by guns than anything else, including fires and car accidents.

Sue Leamy Kies

Dear Politicians,
Please work together to protect our children. If that means banning
assault rifles, providing shooter awareness training, requiring more
stringent background checks for gun purchasers, installing metal
detectors, and making sure guns are securely stored in homes, so be
it! The gun violence in our schools needs to stop. Now.
Passionately,
The Public Good

Chapter 3 – Don't Touch My Stapler!

Begin, be bold, and venture to be wise.
Horace

At 8:10 a.m., my first-hour juniors began to file in, some bright-eyed and bushy tailed; others, not so much. Most of them would soon realize that a seven to seven thirty a.m. wake-up time might require a bedtime earlier than two a.m. However, a few would sleepwalk through the first period of the entire semester.

The first day was an exception. Even the most exhausted, aloof teens could not remain completely cool. It held far more promise than New Year's Day ever has. It was the only day when perfect attendance prevailed, everyone had an "A," everyone behaved, everyone was well-groomed, and—everyone was happy to be there—if only to see their friends again, show off their new school supplies, and don their new outfits.

While tidying up in June at the end of last year, I found a half-empty milk carton stashed behind a bookshelf, and a petrified banana peel between the filing cabinets. Now, thanks to the summer cleaning crew, my classroom smelled of freshly waxed floors, janitorial cleaning supplies and enticing lessons. And, the white boards were white, almost glowing. Gone were the cloudy smears of leftover notes and student graffiti. Images of William Shakespeare, Emily Dickinson, and Henry David Thoreau joined Mark Twain on the walls for literary inspiration. My books and handouts stood at attention on the front table, and neither my students nor I had lost or misplaced anything—yet.

After filing in, the students grumbled about the seating chart as they found their assigned seats. We then reviewed the syllabus of topics, units, and requirements. The first few years I taught, I'd included a lengthy list of do's and don'ts, complete with the detailed consequences for not complying. A few years down the road, it occurred to me that there would always be those rascals whose primary goal was to disrupt my class. Why, then, was I providing them with an itemized list of the very things that irritated me most on the first day?

I decided on one rule, one word, that covered it all. Often, I would play the song by the same name as they walked in the door. Aretha even spelled it out for them: R-E-S-P-E-C-T!

"Respect me and respect each other," I told them. "If you don't, I'm going to do *something*." I liked the ambiguity of *something*. It gave me the opportunity to call the infraction like I saw it and mull over the resulting consequences. And, it gave them time to fret about what those consequences might be. This was a concept I learned at a Love and Logic class with Jim Fay the previous summer, and over the course of the year it proved helpful.

I reminded them that the rule also included respecting other peoples' property. Particularly, my automatic stapler.

"DO NOT TOUCH MY STAPLER," I said, staring them down. "If you touch it, you can bet I'll do *something*—like take away your class participation points for the entire week, call your parents, or make your life miserable in ways you cannot imagine. Again: Do NOT touch my stapler. If it runs out of staples, tell me and I will refill it. Under no circumstances may any of you touch my stapler. Got it?"

Most nodded compliantly at me, the wacko woman ranting about her stapler. I could see the wheels turning: *Man, it's just a stupid stapler. This is going to be a long year. I wonder if anyone else teaches Junior English?*

The day it arrived several years ago, I slid it out of the box and carefully removed it from the Styrofoam packing material. It was black, beautiful, and sleek. I was not a technology nerd who craved every new gadget, but, this stapler—it awakened the geek in me. I plugged it in, grabbed a couple of scraps of paper from my desk and fed them into its jaws.

What an invention. A stapler with initiative. If only I could activate this attribute in my students.

Wham! (I flinched.) Then I turned the papers around and tried it again. Wham! Wham! Wow. It magically sensed the sheets of paper and smacked down, attaching them with the utmost of precision. What an invention. A stapler with initiative. If only I could activate this attribute in my students.

Previously, I'd ordered at least one new stapler every spring because none could withstand an entire year of sixty to eighty seventeen-year-olds who didn't just staple paper, but backpacks, tennis shoes, pencils, folders, jeans, milk cartons, orange peels, the wall...each other. Anything and everything was staple-able in their estimation. Anything. And then, when the stapler inevitably wouldn't work anymore, they intoned those well-intentioned, exasperating words: "Don't worry, Mrs. Kies, I can fix it for you."

Countless too-young-to-die staplers went to their dumpster graves at the hands of some overconfident students who disassembled them and couldn't get them back together again in working condition. If the stapler failed to function after their adjustments, the repairers reacted: BAM! BAM! BAM!, slamming down overlapped palms like zealous EMTs performing CPR. Later in life these same students who thrived on knowing how things worked—how a pencil sharpener sharpened, how a toilet flushed, how a car ran—would invent something grand or be able to fix anything. But, in my classroom, they would never again touch my frickin' stapler. Hence, my new no-touch model. I taped a bright orange Post-it on top: DO NOT TOUCH!

To properly demonstrate the use of the stapler, I placed it center stage and slid in a couple of sheets of scrap paper. I beamed with pride as they gasped in awe. "That's scary," Jessica said from the front row.

Dear Stephen King and other masters of horror:
If you want to frighten teen audiences, consider arming your antagonist with an automatic stapler
instead of an ax or a chainsaw.
Signed,
An Experienced High School Teacher

I informed my students that this state-of-the-art appliance cost a whopping fifty dollars of my ever shrinking teacher budget. Once again, I grilled them: "Whose stapler is this? What are you NOT going to do? Ever?" They answered obligingly, in unison. Any teacher will tell you the first day of training is most impactful. *Will the stapler withstand this last year?* I wondered. I hoped so. It would be nice to pass it on to my successor.

On *my* first day as a student at Platteville High School in 1968, Dad drove our Chevy sedan across Water Street and up Madison. On the left, two high metal lids rose in the air, capping the gymnasium and the library loft. He drove around the circle in front and stopped at the entrance. "Have a good first day. Remember to be friendly and speak to everyone," he said, waving and smiling at every passerby. To my embarrassment, he practiced what he preached. I scooched down in the seat. This was not the first time he'd coached me on his primary rule of small town etiquette.

"Right, Dad."

I got out of the car and searched the faces for any of my familiar St. Mary's Grade School classmates. For the most part, I was excited to be there—except for a looming dread of phy-ed, what we called physical education class. At St. Mary's we exercised at recess playing vigorous games of red rover, dodgeball, frozen tag, or rope skipping. But now we were required to wear red onesies from Gipp's Smart Apparel so we could partake in a bona fide physical education class. The jumpsuit sported snaps up the front, an elasticized waist, and a button-down collar. Mom placed my name on the left side with iron-on black letters she purchased from the dime store on Main Street.

I was ecstatic that we'd be playing field hockey, softball, and badminton, as well as completing units in archery and gymnastics. This was hi-tech compared to the red rubber kickballs and jump ropes we had at St. Mary's. This all came with one huge sticking point: communal showers. Eight years of parochial school modesty had not prepared me for showering with girls I had never even met before, let alone those I'd been completely content knowing with their clothes on. In avoidance of sin, I'd never seen a completely nude body other than my own. I had two brothers, nine and eleven years older, and my parents did not subscribe to *National Geographic Magazine*.

With much trepidation on that first day, I shed my chic onesie and underclothes and walked to the shower room. A few floor-to-ceiling poles with shower heads sprang from the center of the tiled room and more protruded from the walls. Trying my best to appear nonchalant, I was flabbergasted at the scene in front of me. A group of naked classmates stood in the middle of the room and struck up casual conversations, laughing and frolicking like nymphs in the rain. Maybe summer camp had accustomed them to communal showering? Maybe their families were more Bohemian and less Puritanical in their attitudes toward nudity at home?

I could tell others felt self-conscious too. Making no eye contact, we scurried into the shower room, snatching a towel on our way out, and covering up in haste like Eves with our fig leaves. There was only one exit, and our phy-ed teacher guarded the threshold to ensure we had scrubbed sufficiently and check off our names on her clipboard. Thirty-something, with a short, sporty haircut, she dressed in shorts and a polo shirt like a sportswear model you'd see in professional golf or tennis magazines.

When my fellow inhibitionists discovered that having our periods garnered a partial shower in a private stall, we became a healthy bunch of menstruators. Our time of the month lasted a full week, or longer if the teacher became lax in tracking our cycles. It was the only advantage to getting my period that I had, or ever have, experienced, and I made sure to capitalize on it.

Like most locker rooms, a bench ran down the middle of each row, creating another compromising endeavor. How does one get dressed without simply dropping the towel and becoming a spectacle yet again? I observed how some girls slipped on their shirts and panties before removing the towels, and then slipped on their bras under their shirts. Where did they learn these tricks?

There was this one girl, Audrey. Mind you, I was too concerned with my own self-consciousness to notice much, but this girl, even as a freshman, had beautiful Venus-like breasts, full and round, the picture of lovely, budding womanhood. I admired them, not in a creepy way, but in a way that made me wish they were adorning my own chest. She seemed so comfortable with them and with her body.

After we were clean, checked off, dried, and dressed, it was time to vie for prime primping space in front of the wall-sized mirror. We had five minutes to redo our look of the day. We amicably shared makeup, combs, and brushes. The fumes of deodorants, perfumes, and aerosol hairsprays sent us into a stupor that lasted through our second period class.

For most of my teaching years at PHS, I had a room with a large window. I remember debating on whether to place my desk across the room so I could look out at the row of maple trees, or in front of the window where I could feel the warmth of winter rays and the touch of cool breezes. I opted for the latter.

Though a definite plus, this was not the most important advantage to that window. I had despised the mandated showers in phy-ed class as a student, but on becoming a teacher my perspective changed. I'm not sure when and how it happened, but students were now spared the embarrassment of the communal shower. Yes, they slipped into different clothes for gym class, clothes that they were supposed to take home and launder every week. But, alas, they were forgetful teens, and those gym outfits were lucky to undergo one wash and rinse cycle per year. The new sweat combined with the old sweat embedded in the clothes, which in turn transferred to their body. Ugh!!

This was another reason the first day of school rocked: everybody smelled good.

Morning classes finished, I hustled to the staff lounge refrigerator to retrieve my Edgar Allan Poe lunchbox. This was a gift from three of my former students, Courtney, Caitlyn, and Hillary, who showed up at my door the previous summer, brimming with smiles. They'd found the lunchbox while browsing at an eclectic store on a road trip to Iowa. It was midnight blue and adorned with images of Poe, along with a black cat and a raven, two of his most sinister characters. They said it made them think of me. I was honored.

The fridge was remarkably clean, thanks to Cathy, the good

Samaritan who removed the food that had copulated, multiplied, and died there at the end of last year. We ate and visited for fifteen minutes, then did the Stupid Quiz (Super Quiz) from the *Wisconsin State Journal* for the last ten minutes. We routinely shouted out answers when we knew them. If we didn't, Mark, the designated reader for that lunch period, pantomimed hints, arms flailing and hands aflutter, until we guessed the answer. Somewhere along the way, Friday became "Effing Friday." On this day the quiz answer had to be preceded by the f-word or it didn't count, something like the question rule on *Jeopardy*. A welcome release, our raucous laughter often escaped the closed doors of the Teacher's Lounge.

On the first day, I repeated necessary explanations six times, once for each class. Combine all that talking with the onset of fall allergies, and my voice gave out as it did every year. Out of this malady came a solution: the Song Speech. The next day students would be introducing themselves to me and the class by selecting five songs and explaining the sound track of their lives thus far.

Complaints abounded. "Aw…a speech on the second day? Do we have to?" And the quintessential of all teen gripes, "This is dumb!" I'd discovered from past years, however, that once they got in front of the class armed with their favorite songs, even the shyest of students performed the feat with little assistance.

"What does this have to do with English class?" Jack asked. There is always that one student. I explained that the song lyrics were poetry set to sound. During the last few minutes of class, I looked over their shoulders at the speech planning sheet I had given them. Thus far, choices ranged from K-Pop to Weird Al Yankovic and AC/DC to Rascal Flatts and Taylor Swift. This would prove to be an interesting year.

At the end of the hour, I modeled the assignment. I introduced myself and named each song, followed by a brief explanation of its significance in my life:

"'Mary Ann' by the Merrymen is my first song. I always requested this tune from the band at a supper club when my parents and I went out to eat on Friday nights. It's happy and upbeat, about a young woman who sifts sand on the beach and everyone loves her. As a youngster, I tended to be a romantic.

"My second song is 'I Am a Rock' by Simon and Garfunkel. I remember sitting on the kitchen counter at home to get closer to the radio. I loved the melody and harmony, though the lyrics are about isolating yourself to escape the pain of relationships. So much for romanticism, I guess.

"'Mrs. Brown You've Got a Lovely Daughter' by Herman's Hermits is my third one. This song is about unrequited love, to which I could relate in grade school. The boy I liked didn't know I existed. A few years ago my husband and I saw none other than Peter Noone, Herman himself, in concert in Dubuque. What I wouldn't have done to do this as a thirteen-year-old!

"'Piece of My Heart' by Janis Joplin is number four. This song on the album *Pearl* awakened the blues in me when I was a sophomore. I love the soul she put into her songs. It's not good that she is allowing her heart to be broken over and over again, though. No one should let themselves be a doormat in a relationship. Remember that.

"And, my last one is 'I'll Follow the Sun' by the Beatles. It's one of my favorite songs by my all-time favorite band. What can't the Beatles do when it comes to music? They are masters. The opposite of 'A Piece of My Heart,' this tune is about following what makes you happy. Doing this is a choice, and I find it to be good advice.

"Thank you for listening," I said at the end. "Saying 'thank you' is important," I stressed. "It is polite, and it is the audience's cue that you are finished with your speech and that they should clap."

They clapped, and I bowed.

At the start of sixth period one young man entered and approached my desk, smiled, and shook my hand. "Nice to meet you, Mrs. Kies. My name is Brett. I'm really looking forward to your class. I've heard so many good things about you. Say, did you read any good books this summer?"

You've got to love the schmoozers. The contemporary Eddie Haskells. They applied verbal grease like butter on toast. Clever boy. Asking the English teacher if she'd read any good books. I had to give him credit. No other student had ever asked me that on the first day.

"Nice to meet you, Brett. I did read some good books. How about you? What did you read over the summer?"

"Me? Tons of books. Tons!"

"For example? Any particular title or author you like?"

"Too many to mention, really. Uh, er—yeah. By the way, did you really throw a puppy out a window?"

That first few days of school could be revealing in so many ways, yet so completely...incomplete. It was in the long haul, the day-to-day touch with my students, the one hundred seventy-eight days to come, that personalities, learning styles, talent, humor...and occasional conflict will present themselves. I couldn't wait to see who this year's roster brought me!

Chapter 4 – Homecoming and Hormones

All of life is education.
Henry David Thoreau

The workday rhythm after the first days became second nature: up at 5:00, eat cereal and fruit, drink a cup of hazelnut coffee, skim through two newspapers, correct homework, shower, pack a lunch, and leave for school by 7:20 a.m. The wintertime drudge of leaving and coming home in darkness was fast approaching.

I looked out the bathroom window into the dark October morning. What the heck—snow? Then I looked up. Oh. That's right. It's homecoming week. Streamers of white tangoed in the breeze in the branches of our oak and walnut trees. Shredded paper blanketed the ground. Though I would never admit this to the perpetrators, it looked sort of pretty, like a party waiting to happen. However, tomorrow's rain was sure to transform any hint of beauty into clumps the color and texture of a fungus.

On the drive to school I marveled at the makeovers of other houses. This toilet papering tradition began sometime after I graduated in 1972 and before I became a teacher in 1991. As teens, my classmates and I had not been schooled in this activity. Now, during homecoming week, the majority of students became three-dimensional artists, their monochrome masterpieces revealed in the morning light.

During the month prior to homecoming, students stock-piled their stash little by little so as not to seem conspicuous. Soon, every trunk in the PHS parking lot was as stuffed as a teddy bear's belly. On the plus side, this provided an added safety feature in the event of any rear-end collisions.

Before rising to a position as a University of Wisconsin-Madison sports coach, one of our esteemed parents led our local collegiate team. This coach and dad loathed this mischievous practice of toilet papering people's homes...so much so that he enlisted the help of the police to patrol his neighborhood during homecoming week. As is the way with human nature, especially teenagers, papering his house became the pinnacle of achievement among PHS students. Coach corralled many a TP-er in his garage for a passionate heart-to-heart about the honor code of respecting a man's property as he'd learned growing up. Our son and his friends, classmates of Coach's son, were the recipients of at least one such lecture.

In the mid-1990s when I was student council advisor in charge of planning homecoming, Coach's eldest son was elected to that year's court. His second youngest daughter reigned as miniature queen. Coach refrained from the festivities the night of coronation in order to patrol his yard because he knew kids would expect him to be gone. That year, his defense strategy was effective.

The following Monday I was doing a lesson on Edgar Allan Poe's "The Raven" to capitalize on the mood for the upcoming Halloween holiday. We were discussing how the raven in the poem represented the spirit of the narrator's lost love, Lenore. Andy, whose forte was derailing class discussions, said, "You know why Cameron isn't here today?"

Knowing laughter tittered through the classroom.

"Is this something that can or should be shared?" I asked. He nodded and took it as his cue to proceed.

"Well, you see, some people I know were dressed in black, flinging rolls of you know what in—you know who's backyard—when somebody yells, 'Cops!' So, Cameron makes a quick get-away and runs across the yard and down the street and ducks into the backseat of his friend's car."

At this point Andy broke into fits of laughter, and Jason helped out with the story: "After he shuts the car door, Cameron says, 'Step on it, moron! What ya waitin' for?' But, when Cameron removes his stocking cap and looks up at the person in the driver's seat—it isn't his friend behind the wheel."

"It's Officer Meyers in an unmarked police car!" Aaron said, delivering the punchline.

This lent a far more upbeat tone than usual to the study of Poe. I made a mental note to capitalize on this in the future. Imagine the creative ideas that would surface if I'd encouraged them to write their own rendition of *The Raven.* "Once upon a homecoming cheery, while TP-ing in a hurry . . ."

When Coach and his family moved, they sold their house to the newly hired high school principal. Quite the legacy, indeed. You can imagine the gallery of white he witnessed every morning during his first homecoming week in Platteville and every homecoming thereafter.

The new principal took a less defensive approach to TP-ing. Instead of making it a challenge, he cleaned up the mess when they were finished and figured they would tire of it when they got no reaction. Many teachers and parents, however, became fed up with the messes and complained that the whole toilet papering nonsense was getting out of hand.

To keep the peace, the principal announced over the intercom on Monday afternoon of homecoming week: "I know you're all looking forward to the festivities coming up, and that's good. But remember, toilet papering or even being on someone else's property without permission, is considered trespassing and can result in getting a ticket. If you are going to take part in this activity, you need to make sure it's okay with the

31

homeowners or you risk getting ticketed by the police. Have fun but be safe and law abiding too."

After the announcement, a student asked, "So, Mrs. Kies, how do you feel about toilet papering? Do you care if we beautify your yard?"

"Someone...maybe it was you...already beautified it last night. You can come clean up the decorations today after school, okay?"

"It wasn't me. Really." He held his hands in the air, a mugshot of innocence. "We did do Mr. Kennedy's house last night. He was hiding behind his house and sprayed us with the hose. It was awesome!"

In my day, homecoming was a fanfare of tradition. A pep assembly, skits, and a bonfire preceded the all-important dance following the game on Friday night. Girls back then were expected to have dates to go to the dance. And, it was expected that the boys did the asking.

In my sophomore year of high school, Kevin, a boy I began to like the previous summer at band camp, asked me to go to homecoming. Well, not really asked. He wrote it in a note. He often wrote me notes, folding them like origami lockboxes so no one could open them without being detected. He gave them to a friend who placed them in my awaiting hand. I would write back to him to be delivered in the same manner. By today's standards, this was a labor intensive communication system. Texting would have made it a lot simpler, though I truly believe that receiving a handwritten note from someone who *likes* you is much more personal than a text.

That weekend, my mother, who was as elated as I was about my invitation to the dance, took me shopping for fabric and a pattern for the dress. For years, we collaborated on clothing in this manner, including prom dresses and eventually my wedding dress. She not only saved money, but I gained a wardrobe piece unlike anyone else's. I chose navy blue velvet. She cut out the fabric, making sure the nap all ran the same way for the dropped waist pattern with a flared skirt. The contrasting pointed collar and buttoned cuffs emerged from a swath of white sateen. I did my part in covering the buttons to arrange down the front.

On Friday night, Kevin, his hair combed into the fashionable Beatle's style, rang the bell right on time. He handed me a box containing a lovely white chrysanthemum corsage, and I introduced him to my parents. After Mom helped me pin on the corsage amidst some uncomfortable small talk, we left for the dance.

We made the mile-long trek on foot; I in my velvet dress and low heels and Kevin in dress pants, shirt, and tie. Both my parents and his older sister had offered to give us a ride, but we declined. We thought riding with them might be awkward. Of course, walking all that way in dress clothes wasn't awkward at all.

"So, how do you like Miss Rassman's English class," I asked, trying to stir some conversation.

"I liked that project we did a few weeks ago, you know, the one where we worked in groups on those presentations?"

"Yeah, that was fun."

The clouds blocked any light from the moon and stars, a perfect opportunity for him to take my hand. But, he didn't. I guess I could have taken his, but I was shy too.

After another block of silence, I asked, "Is your sister going to the dance with her boyfriend?"

"Yeah, she is."

We exchanged a few more banal pleasantries. He said he liked my dress. I said thank you. Our conversation was as sparse as saplings in a desert. Without a paper and pen, we didn't know how to communicate. My students have told me that this happens with habitual texters. They sit in the same room and text each other rather than talk.

We walked up Madison Street to the high school and entered the commons area where homecoming dances still take place. Now, students often go in groups, decorations are minimal, and a disc jockey presides. That night, Moonflower Vine, a great band made up of five of our classmates, provided the tunes. Kevin and I danced to almost every song, the proof showed in the handprints on the back of my velvet dress. In between songs we had some punch and talked to other classmates.

Afterward, we took the same route home. While we were saying goodnight on my front steps, I thought maybe he'd kiss me. Then his friends drove up.

"Hey, Kevin, you comin' or what?" one of them yelled.

"Yeah, hurry up and kiss her and let's go!" yelled another. Hoots of mockery projected from the windows of the car. Talk about ruining the moment.

"Sorry about that."

"It's okay," I said. "You'd better go so they don't wake up the neighborhood." I knew my parents were alerted by now and probably watching through the window. We said our polite goodnights and told each other how we'd had a great time. He smiled and gently squeezed my arm, then hopped down my steps and into the car with his friends.

"Chicken! Why didn't you kiss her? You're such a big chicken!" I heard as they drove away.

A few weeks and a few more notes later, the relationship with Kevin ended. In writing, of course. Sweet, shy, and a good dancer, he wrote lovely letters. When we were seniors, Kevin began dating a girl from the class behind mine. They ended up getting married. They had a smart, spunky daughter, and I was privileged to have her as a student when she and her mom moved back to Platteville. Sadly, when she was a little girl, Kevin died in a construction accident while at work.

Life, as we all find out eventually, has no regard whatsoever for fairness.

* * *

During my first year teaching at PHS in 1992, Mr. Trickel, my former senior English teacher, was now the principal and my boss. Notoriously *old school*, he believed that freshmen coming in at the bottom of the pecking order had to earn their stripes. As luck would have it, my classmates and I had lockers in the hall outside his room freshman year.

"What's all the noise out here? Where are you supposed to be? Wherever it is, get there! Vagabonds, nothing but vagabonds," he mumbled, ducking back into his room: the bear retreating to his cave.

I had steered clear of him until Senior English. Pleasantly surprised, I found his class to be my favorite. Delving into the psychology of the characters in literature was his strong suit. When teaching *Return of the Native* by Thomas Hardy, which was set in the mid-nineteenth century, he used Eustacia Vye and her suitors to instruct that, universally, the human desire for something or someone supersedes the pleasure of its actual attainment. He illustrated this point by sharing his unfulfilled but fulfilling ongoing fantasy for a date with film star Raquel Welch. During the *Macbeth* unit, he dressed head to toe in Shakespearean attire, encouraging students to do the same. Why he ever wanted to leave all that fun and become a principal is beyond me.

The year I began teaching full time, 1993, Mr. Trickel was under the gun to find someone to take the extracurricular position of student council advisor. As a newly hired teacher, I had to prove my mettle. It was his way of testing me, a freshman teacher.

When I attended PHS, the student council addressed the effect of school policies on students. Over the years, the organization had evolved into more of a social council. The primary duty of the advisor now was to orchestrate and oversee the designated homecoming spirit dress-up days, bonfire, pep assembly, and presentation of the court at the Friday night football game. The dance on Saturday night was the culmination of all the hoopla.

During that first year, student council members voted to include some fun outdoor activities after the pep assembly, including a powder puff football game and a car smash. The student council president asked her brother if he would donate an old wreck of a car he had sitting around for parts. He hauled the body in on a flatbed and deposited it in a grassy spot behind the school. For a mere one dollar students could whack the car three times with a sledgehammer to see how much damage they could do.

The tickets for the car smash sold like firecrackers on the Fourth of July. A responsible previous PHS graduate, the student council president's brother removed the windows to prevent flying glass and roped off the car smash area to keep spectators at a safe distance. That afternoon cheers rose in encouragement when someone made a particularly damaging dent.

A number of students submitted their tickets and gave the car their best shot with the hammer. Then, a student, a sturdy football tackle, climbed onto the hood of the car and took his first of three swings at the roof. Crunch! Crunch! Nobody said participants couldn't stand on the car, but it looked perilous to me. Before I could do or say anything, he was getting ready for his third shot. "Be careful!" I yelled, praying he wouldn't fall off and break his neck.

"Come on, you can do it! Give it all you've got! Yeah! Slam it!" He had the crowd going. "Put those muscles to use! Go for it!"

Adrenaline flowing, the student expelled a prolonged grunt and heaved the sledgehammer for the slam of all destruction. At the height of the swing, the top of the arc, somehow the iron head dislodged from the handle of the sledgehammer. The crowd gasped. Our eyes followed its trajectory over us to where it landed on the ground with a thud.

The student looked at the headless handle in his hands. "What the..."

It took a few minutes for us to register how fortunate we had been. If the student had been on the ground level with the crowd instead of on top of the car—or if someone had been standing where the chunk of iron had landed—yikes! I cringed at the thought.

On Saturday night the homecoming dance presented a different set of problems. The student council and I spent the afternoon decorating the commons area with red, white, and silver balloons and streamers. We went home and changed for the dance, and some of the girls went to the salon to have their hair styled.

That night the DJ got things underway and all was going well. Students began moving onto the dance floor, when a female student approached me with concern. "Mrs. Kies, isn't that supposed to be one of our chaperones?"

I followed her gaze. Our twenty-two-year-old choral instructor was standing in a dark corner with her date. She was wearing a black off-the-shoulder mini-dress and that *pensive, sexy* look that seems to come so naturally to Victoria's Secret models. Her date's face was buried in her neck. When he emerged, we noted a bit of an age gap, as he resembled a distinguished and graying Richard Gere.

Was I supposed to do something about this? What would I say? You need to stop making out right now? Save that stuff for after the dance? Get a room? They were both adults, though not best role models as chaperones for a teen dance. I decided to ignore it in hopes they would cool down as the dance went on. Or, maybe they would leave for a while and come back less bothered?

The instructor taught at PHS for two years. Along with her homecoming chaperoning debut, she directed and presented two top-notch musicals. The stellar singing, acting, and the costumes displayed her ability to put on a show. She also conducted memorable concerts. Every time she leaned forward on the podium to cue the trumpets or emphasize the upbeat, her mini skirt rose in time to the music. It made sense that she left teaching to pursue a career in theater and entertainment. It was obviously her true calling.

Students chose the DJ for the dance. When he played the remake of the hit "Mony-Mony," originally recorded by Tommy James and the Shondells, my foot tapped and my head bobbed. I recalled dancing to that very song in that very room years ago. The dance floor filled and students were loving it. Maybe times hadn't changed that much after all.

Then—the chorus to the song began. During the interlude between the repeated phrase "Mony-Mony," dancers began thrusting fists in the air and shouting. *What are they doing?* Students gave me sidelong glances, like my own kids when they were doing something they shouldn't be doing.

Elizabeth, the orchestra teacher not long out of college, was standing by the office door. I figured she'd know, so I approached her. "What are they yelling?"

"You probably don't want to know," she said.

I listened again as the chorus repeated. "Are they chanting about...getting effed twice?"

She nodded.

Participants waved arms in the air and yelled out the profanity in animated glee. I imagined the principal strolling in at any moment to check on the dance, the f-word funneling from the commons through the halls. I made my way over to the DJ, raising my voice above the clamor: "If you want to see your paycheck at the end of the night, you WILL NOT play that song again tonight

38

under any circumstances. Okay?"

The following year the student council representatives opted to have a "Kiss the Pig" contest to raise money for the local food pantry. I was relieved. This sounded far less menacing than a car smash. Various faculty members were nominated, and, with their approval, their names and pictures were placed on large jars in the commons so fans could deposit money in the container of the person they wanted to kiss the pig at the homecoming pep assembly on Friday.

The local newspaper and radio station had announced the week's activities. Whether due to this publicity or an informer among us, PETA (People for the Ethical Treatment of Animals) got wind of our contest. And, they weren't at all happy about it. A few of their representatives showed up outside our school with signs and a news crew a day before the kissing ceremony was to take place. They questioned and confronted students entering the front door. Because they were backing up traffic at the school entrance, the local police got involved and told the PETA people they'd have to move their protest further away from the school. So, they moved to the driveway entrance, waved their signs, and shouted: "Spare the pig! Spare the pig!"

"I don't get it," a student council member, said. "The pig is going to get fat and get slaughtered, right? And PETA doesn't want him to get kissed?" She was puzzled and somewhat agitated, as were other members of our agricultural community. However, some PETA sympathizers in our midst believed that the kissing contest put unwarranted stress on the baby pig.

After some consideration, Mr. Trickel allowed the contest to proceed.

Weeks before, one of the student council members had talked to a student whose parents raised pigs on a farm outside of town. He made arrangements to pick up the little oinker in the afternoon and return it right after the pep assembly. Something came up, and none of the students were able to fetch the pig. They asked me to do it. My husband and I used to farm, so I knew from experience that the most threatening aspect of a pig was its odor. I didn't want my chauffeuring duties to cause our vehicle to reek like a decomposing body for the next year. But we couldn't have a kiss the pig contest without a pig.

That afternoon I drove the winding road out to the farm southwest of town. The owner obliged in helping me pick out an appropriate, cute, wiggly, little piglet. We put Wiggles, as I came to call him, in a cardboard box with some straw. He let out a few squeals, then quietly settled into his nest on the drive to school. I buzzed along at a good clip so Wiggles' *eau de poo* fragrance wouldn't permeate my vehicle.

After arriving at school, I looked for a place to put Wiggles until his romantic encounter at the assembly. The janitor said that the bathroom in the main office might work because it was tiled and pretty much pig proof. I put the box on the floor and opened the top so Wiggles could get his bearings. I filled a small bowl with water in case he got thirsty and left to watch the pep assembly.

When it came time for Wiggles' debut, I returned to the bathroom to fetch him. In that brief period of time, he'd escaped his comfy house, spilled his water, and pooped and peed all over the floor. Holy hog manure, it reeked in there! The PETA people would have been proud of that spunky little swine. His little cloven feet were caked with his own crap that he'd tracked all over the tile. I wiped up the floor and washed the pig as best I could. Hoping for no more excrement mishaps, I tucked him under my arm and carried him to the gym.

His cuteness elicited a chorus of "Aws." Then, as if on cue, he let loose with what I chose to interpret as squeals of delight. I handed Wiggles to the student council member who held him gently while the vice principal, the lucky winner of the contest,

40

planted a big smackaroo on his stinky little head. The audience laughed and applauded. Wiggles was a star, albeit a putrid one.

After the assembly, I drove Wiggles back to his home on the farm without any mishaps. I imagined him boasting to his littermates about his getaway—the fast limo ride, the comfy straw-filled coach, and the posh hotel with tile floors and a big white swimming pool. He'd surely tell them about the raucous rock concert where some groupie kissed him on the noggin, making his peers envious and surprised to see him return. Round trip excursions from the farm were rare in the swine world.

Dear Advisors of Activities,
Never underestimate your students' uncanny ability
to draw you in to their hare-brained ideas that
could cost you much grief and possibly your job.
If it sounds like too much fun to be true, it probably is.
Glad I Survived,
Mrs. Kies

* * *

After five years as student council advisor, I was happily replaced by someone who relished the thought of planning homecoming. Ka-ching! A win...win! This freed me up to become a regular participant in the faculty/staff skit, a fun tradition during Friday's pep assembly. Our lives were plenty busy with the usual meetings, duties and keeping students on task, but this skit was a rare chance for us to have a bit of fun together as a staff.

One of our favorites was "Toy Glory," in which the main character Sandy won the Homecoming football game against the nasty opponents with the help of sidekicks Goody and Fuzz. I played Bo Sleep in the original version, but four years later I played the villain Aunty (Anti)-Dismee in the sequel. Our rendition of "Shiverdance" featured a group of us teachers and staff doing intricate step dancing to Celtic music with our arms Saran-wrapped to our sides to make sure we didn't move them. We also wrote up a script using the characters from *Gilligan's Island*, and in more recent years choreographed hip moves to "What Does the Fox Say?" and "Gangnam Style."

One year we canceled our skit because several students got carried away with toilet papering the PHS football coach's home. They broke lawn ornaments and trampled landscaping, making a shambles of his yard. Student council members begged teachers not to nix the skit because of the behavior of a few numbskulls. They said the student body looked forward to our participation "more than anything in the pep assembly." Wow. We had no idea we were so popular.

The next year the theme was "We Will Rock You." We decided to keep it simple and capitalize on the obvious connection by lip syncing along with notable songs. Teachers and staff members who wanted to participate could get their act together on their own; no lengthy rehearsals necessary. Miss Schober had access to the costume closet, which was used for musicals and plays, and rock stars were born! We practiced a couple of mornings before school that week, so Mr. Clark, the guidance counselor, could act as emcee and tie all the acts together.

Mrs. Callahan, clad in a not-too-short skirt, fish-net stockings, and funky wig, performed the best school-appropriate Tina Turner moves in the business to "Rollin' on a River." I fulfilled a lifelong dream and wore a mop-top wig, wire rimmed glasses and suit to rock out with me band mates Paul, George, and Ringo (aka three of my illustrious colleagues) to "She Loves You, Yeah! Yeah! Yeah!" We had to be careful that our wigs didn't fly off when we shook our heads and wailed in unison, "Oooooooh!"

Dr. Jacobson was Elton John, sporting a white sequined cape and big glasses, singing "Don't Go Breakin' My Heart" with Kiki Dee, a.k.a., Mrs. Chandler. Our choir teacher, Mrs. Armstrong, modernized the set with Madonna's "Vogue." We also had an appearance by the meticulously choreographed Supremes and a bat-biting Ozzy Osborne.

The showstopper came when Mr. Kennedy donned a skirt, stockings, and bra-like top stuffed with two oranges, showcasing his hip-swinging dance moves to Lady Gaga's "Born This Way." Students lost themselves in laughter to the point of tears, and Gaga got a standing O.

Over the weekend, however, complaints found their way to Dr. Jacobson. Concerned students said it demeaned women to have a man cross-dressing and making a spectacle of himself in women's clothing. No complaints surfaced about how Mrs. Lipska and I dressed as guys and imitated John Lennon and Paul McCartney. Dressing in drag brought lots of laughs along with lots of controversy.

Over the years, the cross-dressing skits at PHS made their way to hitherdom, along with kissing pigs and smashing cars. Times changed and we evolved, becoming more sensitive to people and piglets. And that's a good thing. In my last year of teaching, we resurrected the "Toy Glory" skit because none of the current students had seen it before. It was fun and inclusive and pleasantly anticlimactic—a good way to go out.

Chapter 5 – Just Hormones

Don't let schooling interfere with your education.
Mark Twain

I opened a student's copy of *The Scarlet Letter* to verify the number of the book for check-in purposes, and there, drawn inside the front cover, was a depiction of a huge barrel of a gun. Why would anyone at PHS be drawing a gun in a book? Platteville was not a hub of gang-related activity; though, like any high school, we had our share of disgruntled kids. Remember the three bomb threats in one year? But—a gun?

I dismissed the image as a fluke. Then I came upon it again. And again. I must be missing something. I examined the doodle from different angles. Finally, it occurred to me. These weren't guns at all. I was embarrassed by my gullibility. I did not remember this doodle from my high school days, though I did recall some kids wrote nasty add-ons next to people's names in textbooks, like "...is a slut," or "...eats shit." Or, they filled in a fake name in the space provided, such as "Ben Dover" or "Mike Hunt." But this?

Once I saw the symbol for what it was, I began to see it everywhere. On folders, desks, assignments. Had it been there all along? Had I been stupidly oblivious? Was I experiencing the Baader-Meinhof Syndrome where now that I noticed it, it seemed an obsession? I had a caricature of Shakespeare hanging on the wall by the pencil sharpener. One day I saw that Will's anatomy was showing through his knickers. Considering the often bawdy nature of Shakespeare's writing, he likely would have been proud of this appendage.

But still. This is school. Penises are not supposed to be part of the décor.

And it wasn't just drawings. These pubescent artists used all mediums, including poster putty, the whitish gray, pliable, sticky stuff I used to attach posters to the wall. I began finding tiny putty penis sculptures hanging around the room. On the wall near the light switch, on the white board, on the bulletin board near the door.

The frequency was real, not my imagination. They *were* obsessed. One would think that after almost sixteen years living with this anatomical feature, boys would be accustomed to it and not so driven to create crude replicas. All males have them, for heaven's sakes, and all females by this point know boys have them. While writing about this phenomena for this book, I did a Google search that stated this phallic art was prolific in ancient Greece and Rome as well. Men and boys, it seemed, had been enamored with depicting their penises since the time of cave drawings.

I needed to address the problem before it got even more out of hand. "Look, I know some of you like to doodle, and I realize at your age you are at the mercy of your hormones," I said one day, "but I've had it with the penis drawings and sculptures all over the place. It's inappropriate, and I don't want to see any more of them." They responded with giggles and grins. "Let's be mature about this, okay?"

They were surprised I used the word penis in my reprimand. I saw no other way than to confront the subject head on, pun intended. And, it helped. Fewer penis sightings occurred the rest of the year.

For a few years my penis speech became a standard yearly lecture to the sophomores. Later in my career I was assigned to teach juniors. Many of them would turn eighteen in the coming year, and I believed—I hoped—they would be more inclined to contain their sophomoric impulses. And I was right. Penises no longer surfaced everywhere, just an occasional pop up. I no longer had to give the speech, just a gentle reminder.

Sadly, even juniors sometimes reverted to their penis obsessions. As a reward for reading, studying and giving stellar efforts, I took my AP Language and Composition class outside to finger paint. We had studied movies and stories where water was the main theme, either in a romantic or realistic or naturalistic way: Hemingway's *Old Man and the Sea*, Melville's *Moby Dick*, Crane's "The Open Boat," and the film version of Norman Maclean's *A River Runs Through It*.

We took the paints, water, and paper to the sidewalk outside my room. Their objective was to create a piece of art with water depicted in a way that represented one of the stories we studied. They needed to be able to explain to the class whether their work conveyed *romanticism* (exaggerated themes, primarily happy and good), *realism* (themes representing both good and bad) or *naturalism* (themes of striving to overcome nature) and why.

The sun was shining, and the air was just-right warm without being too hot. Students sprawled on the sidewalk engrossed in their work, choosing the different colors, experimenting with various textures and techniques to portray the essence of the stories. Shelly chose the vibrant hues of a sunset over the water from *A River Runs Through It*. It only needed Brad Pitt's face in the foreground to be a masterpiece. Jeremy splattered his white paint Jackson Pollock-style, which represented naturalism, as if a storm were churning up the blue waves in Stephen Crane's "The Open Boat."

I walked down the sidewalk, commenting on their creations and engaging them in conversation about their work. Then, I got to Nathan. His gigantic gray whale had suspiciously round tail fins and a tiny smile positioned at the tip of the long body. He said it was an exaggerated, romanticized Moby Dick swimming in the ocean, pleased with himself for escaping Captain Ahab.

And just when I thought junior boys were beyond this immaturity. (Deep sigh.)

* * *

Some of the best suggestions for curriculum additions, especially movies and projects came from the students themselves. It made my day when they saw connections between what we studied in class to current movies, trends, and history. They were applying their knowledge, and that, after all, was my ultimate goal: to awaken their thinking about the timeless universality of humans and the world we cohabit.

Years ago a student recommended watching the Robin Williams movie *Dead Poets Society* to illustrate transcendentalism and the works of Henry David Thoreau and others of the romantic movement. It portrayed the transcendental concepts of seizing the day, learning from nature, and trusting one's inner voice, so perfectly that I used it every year until I retired.

The tradition of having a transcendental day to honor Ralph Waldo Emerson and his friend and student Thoreau began in a similar manner midway through my teaching career. After reading parts of Thoreau's *Walden* and Emerson's essays about nature, one of my female students proposed we do something "transcendental" and unconventional in the authors' honor.

"Thoreau believed that in changing it up now and then by taking a different path to the pond, right?" she said. "Why don't we go outside and build a snowwoman instead of a snowman?"

Six inches of snow had fallen the day before. According to the forecasters, more was on the way. Later that day we would be released at 1:30 due to heavy snow.

It seemed like a great idea. Students went to their lockers to gather coats and mittens. It was about thirty degrees, making the snow a perfect packing consistency. One group began with small snowballs, rolling the biggest one around until it picked up so much snow that three of us could barely push it. I helped them lift the mid-sized one on top of the first, packing snow around the middle to secure it. The smallest one became the head. Another group of students worked independently, which was also transcendental, they told me. They chose to make their own unique snow creation and rolled their snowballs around until they were gigantic.

"Trying to outdo us?" I asked. "You're going to have a hard time getting those stacked on top of one another." They continued working, laughing at my observation. Out of the corner of my eye I saw smiles creep over the faces of the students in my group. But I focused on our project. One student in my group retrieved the colored markers from my room, and we added features to the face of our snowwoman—eyes, nose, and mouth—and pink cheeks. We named her "Emily" after Emily Dickenson who wrote poems that were inspired by themes in nature. We used clumps of dead grass for the hair and stuck in sticks for the arms. She looked distinctive and lovely in her long white frosty dress.

During passing time in the hall after lunch, the senior English teacher said, "That's quite the snow sculpture your students made out there. Do you think they'll get in trouble for it?"

"Trouble? It's a snowwoman...in honor of Emily Dickinson."

My colleague led me to the window in her room and pointed at the two gigantic snowballs juxtaposed at the base of the flagpole. In that moment I promised myself I would never again underestimate the entertainment value that adolescents placed on phallic symbols.

Another instance of literary inspiration occurred when my juniors studied romanticism. We read the stories "The Devil and Tom Walker" by Washington Irving, "Quitters, Inc." by Stephen King, and "The Open Window" by Saki, a.k.a. H. H. Munro. They seemed to grasp the idea that romanticism isn't only the traditional lovey-dovey, mushy stuff of movie romances, but *exaggerated* elements, as in supernatural happenings, good versus evil, emphasis on nature, symbolic names, and, above all, a happy ending. "Quitters" was their favorite. They were familiar with the work of Stephen King, and the primary theme of the main character trying to quit smoking was relatable, if not personal, for many.

My student Jessica suggested we watch the film *The Notebook*, as it exemplified many of the elements we'd discussed. Her peers rallied in agreement.

"I'll think about it," I responded. My husband and I saw *The Notebook* in the theater. We enjoyed the story as well as the actors. I didn't recall any supernatural happenings, but it contained exaggeration and natural elements—and a perfectly choreographed ending.

"We'll watch it on one condition," I told them. "You will be expected to recognize and give examples from the movie of the romantic elements we studied."

"Yeah, yeah. We can do that. No problem."

Most everyone enjoyed the film and recognized the elements; notably, the scene where Noah takes Ali out in the boat to look at the swans. Nature is trumpeting its glory. The imagery of the water and trees and swans reflects the feelings swelling between them. Then the storm rumbles in, rendering the tension of Ali being engaged to someone else. And then the rain falls and they paddle to the dock and run to the house where Noah carries her inside. They begin tearing at each other's clothes. Students were rapt. The intensity of the scene became uncomfortable, but the camera cuts away at just the right moment to avoid an R rating.

To ease the tension, Jessica blurted, "What are they doing, Mrs. Kies?"

"They're going swimming," I said, the first *appropriate* answer that entered my mind. "You can't go swimming with your clothes on."

For the remainder of the year, "swimming" became the class code word for having sex. When we read *The Scarlet Letter* and made reference to Hester Prynne and Arthur Dimmesdale's tryst, Mitchell said, "You mean Reverend Dimmesdale and Hester went swimming?"

One day in the midst of a discussion the day before prom I snatched a teachable moment and extended the metaphor: "It's never a good thing to let anyone talk you into going swimming if you don't want to...and...when and if you do decide to go swimming sometime in the future, remember to be safe and wear a life jacket."

Like the students, I would occasionally come across a movie that complemented our literary studies. Rather than read a story and show the film rendition of that same story, I preferred to find a visual aid that conveyed the themes and engaged visual learners.

After we studied Hemingway stories, like *Old Man and the Sea* and "Big Two-Hearted River," I often showed the film *A River Runs Through It* (1992). *A River Runs Through It* is based on the autobiographical novel by Norman Maclean and exemplifies how water, as in the stories we read in class, provides a living, food, and lessons about life for the main characters. Set in the 1920s, the time period is also apropos. The character of Paul Maclean, Norman's brother, resembles Hemingway in many respects. He's a writer, a risk taker, a tough guy, a lady's man...and he loves fishing.

Robert Redford narrates the film. The first time I showed the movie in the late 1990s, I commented that the actor who played Paul was pretty cute and looked like he could be Robert Redford's son.

"Mrs. Kies—you know that cute guy is Brad Pitt, right?" asked Maria. "He's hot...and famous. But who is Robert—

Renfield, anyway?"

My comments on an actor's attractiveness surprised my students. Like when they saw me at the grocery store buying food to eat or at the drug store picking out shampoo. That week, and for several years thereafter, students showered me with Brad Pitt photos. Brad with long hair, short hair, blond hair, streaked hair, brown hair. Brad with his shirt on, shirt off, smiling, smirking. Brad alone, and Brad with his various love interests.

There was no getting around it, he was beautiful. "One can't throw beauty like that away," I said and added each on to the wall by my desk. Students were proud to contribute to what became known as my shrine to Brad, and I couldn't disappoint them, right? After a few years, the entire wall by my desk was plastered with Brad pics.

Alas, time passes, and things change. None of us are immune to it. Even Brad.

Alas, time passes, and things change. None of us are immune to it. Even Brad. During my last year of teaching, a student looked at the wall of pics behind my desk and asked, "Who is that guy in all those photos, Mrs. Kies?" I looked at her in disbelief. For years now Brad had peered over my shoulder as I had graded papers and planned lessons. Was I becoming passe? On the day I retired, I used my phone to take a picture...and then threw them all away.

My favorite poster titled "Renaissance Minstrels" hung above a bookshelf behind my desk. It portrayed the Beatles: John, Paul, George, and Ringo, sitting around a table chatting it up and wearing Shakespearean garb. Students who approached my desk often asked who these guys were too. Really? Maybe there should be a class on pop culture literacy.

I tried to do my part to enlighten students about the Lone Ranger and Tonto, and they filled me in about Sponge Bob Square Pants.

* * *

We were a third of the way through the year. My Brad wall was looking fine as can be and my stapler was intact, though Jessica still jumped and squealed every time she used it. Maybe she had aichmophobia (fear of pointed objects).

Thankfully, no one had mentioned the puppy incident in a while. I could only hope that story had run its course and I would hear no more about it.

PART II–EDUCATING ME

Chapter 6 – Jane's World

Reserving judgment is a matter of infinite hope.
Nick Carraway in F. Scott Fitzgerald's *The Great Gatsby*

My first job out of college in 1992 was as a teaching assistant to Jane, a special education teacher at PHS. Jane, if you remember, was the teacher who fell asleep and began to snore in the auditorium during the superintendent's delivery of data during a district inservice meeting. John Erickson, the Director of Special Education, said the aide position paid about $9,000 per year. A sad pittance for anyone, and here I was, a recent college grad. At this time, full-time teachers were earning $21,000. Oh, well. At least the job provided health care benefits for my family and me. I hoped to prove myself and nab an English teaching position when one opened up at PHS or the surrounding area.

Jane was an ED teacher. ED stood for Emotionally Disturbed, which meant that students with this designation had been determined to lack the ability to form and maintain relationships with peers and teachers. Eventually, that term changed to EBD, emotional behavioral disability.

I was a bit skeptical. I'd heard stories. Not about the kids. About Jane. Like the day the women faculty members went out for lunch at the Timber's restaurant where diners were routinely entertained by Bob Velzy playing a custom-made pipe organ. People came from all over the tri-state area to see and hear this one-of-a-kind instrument.

The volume that day was so loud the women couldn't hear each other while chatting. And Jane had come to chat, not to hear the organ. When Bob finished his song, Jane politely asked him to turn down the volume. During his next set when the chords again assailed their eardrums and drowned out their conversation, Jane took direct action and unplugged the organ from the outlet.

In looks, Jane matched her name: plain. Attractive, but unassuming, she wore no makeup or jewelry. Clad in jeans, T-shirts or sweaters, sneakers or Birkenstocks, depending on the season, she kept life simple. Her dark curly hair was clipped into a practical bob, and wire rimmed glasses framed mischievous blue-gray eyes. Tell Jane a joke, especially a raunchy one, and her body folded into a full-bellied guffaw, echoing down the hall and around the corner to the library.

I found that Jane's room was better than any college class I'd taken in learning how to deal with students. A model of extraordinary patience and skill, she knew how to bond with those who carried around weighty chips on their shoulders. Her students' moods were sporadic, volatile, and contagious. If one of them came to school hungover, tired, or just plain pissy, the rest followed suit until another front blew in. I knew if I could learn to manage these students, any future English class would be a leisurely stroll down the hall.

Jane was genuine but blunt, a sort of left-wing Dirty Harry. Though she was a tiny wisp of a woman, a full-fledged gale couldn't rock her philosophical boat. In her youth she accessorized her formal prom dress with stylish combat boots. Out of concern for soldiers and people in general, she protested the Vietnam War and took on any cause that championed the downtrodden. She'd joined the establishment as a special education teacher to try to help all kids be the best they could be. She understood their disillusionment with life and authority figures. The calling suited her, and she was good at it.

Administrators could never figure out the least disruptive place in the school for Jane and her students. Every few years her room assignment changed. The year I was her aide we occupied the now abandoned lab where I'd taken General Science with Mr.

McIntyre as a freshman. This was deja vu. The same glass-doored storage cabinets lined the walls, and the two sinks remained, one in the back of the room and one in front. Even the tables were configured the same until Jane and I moved them around.

Prone to exploring boundaries, our students immediately turned on each Bunsen burner valve upon entering the room. To their dismay, they discovered the gas supply had been shut off. Morning light spilled onto the black-topped tables from the large eastern window. In the winter, we all donned our coats when the arctic air snuck in through the cracked seals that hadn't been repaired or replaced, probably since I sat in there for General Science.

Out of our ten students, five stayed with Jane and me for the entire day. Others, depending on their emotional capabilities and IEPs (Individual Education Plans), attended some regular classes when appropriate for their needs. This educational strategy was known as utilizing the least restrictive environment. Our curriculum for those with us all day included a life skills unit, part of which was to teach healthy eating and living. Every Monday we planned a menu for Thursday and then went shopping on Tuesday or Wednesday.

One day Casey, Sam, and I hopped in the school van to purchase the list of supplies from the local supermarket for our meal of lasagna, salad, French bread, and cake. Jane and the rest of the crew stayed to clean and ready the kitchen we used in a trailer behind the school. This trailer, at one time, had been used to teach vocational skills for those hoping to get jobs in the hotel or restaurant business.

Casey, an intelligent, sandy-haired young man, was not too keen on completing school work. Often aloof, he slept whenever he could get away with it. He seemed to struggle with depression. He and Sam lived in the local group home, the establishment where the courts sometimes opted to send teens after they had accumulated minor offenses in cities like Milwaukee or Madison.

Chris, the group home manager, said judges preferred this placement route rather than Juvenile Hall in order to facilitate rehabilitation. Surrounded by cornfields, our small community challenged the comfort levels of the young men who were accustomed to the anonymity and temptations in the city. Separated from their bad-influence friends, they would have to look harder to find mischief. The group home promoted structure, something their homes often lacked: household chores, budgeting money, and peer support were skills that were stressed.

The counselors, usually college students working on education or counseling degrees, supervised the residents and tracked their school performance and behavior. A point system allowed the teen boys privileges and home visits if they complied and did their assigned chores. Oftentimes, they might come close to earning enough points for a home visit, then blow it by doing something stupid.

Early on, Jane explained to me their tendency of self-sabotage. If they got a poem published in the literary magazine or got a good grade on their science test and you gave them a compliment, they balked. The feeling of accomplishment was foreign and frightening. They seemed to believe if they succeeded, they'd somehow sold out. If they weren't that "bad kid" anymore, then who were they? And, what big things would people expect of them now that they were seen as being capable?

At the supermarket I wheeled the cart down the canned food aisle looking for tomato sauce. Casey walked well ahead of Sam and me, scouting for the best product for the best price. At least

57

that's what he said he was doing.

"Hey, here's some good spaghetti sauce!" he said, bending and pointing to a jar on the bottom shelf. As he did so, his fashionable baggy jeans slipped from his hips and fell to his ankles. There, in the middle of the canned food section of the grocery store, with several patrons bearing witness, Casey bared his undie-less white butt for all to see. Sam busted a gut laughing.

"Sorry," I said to the woman beside me. After he yanked up his drawers, I latched onto Casey's arm and marched him to the front of the store. I pointed to a bench in the entryway and ordered him to sit and wait for Sam and me to finish shopping, threatening some lame, shoot-from-the-hip consequence. Like, "Don't move or you'll never be able to go shopping again in your lifetime."

When we got back to school, I asked Jane, "What would you have done in a situation like that?"

"Well, I guess you've been properly initiated to shopping with the boys," she said amid snorts of hearty laughter. "You did fine. And, you're right. He won't be going on any errands again any time soon."

I was stymied. What had Casey's mother or father done at times like this? His family, unlike many of the other boys, was affluent. He dressed well and was not in need of material things.

Jane tried to help me understand. "Each student has his own set of circumstances. There's no standard pattern and no standard solution. I try to leave the in-depth analyses to their counselors and psychologists. Our job is to try to teach them what we can about successfully getting along in the world. The problem is, we get them late in their development and we don't have them very long."

As situations presented themselves, Casey calculated on how to capitalize on them. He was smart and played the system. In contrast, Sam reacted impulsively...to everything. His red hair, brown eyes, freckles, and bounding interactive nature reminded me of a puppy. Not as physically attractive as Casey, Sam made up for it with his boyish charm. One day I teased him about his freckles. He chased me around a table in the classroom, pretending to be angry. From then on, I was his pal. At the other end of this childishness crouched his anger. He was like the Seven Dwarfs combined into one person. You never knew which one you were going to encounter: Happy, Grumpy, Dopey, Bashful, Doc, Sleepy or, during allergy season, Sneezy. Now, I recognize that he probably had what doctors diagnose as bipolar disorder.

One day Casey and Sam were putting together a picture puzzle of a castle during their free time. Sam saw a piece that he thought would fit into the moat. He reached for it, but Casey anticipated his intention and beat him to it.

"Hey, I was going to use that piece," Sam said, his face flushing so red it muted his freckles.

"I don't see your name on it," Casey said, turning the piece over in his palm.

"Give it here, moron!" Sam yelled, stomping his foot on the floor and holding out his hand.

Casey looked him in the eye, smiled, and put the puzzle piece in his pocket. His smirk said it all: *Make me. I dare you.*

He knew Sam couldn't resist the taunt. The argument escalated until Sam was shouting obscenities.

"Hey, guys, cut it out, okay? Chill," I said, though no one on this planet ever calmed down when told that.

Sam picked up two fists of the puzzle pieces, threw them on the floor and jumped up and down, screaming, "You effing took my damned puzzle piece! You effhead, give it to me!"

Jane left the other students she'd been talking to and came to the rescue. "Hey, Sam. How about we go for a walk outside? It's nice and sunny today." She motioned toward the door. With some gentle urging, he left with her, spewing additional vulgar names at Casey over his shoulder. Jane, the guru of calm, provided Sam with the opportunity to de-escalate and save face.

"Don't you have anything better to do than aggravate people?" I asked Casey after they left.

"No," he said. "Don't you?"

Jane was always on the lookout for ways to give the boys positive experiences. So, when Chris, the group home manager, asked if we'd supervise the boys in painting the cement block walls in the basement, Jane jumped on it as a lesson opportunity for art class. After covering the floors, old pool table, and couch with discarded sheets, the boys wielded rollers to apply a base coat of white to two of the walls.

For content, they decided on attempting murals from J. R. R. Tolkien's *The Hobbit.* This was before the movie *Lord of the Rings* made it to the screen. Jane and I read them the character descriptions from the book so they could render the images. Jason was artistically talented and drew the initial sketches they agreed upon: the hobbit Bilbo Baggins sitting by the entrance to his tree on one wall and the bearded wizard Gandalf in the midst of casting a spell on the other. Jane and I and the boys filled in Jason's outlines with brightly colored paint. When finished, we proudly signed our work.

Years later we discussed Tolkien in one of my English classes. Afterward, one of the group home students told me about the murals on the basement walls at the house. "Oh, my gosh!" I said. "Are they still there?" I told him if he looked closely at the signatures of the artists below Bilbo Baggins' tree, he would recognize two of the artists' names: Jane's and mine.

Jane had a friend who led spelunking expeditions in area caves. She thought this would be a good bonding and learning experience for our students, so she gave Jeff a call and set up a day and time. Jeff warned that it would be a damp and dirty adventure. So, attired in old jeans, sweatshirts and shoes, we boarded the van. It was a sunny fall day as we met Jeff at the mouth of the cave. He outfitted us with hardhats and flashlights and told us we would be safe as long as we listened to him and followed his guidance. All heads nodded in compliance. Were these really our students? Jane and I traded surprised looks with each other.

The opening of the cave was low. Jeff demonstrated a crouching position and told us at one point we'd need to lower ourselves into a belly crawl. "If this sounds too challenging, no pressure. You can wait outside and enjoy this beautiful day. What do you think?"

Jane and the boys didn't hesitate for a moment. I do not like small spaces. The horror of being shut up in a box, put in a hole in the ground, and covered with soil has led me to opt for cremation. However, the fear of missing out on the caving adventure outweighed my claustrophobic worries. Following our leader Jeff, we slid on our butts down the slope to the opening, folded into a crouch, and in ten yards or so, dropped to our bellies. Like soldiers in training, we navigated the underground obstacle course. Bringing up the rear, I inched along, my hardhat bumping the ceiling with each wiggle forward. I couldn't help but think about how one minute shift of the earth could make us into a human pâté. But there was no going back now. How would I ever turn around?

We made it to what Jeff referred to as "the BIG room" and stood up. He said to be quiet because we didn't want to disturb the bats hanging on the walls and ceiling. *Yikes!* He used his flashlight to show us our cohabitants. The boys gaped in awe. Oh, great, tight spaces, now bats. Once, when my husband was not at home, a bat emerged from nowhere and swooped throughout the house. I crawled to the nearest door to escape, leaving my children inside to fend for themselves.

Jeff led us down a corridor off the big room to a place he

called "the mud room." To get into the mud room, one had to butt-slide down a flat rock to land in the six inches of mud at the bottom. Again, Jane and the boys wasted no time. Their fun-filled shrieks drifted to where I was happy to remain at the top. When they tired of splashing in the goop, I offered a hand to help pull them up the slippery rock while someone gave them a boost from behind.

Before making our way to daylight, we sat cross legged in a circle on a level spot on the floor just off the big room. Jeff shined his flashlight onto his face and told us all to stare at him for thirty seconds. When he turned off the light, no matter where we looked, his facial features still glowed eerily in the pitch dark.

On the ride home, the boys relived their adventure as if they'd just visited Disneyland. They took prideful joy in calling me a wimp. "Yeah, someone was too chicken to go into the mud room!" For days and weeks thereafter, they recapped every detail of the experience to anyone who would listen. Jane scored big with this activity. The bonding that occurred that day got us to the end of the year. Almost.

Because the cave adventure had been such a success, one day Jane and I took our five full-time students on a walk in the woods near the school for science class to observe the flora. A small stream cut through the land supporting wildlife and vegetation galore. Their assignment was to gather plant specimens to bring back to the classroom to identify. Each student would research and do a presentation on at least one plant.

Three of the boys hailed from an urban setting, so we warned them not to touch the shiny, three-leafed ivy plant variety. We even showed them a picture of it. Jane knew this warning might be taken as a dare. Her warning, like mine, didn't carry the same authority as Jeff's. She figured we'd done our part in educating them. If they broke out from a blistery poison ivy rash, they'd know better the next time. "Experiential learning," she called it.

We crossed the road and walked on the soft bed of needles under the grove of well-established pine trees to the stream where we thought the variety of vegetation would be most plentiful. It was a warm day, a few weeks before school adjourned for summer.

"I wonder if there are any 'shrooms around here," Sam said.

The other four guys laughed. "Not the kind of 'shrooms you're talking about," said Jake.

After some wandering through the woods, Sam found a mushroom. He held it in front of his mouth as if to take a bite.

"Not a good idea, Sam," Jane said. "Most mushrooms around here are poisonous, sometimes deadly."

"What about morels?" Sam asked. "Want a 'shroom, guys?" He held it out to them.

"Yeah, I bet you'll get high on that," Casey said.

When the guys didn't take him up on it, Sam upped the ante. "Here goes!" He stuffed the entire mushroom into his mouth. Jane, always cool and in control, was livid. I'd never seen her mad before. Fueled by fear, she told Sam how stupid he'd been and quickly led the way through the pines across the road to school. A call to the school nurse led to an immediate call to Wisconsin Poison Control. (This was before cell phones and Google searches.) Would he get sick? Die? Should we rush him to the hospital? We imagined the next-day headlines: *PHS Student Eats Poison Mushroom, Dies: Teacher, Aide charged with negligence.*

Jane had had the wherewithal to pick up one of the mushrooms and put it in her pocket. She described it and where we found it to the attendant on the phone. It turned out to be one of the few nonpoisonous mushrooms in the area, besides morels. Sam was lucky, but it didn't seem to faze him. He'd created this drama and received attention. In his mind, the risk was worth it.

Not long into the year, I realized that the term education experts gave to our students, "at-risk," described more than their high school graduation potential. It applied to their personal lives as well. That same year, Jason bragged to buddies about the pellet gun he brought to school and stored in his locker. This was before Columbine, but bringing a weapon to school was not an acceptable thing to do. He said he'd brought it to sell to a friend, but the principal and the school board were not impressed with his entrepreneurial efforts. He was expelled.

Another student, Zach, resided at the group home because he was an inhalant addict, often stealing gasoline, white-out, glue, or whatever he could get his hands on to get high. He was tall, bright, and handsome, but also unpredictable and unmotivated. He was adopted as a baby and, according to his parents, had always posed significant behavioral challenges. He told me once that he was sent home on the first day of kindergarten for taking off his shoes and peeing in them in the middle of the hallway.

For about a month, I worked one-on-one with Zach. We tackled algebra first. For a break, and as incentive, we would tip a couple of empty wastebaskets on their sides as goals and play some indoor hockey. He had seen *Above and Beyond*, the 1990 biopic about Wayne Gretzky, and idolized him. The strategy worked for a while. He completed assignments and we moved on to science. This time as a reward I helped him make a cake for one of his group home friends. He decorated it himself. *Happy Birthday, Michael!* he inscribed with runny blue icing.

One day Zach didn't show up for school. He'd been on a roll as far as attendance and work completion, so this seemed weird. Later that day the school psychologist said that Zach had been sent away and would no longer be attending PHS.

"But why?" I asked. "He was making progress, succeeding." The school psychologist reiterated Jane's warning to me that ED students often sabotage their own success out of fear of the unknown. A few days later I found out the rest of the story. Zach had hung a cat by the neck in a tree behind the group home.

I was so disappointed. Disappointed that Zach was unable to embrace the progress he had made personally and academically. I was also shocked. Shocked because in the four weeks I'd worked with him I had not seen any indications that he was capable of violence, let alone hanging a cat.

Three of our part-time students died a few years after graduating, or at least when they should have graduated. One young man was found dead from a drug overdose. Whether accidental or intentional was unknown. Two others perished in separate drunk driving accidents. And, Zach, too, passed away in his twenties from the results of inhalant abuse. This past year I read about another of the five boys Jane and I taught that year. He died at the age of forty-seven after serving time in a Dubuque jail. I don't know what happened to Sam and Casey. I can only hope they found a peaceful way in the world.

That year was transformative. Teaching students and caring about them can make a difference in their lives, but that difference is not immediate, not always successful, and seldom easy. By the time a student is in high school, habits are well established, especially the bad ones. Later in my career, while teaching English, I often thought of those young men, my first students, especially when teaching about Henry David Thoreau. "The mass of men lead lives of quiet desperation," he wrote in *Walden*. I would add that some men and women through no fault of their own are much more desperate than others, and some much less quiet about it.

65

Chapter 7 – The Best We Can Be

Time flies over us, but leaves its shadow behind.
Nathaniel Hawthorne

After working with Jane that year, I was fortunate to land a part-time English teaching position at PHS which evolved into full-time in 1993. Yay! About ten years into this position, I headed for the teachers' lounge on a snowy, December day for lunch. Three men outfitted in camouflage greeted me at the door. One smiled and presented me with a brown paper bag.

"Thank you," I said. Each staff member who entered got the same.

"What's this for?" Brian asked. Brian was known for asking the questions at faculty meetings that we all wanted to ask but didn't.

"It's a little something to show our appreciation for the great work you all do teaching our children," the tallest one said. "Enjoy!"

We all knew there was no such thing as a free lunch. But food was food, and we pounced upon it like prey whenever it appeared in the teachers' lounge. Anything sitting around was fair game, so we often stooped to hiding our snacks for fear of losing them to hungry peers. John's large bag of chips had disappeared a few weeks before, and we'd been eying each other with suspicion ever since.

I tore away the waxy wrapper and bit into the sandwich, opened my chips and set the cookie aside for dessert. A few minutes later, Jane wandered into the lounge. "Thank you very much," she said, taking the sack. She made a quick assessment of the situation. Instead of sitting down, she began loading up on as many lunches as she could carry. "Thank you," she said. "My students will appreciate these."

"Ma'am, these aren't for your students," the balding recruiter said. "They're for you—the teachers—"

"Oh. No, thank you. I brought my own." After two trips of deliveries to her students, Jane retrieved her lunch from the refrigerator and sat down in her usual place at the end of the table.

As anticipated, the recruiters transitioned from benevolent food providers to presenters. Using a laptop, they flipped through PowerPoint slides projected on to the wall as we devoured our food. The shorter recruiter did most of the talking, while his two muscular cohorts stood on either side of the table, their hands clasped behind their backs.

The speaker began outlining the exceptional educational opportunities and benefits the military had to offer. Meanwhile, Jane initiated conversation as she did every day, as if the recruiters were pictures on the wall. "Please pass the salt. Oh, and the pepper would be good, too. Thanks. Has anyone met the new student yet? I believe he's from Cuba City."

The recruiters gave Jane a three-way version of *the teacher look*, which translated: *We're talking, lady. Shut the hell up, and cut it out already!*

She paid them no heed, and they picked up where they left off. Jane reached for a napkin, deftly nudging the computer screen sitting on the table. The presenter kept talking and repositioned the monitor. This exchange of maneuvers occurred a couple of times. The two recruiters took their hands from behind their backs and crossed their arms over their chests.

"Sir, this is our lunch time," Jane said, breaking the stalemate. "We get twenty-six minutes, and we don't want to spend it listening to you." Her tone was soft, and her hands accompanied her words in delicate, meaningful movements. It was in this same manner she talked to her most difficult students.

We all nervously nibbled our cookies. It was like witnessing a car accident—not pretty but impossible to look away or leave. Part of me wished Jane would be quiet to avoid conflict, and the other part admired her chutzpah and secretly cheered her on. None of the rest of us had the spunk to challenge these guys who had successfully bribed us with food and ambushed our lunch time.

"Ma'am, other people may want to listen," the presenter said. "If you don't, that's okay. You can go somewhere else to eat."

Danette's foot tapped mine under the table. We exchanged knowing looks. That silly fellow. He had no idea that Jane the pacifist could become as impactful as an M16. With no biological children, her students were her kids, and her maternal instincts were as fierce as a mother bear. She objected to the glittering promises some recruiters routinely made, luring her kids with free pens and trinkets into a life that they were not ready for emotionally, intellectually, or physically.

She dabbed her mouth with a napkin and placed her hands in her lap. "Me leave? I beg your pardon? This is *my* workplace, *my* lunch, *my* time. I'm not going anywhere. There are plenty of other rooms in this school where you can do your presentation for those who wish to attend. Now, if you don't mind, I'd like to eat in peace." After having her say, she continued to eat and visit, nixing any further debate on the subject.

Not everyone in the lounge agreed with Jane's tactics. But no one said anything. With no backing, the men said a few closing words and packed it in until the second lunch period. No doubt, praying that Jane wasn't available or hungry enough to eat twice that day.

Jane retired at the end of 2011 after Wisconsin's Governor Scott Walker instituted Act 10, also known as The Budget Repair Bill, doubling what teachers paid toward their insurance and retirement benefits. (More about Act 10 and the devastating effect it had on state workers' lives, communities, and professions is coming up in Chapter 15.) After crunching the numbers with the help of the superintendent at the time, Jane found that the additional money taken from her check would reduce her earnings to the point where retiring was not only beneficial...but necessary. She and her husband would need the retirement package offered by the district to continue running their horse farm outside of town where Jane cared for her own animals and any needy animals that came her way. Jane and her husband soon became certified to care for mentally challenged adults in their home. She continued to attend yoga class twice a week, and I had lunch with her on occasion.

Then, Jane got cancer. Pancreatic cancer.

She said she'd always pictured herself living into her eighties, sitting peacefully in her rocking chair on the back porch with her husband and animals. She took treatments and fended off the inevitable as best she could for almost two years. Naturally thin, she got thinner. She lost her hair—but not her sense of humor. Before she became too ill, friends hosted a benefit to help with medical bills. Also, her most recent teacher's aide, Cathy, organized an evening Mississippi River cruise in her honor. Jane loved it. And she loved us. We know because she made sure to tell each and every one of us that evening.

One day after yoga class, I was talking with one of Jane's special education colleagues. "I visited Jane yesterday and wanted to cheer her up. Instead, when I left, I was the one who felt cheered up by her. How does she do that?"

Friends and family brought Jane food and cards and stories to show support. But, Jane flipped the script. One day my husband and I drove down the lane to Jane's farm south of town bearing fresh eggs from my backyard chickens, homemade cookies, and books. A throng of dogs announced our arrival, greeting us with wagging tails and gentle nose nudges. Jane let us and the dogs in, thanked us for our gifts, and offered us a seat in the living room. After sniffing us sufficiently, the dogs plopped on the floor at our feet. Except one, Jane's favorite, who cozied up to her on the couch for some much appreciated ear scratching. A couple of cats wandered in and checked us out too.

Jane told us about the pleasant young man who'd administered her last chemo treatment who noticed she was reading *Calypso*, the David Sedaris book I'd lent her. He told her he found Sedaris hilarious, too, and looked forward to reading that one. Just then, Jane pointed out the window, her laugh erupting with pure authenticity. "Look! See Donnie?" she asked. "Listen. He can't sing a lick." Donnie was one of the special needs adults living with Jane and her husband. Astride the four-wheeler, he was bumping along in the field wearing earphones shouting out the words to his favorite songs at the top of his lungs. We listened. Jane's laughter was not unfounded. Donnie's driving far surpassed his singing ability.

The dogs escorted us back to our car. Jane stood in the doorway waving, and we pulled away with big smiles, light hearts, and a book about raising chickens.

The last time I had lunch with Jane, we met at Steve's Pizza Palace in Platteville. We talked about old times and old students and laughed like it was yesterday. Afterward, we went to her car. She opened the trunk and handed me the books I'd lent her. She also bestowed upon me her yoga mat. She was always giving. I miss what Jane gave to the world. I miss her kindness and love, her wisdom and wit, and, above all, her ability to savor the good in people and her bravery to challenge the status quo.

Jane's body left this world on Tuesday, February 16, 2021, at the age of sixty-eight. Her spirit lives on in all teachers who work with students who have special needs.

Dear Teachers and Staff
I know you are busy. Very busy. Too busy.
On those occasions when students badly need
discipline and boundaries, please try to model
your instruction with patience and kindness like Jane did.
Signed,
Jane's Friend

Chapter 8 – Young Rascals

"Whadda ya gonna do?"
Tony Soprano

It's true. English teachers have no life beyond grading papers, assigning classic novels, and making sure the world speaks in grammatically correct sentences. We tend to be a ridiculously optimistic lot who search for creative ways to promote the importance of reading, writing, thinking, and communicating. To accomplish these goals, year after year we attempt to expose our pupils to cultural perspectives and language from literary classics, like *Huckleberry Finn, To Kill a Mockingbird, The Scarlet Letter*, and *Romeo and Juliet,* etc. Remember these? We adore these works, their authors, their messages. Why shouldn't our students? Why shouldn't everyone? Don't you?

Whenever I announced to the class we would be reading a classic novel, complaints resounded shrill and sure like disgruntled cats yowling: "Why do we have to read this? Can't we read something written in this century? A good book for a change with words we can understand? Who decides what makes a classic book? A room full of English teachers? No wonder."

My response to the first question evolved. "Because I said so!" seemed lazy, so I developed something more refined: "Classic literature mirrors what people have thought, observed, and experienced through the ages. It helps us gain understanding about eras and cultures beyond our own, so maybe we can avoid their mistakes. From it, we gain insight and compassion into what it means to be human."

Though I deemed this defense to be on point and eloquent, it failed to crack the hard nuts. Some didn't bother to pretend to read and brazenly strolled into class with the Sparknotes app open on their phones. At least they were reading something. Even if it was at a sixth grade reading level. Then there was always that one kid, like Josh, who puffed out his chest and announced to the class, "I've never read an entire book in my life, and I get by just fine."

I mentioned that this wasn't something one should go around bragging about. He heeded me not.

"I always get B's on the tests by listening in class," he said.

How could I effectively explain to him that it is not the grade that matters but the skill, knowledge, and cognitive development that happens in the process of reading? Why did getting students to read have to be a game of bribes and punishments? In my first year of teaching *Huck Finn* to juniors, I assigned the first six chapters. They were short chapters, only a few pages each. I told students there would be no study guide, and they applauded. I was such a virgin teacher then. I thought their approval was a good thing. On the day the reading was due I arranged the desks in a big circle in anticipation of the lively face-to-face book discussion to come.

I started it off with the first question: "What did you think of how Huck tricked Miss Watson by sneaking out of the house?"

They all stared at the cover of the book on their desks.

Crickets.

I tried another approach: "What did you think of the requirements to get into Tom Sawyer's gang?"

No one looked at me for fear I'd call on them.

More crickets.

"How many of you did the reading?"

Resounding crickets.

I suspect the few who read didn't want to risk saying so for fear of being ostracized...or smacked over the head by their peers. A couple piped up and said they didn't like the book, and

73

that's why they didn't read.

"That's like saying you hate fish tacos without ever trying them. It's okay if you don't like the book. I'm fine with that, but in order to voice a valid opinion, you have to read it so you can be specific about your dislikes. We call it a critique. We learn to back up our opinions using evidence."

Out of necessity, I began to give daily reading quizzes to motivate the unmotivated.

Another complaint stemmed from the fact that most of the classics weren't real. They were fiction. "It never really happened," said Malcolm. "Why would I want to read about it if it's not real?"

"Do you watch TV programs or movies?" I asked. "You know that *The Sopranos* and *CSI* may be based on reality, but they are fictional, right? So are most movies."

"If you assigned stories like *The Sopranos* and *CSI*, I might actually read them," Ron said. The class snickered but concurred with fervent nodding.

Touché.

This revelation spurred me to incorporate some contemporary and nonfiction reading into my curriculum. As I previously mentioned, one of my colleagues recommended "Quitters, Inc." from Stephen King's *Night Shift*. It's a gritty story about an organization that implements mob-like tactics such as electro-shocking spouses to get its customers to quit smoking. Students could identify with the perils of tobacco addiction. And, the dark humor appealed to them. I paired it with "The Devil and Tom Walker" by Washington Irving, written one hundred and fifty years earlier than *Night Shift*. Both authors used elements of exaggeration, symbolic character names, and the theme of good versus evil. "Quitters, Inc." became a favorite and a staple every year.

"Fiction is often more honest than nonfiction," I explained

one day, and we discussed why this might be. Authors writing biographies or autobiographies take into consideration what other people might think or say about their content. There could be repercussions. Will it offend someone? Do I really want to share this personal tidbit? What will readers think of me? What if the person I'm writing about or their family takes offense? Did others see an incident differently?

These decisions color an author's narrative and temper their writing. Authors writing fiction focus on the story without concern for impressions and disclosures of others. Be aware that I contemplated all the above questions while writing this memoir.

One Friday I cleared off the books and notes from my podium. It was my students' turn to stand up front. We'd been reading poetry. If getting them to read fiction was hard, imagine their reaction to poetry! I knew only a few would read poetry on their own without threat of torture, so we completed all the work in class.

We examined literary techniques like alliteration, allusion, and metaphors that authors used to communicate their ideas more clearly. For example, consider the sentence, "The snake slithered down the path." This is good. However, "A slithering shadow, the snake cut me off in the path," conveys the visual image, as well as the author's reaction. We read poems from our literature book by Elizabeth Bishop, Sylvia Plath, May Swenson, and others. For their assignment, students were to use those works as inspiration to write a poem of their own, emulating some of the devices we had studied.

Barry was in my fifth period. He was absent a lot. At least one to two days per week. When he came back, he looked healthy. I considered that maybe he had issues with depression. My goal was to help him get caught up once he got back. He was good at making up his work. How well he completed it—well—that's a whole other topic.

"Hey, Barry, good to see you? How are you feeling?"

"Better, Mrs. Kies. Much better."

"Students are reading their poems to the class today. Were you here when I explained this assignment?"

"Yeah, yeah, I was. I'm finished with my poem. I can read it today if you want."

"Wow, way to go, Barry."

Samantha read her poem about missing her sister who was away at college. Joe, another student, wrote an ode to his dirt bike. Karissa reminisced about her summer crush. Keeping with the spirit of the Beat poets, short for Beatniks, we snapped our fingers instead of clapping for each person.

Barry volunteered to go next. He chose to sit on the stool at the front and read from a piece of crumpled notebook paper. His speaking voice resonated deep and strong with inflection; his timbre, confident and soothing, like a young James Earl Jones. At the start of the year I noticed this and told him that he might want to consider a career in TV or radio.

He said his poem was a riddle and that we should be prepared to guess the answer at the end. He began to read:

I am silver and exact. I have no preconceptions.
Whatever I see I swallow immediately
Just as it is, unmisted by love or dislike.

His peers looked at each other in disbelief.

I am not cruel, only truthful,
The eye of a little god, four-cornered.
Most of the time I meditate on the opposite wall.

Soon, chuckles erupted. Heads turned to where I was sitting in the back of the room. Barry looked up, then continued.

It is pink, with speckles. I have looked at it so long
I think it is part of my heart. But it flickers.
Faces and darkness separate us over and over.

He read the last stanza, and classmates could no longer stifle their laughter.

He looked around confused, as if to ask, *What's going on?*

"Barry, perhaps you misunderstood the assignment," I said. "You were supposed to *write* a poem."

"Yeah, I know. Was there something wrong with it?"

I didn't want to embarrass him. But he had done this to himself. And his peers knew. We all knew.

"I liked it. In fact, the whole class enjoyed it when we read it from our literature book in class on Tuesday. 'Mirror' by Sylvia Plath, right?"

Barry's face reddened as he got up and returned to his seat. After class I approached him to discuss plagiarism and the seriousness of the offense. There were consequences beyond getting a failing grade on the assignment like he was going to get. At a higher level, one could get sued or expelled from a school for doing this.

Barry graduated from high school and eventually started his own DJ business. He now uses his gifted speaking voice to introduce other peoples' songs at weddings and important events, giving due credit to each and every artist he plays.

The following year I met Phil. He was assigned to my Advisor Group, which was similar to a homeroom. He was also in my Junior English class, so I saw him twice a day. At five feet, six inches, with a head of ginger-colored curly hair and a mass of freckles to top off his impish demeanor, performing was his gift. His eyes and physicality projected emotion with ease. For two successive years Phil landed the comedic character part in the school musical. He pulled the audience into his lair of high jinks and delivered lines into their applauding hands.

His theatrics in my room made class more fun than it probably should have been.

One day, with a pile of papers waiting to be corrected and students' chattering getting on my nerves, I snapped, "Be quiet—unless you want to lose all your participation points!"

As he left my room, Phil said, "You seem kind of stressed today, Mrs. Kies. Do you need a hug?"

"Thanks, but I don't do hugs, Phil." This was why I never, not for one second, considered being a K-4 teacher. Those students not only give you hugs but yank on your clothing and cling to your limbs like koala bears until you give them their desired attention.

A couple more times on hectic days, Phil offered a hug. I politely declined. "I appreciate your concern, but I'm good, Phil. Thanks."

"One of these times you're going to give me a hug, Mrs. Kies. Everyone needs one now and then."

After the holiday break, I was sitting at my desk during the Advisor Group. Grades were due the following Monday and parent/teacher conferences would consume two of my evenings. When students realized the A or B they'd envisioned at the beginning of the quarter was in fact a C or D—or worse—they panicked. It was official. Grade-begging season had arrived: "What can I do? Extra credit? Please, there must be something!"

"You're getting the grade you earned," I told them. "Extra credit was due a week ago." Some teachers didn't accept extra credit at all. Smart people.

As I took attendance on my computer, Phil noticed my angst in deflecting the grade beggars. He approached my desk and gave me a pat on the back and a loose hug. "I hope your day gets better, Mrs. Kies," he said. "See you later."

At the end of the year, Phil was leaving my room with the rest of the students. "I bet you're looking forward to summer break." He held out his arms, and this time I returned the hug. In my school days, relationships with teachers were formal. Hugging a teacher or a teacher hugging a student would have been as likely as a snowstorm in July and involved a trip to the principal's office for a reprimand for both teacher and student.

I credit Phil with teaching me to embrace students when appropriate. After hugging Phil, I began holding out my hand or giving a hug to students at the end of the year. And, if someone lost a loved one or went through a hard time, I also offered a heartfelt hug. That human connection, that ability to show compassion in this way can be far more powerful than words. And that's a candid admission coming from a vocabulary-loving English teacher.

One year my teaching assignment included four sections of sophomores and two of juniors, 140 students, give or take a few. One of those sophomores was Joey. He had the physique of a boxer, thick and low to the ground. His arms encased his body like parentheses. His brown skin, the color of just-right toast, was no doubt due to his self-proclaimed Native American heritage and hours spent outdoors. He played trombone in the band. This made him an anomaly. Most students who participated in band and music were self-disciplined, hard-working, polite, and smart. Well, Joey was smart.

"Mrs. Kies! Hey, Mrs. Kies! Come 'ere. I've got a cool trick to show you," he yelled from across the room.

Teachers learn what to ignore and what to address. It takes years of experience to hone, and sometimes we still make the wrong call.

My experience with Joey in summer school a year and a half prior should have told me that ignoring his plea was not an option. I tried anyway.

Teachers learn what to ignore and what to address. It takes years of experience to hone, and sometimes we still make the wrong call.

Making my way amid the rows of my third-hour students, I checked off completed *Fahrenheit 451* study guides. Later I would transfer the scores from my paper roster to the electronic grade book so concerned parents could check grades online to see if their teens were deserving of a social life that weekend.

"Mrs. Kies! Watch this, Mrs. Kies! Mrs. Kies! You're going to love this. Really, you are."

"I'll be there in just a minute, okay, Joey?" I responded, all the while thinking, Yeah right, Joey. What I'd really love is if you'd have your homework done for once—and learn to shut your mouth and not spout asinine, impertinent comments when I'm trying to teach.

Recalling Jane's patience, my inner teacher voice countered: Don't judge Joey like that. So what if he's been a major goofball in the past. So what if he hasn't turned in one assignment on time as long as you've known him. For heaven's sake, give him another chance.

As I checked off their work, students chatted. Sometimes snippets about who was dating whom or who was not talking to whom surfaced. A teacher can learn a lot about her students this way. And, there were those who asked thought-provoking questions about the reading assignment that they never would have asked in front of the entire class, concerned their peers might think them stupid or, heaven forbid—intelligent.

"You're going to love this, Mrs. Kies. It's so cool. Really."

Joey lived in the low-income apartment complex a few blocks from school. A revolving door of authority figures seemed to provide minimum stability to him and his numerous siblings. He now wore a shiny new ankle bracelet so the cops could keep better track of him after he stole and wrecked a car last summer.

I arrived at Joey's empty desk and placed a zero next to his name for the uncompleted assignment. I wanted to shake him and yell: Can't you see if you'd make use of those capable, dormant brain cells enclosed in that numb skull of yours you might be able to get off the merry-go-round to nowhere that you're riding? Oh, and Joey? You really need to go home and take a shower.

Instead, I said, "Okay, Joey, let's see it. This better be good."

"Oh, it is, Mrs. Kies. It is."

Again, I squashed my negativity. *What if he really did learn some sort of clever magic trick and you denied him that bit of encouragement he needed to succeed?* You don't want to be unappreciative of your students' talents and creativity. He might grow up to be a gifted musician or win an Academy Award or a Pulitzer or something. Many students don't perform well within the construct of the traditional school. Look at Albert Einstein and Steve Jobs. John Lennon's teachers yelled at him for doodling all sorts of silly words and drawings on his notebooks. Imagine!

The class and I watched as Joey held a quarter between his thumb and forefinger, making two big ceremonial figure eights in the air for all to see. "Watch closely, everyone, as I make this quarter disappear right before your very eyes."

Hmm. Sleight of hand. Maybe he's got something here. He certainly did enjoy center stage.

Joey made one final sweeping loop in the air for flair: "Now you see it; now you don't." He held the quarter up like a torch...then stuck it quickly and entirely up his right nostril. He then flashed his empty hands as if he'd just landed on the moon.

The room groaned. Eyes rolled. Weak titters circulated. The girl next to him said, "Yckthh!" and slid her desk away from his.

"What'd ya think? Pretty good, huh?" He grinned and removed the quarter.

In retrospect, I guess it's better that I had erred on the side of hope instead of doubt. He'd probably had enough of the latter in his life already. This thought was self-soothing on my part and made me feel better for how gullible I'd been.

Speaking of gullible, it is one of my favorite words, along with moxie, zealous, juxtapose, and others—including swear words. When I shared my philosophy that expletives had their purpose and place in our vocabulary, a few students looked at me in disbelief.

"The purpose and place for swear words is not the classroom or directed at other people," I said. I went on to explain what an emotional release these words could provide. "Nothing feels better than to let loose with a few choice words after stubbing your toe or getting frustrated with technology. Expressing feelings using language is culturally human. Therapeutic even. However, these words are often overused today, to the point where they've lost their impact."

While watching the British television show *Foyle's War*, I became enamored with the phrase, "tickety-boo." Foyle's chauffeur, Samantha Stewart, used the term regularly. "Everything's all tickety-boo here, sir," Sam might say. Meaning, *Everything is good, just as it is supposed to be.* Tickety-boo is far more descriptive and entertaining than "as it is supposed to be." I did a bit of detective work on Google to find out how it came to be. Though its origin is not certain, it may have been influenced by an Indian phrase or a South African song when British imperialists occupied these countries. Due to extensive travel, the world's cultures and languages have collided and evolved.

To explore how geography affects the evolution of language and communication styles, I showed my sophomore classes the video *American Tongues*. This Peabody Award-winning documentary made in 1988 by Louis Alvarez and Andrew Kolker featured interviews with people from all parts of the United States. It examined the origins of American dialects and accents in a humorous way. For example, due to where various people immigrated, on one side of the Hudson River, people tend to say, "Paaark your caaar," and on the other, "Park your car."

In the video, American fishermen on a remote island on the East Coast shared jokes at a local hangout, roaring with laughter at the punch line. The joke teller's dialect was so thick, students couldn't understand a word he was saying. It wasn't only the dialects that were affected by region, but the customs of language discourse as well. In the South, someone visiting another for a specific reason would sit on the porch and shoot the breeze for a while before getting to the point. In the North, people tended to get right to business first, and, if there was time, they'd shoot the breeze afterward.

Right here in the Midwest, there were those pesky, trendy words that crept into students' speech. They began as verbal habits, developed into irritants, then became out-and-out diseases. Like, "like." Or, "literally." I have had students who couldn't say an entire sentence or express a complete thought without using the words "like" or "literally." These words have taken the place of "er, um" and "ah."

Sherry, an intelligent straight-A student, had inadvertently become addicted to the word "like." As she stood in front of the class to give her speech, the word "like" became so distracting that it overshadowed her well-researched content. Afterward, we talked, and she made it her goal to become less dependent on that word as a verbal crutch.

One verbal development that really bothered me was when students said they did something "on accident." Where did this come from? The preposition "on" means "on top of," as in "The books are on the table." Or, as when naming a specific date, as in, "She is running the race on Thursday." One does something *by* accident, not *on* accident." Grrr!

Dear Reader,
Please heed the important language lessons
cited in the previous paragraphs.
Like I always told my students,
you don't want to anger the grammar gods.
Somewhat biased,
The Author

If this seems picky, keep in mind that English teachers savor vocabulary like sommeliers appreciate a finely-aged wine. One of my goals was to convey this love of language to students. For this reason, every Monday morning I wrote five new vocabulary words and their definitions in bright colors on the white board in the front of the room. Underneath them, I wrote a literary term, like alliteration or foreshadowing, and its definition. Over time, I also included a weekly usage lesson focused on common errors I'd found in students' writing, like affect/effect or the proper way to use a semicolon.

These weekly vocabulary lessons were my replacement for Daily Oral Language (DOL). Popular in the 1980s and '90s, DOL was implemented at all levels of the Language Arts curriculum in order to teach basic spelling, usage and grammar concepts. At first I was a proponent. I wrote my master's thesis about the effectiveness of DOL in the classroom. It far surpassed the separate grammar and punctuation units of old because it integrated the concepts instead of parsing them out into separate, non-integrated units.

The problem, however, was that students were expected to

copy the sentences down incorrectly before correcting them. Therefore, students were initially writing down and internalizing incorrect grammar and usage. Students at high school level knew that the first letter of a sentence was to be capitalized and that a period goes at the end of the sentence, yet every sentence required students to correct these errors on every-single-sentence-every-single-day.

I required students to write these correctly spelled vocabulary words in their notebooks. As they did so, I questioned them. "Does the word have a root that is recognizable, as in *servile*, which means servant-like? How many of you take a foreign language? Is the word identifiable because of its foreign language derivative?" For example, we discussed that *amity*, meaning friendship, came from the Latin amicus and evolved into both Spanish and French words for friend, *amigo* and *ami*.

"Have you heard of the book and movie *The Amityville Horror*?" I asked.

"Yeah," said a student. "That title is an oxymoron. Mrs. Soles taught us that term in seventh grade. She said it was one of her favorite words." God bless Mrs. Soles.

My hope was that these lessons would equip students with methods for determining and remembering the definitions of all unknown words instead of cramming the gray matter for the quiz every Friday. However, many resisted expending the energy to write down the words. I told them I'd read about studies showing that taking handwritten notes helps people remember by engaging the body and mind.

Occasionally, I got carried away with my analogies: "Taking notes is just like taking heroin," I said to motivate them. "The knowledge runs up your arm and right to the brain." I quickly added, "Not that I have ever done heroin, nor should you." The next year, when she graduated, a student transcribed that quote in red and blue calligraphy and presented it to me in a 5 x 7 frame which continues to adorn my desk.

"What do we haff-ta learn these for?" asked Vinnie one Monday as he begrudgingly wrote the words in his notebook. "We'll never use them again anyway."

His complaint was meant to be rhetorical. But I explained that the ACT and SAT test preparers recommended these 125 words as those that juniors should know. Using standardized tests to scare students into studying vocabulary is not a strategy I endorse. So, I added, "Don't you want to be able to have the skill to figure words out from context? What if someone uses them? Don't you want to know what he or she is talking about?"

"No offense, Mrs. Kies, but normal people do not use these words," said Jessica. The class laughed and nodded in agreement.

I made the mistake of getting defensive: "Of course, they do. Just last night Len, the older British judge on *Dancing with the Stars* used two of them. He described one of the dances as *ephemeral*, and said another dancer's technique was an *enigma*."

"What is *Dancing with the Stars*?" Jessica asked. "My grandma is always talking about it."

For the vocabulary quiz on Fridays, I pronounced each word for them, and they were supposed to write it correctly spelled on the lines provided for two points each. Below that was a paragraph. They would insert the appropriate words in the correct blanks for two more points each. At the bottom of the page, they defined the literary term and corrected the usage example for a total of four points. They got one point for placing their names on the quiz. That was a total of twenty-five points.

At the beginning of the year, I had them do the math to see that twenty-five quizzes at twenty-five points each came to a total of 625 points, approximately the same amount of points as three unit tests. I hated boiling the curriculum and their education, which I saw as more important, down to a pile of points. But, some students responded to this motivation, so I used it to my advantage.

As my student Vinnie came into the classroom one Friday, I handed him a quiz and said, "Make sure you don't look at the ceiling, okay?"

"What?"

"Don't look at the ceiling."

"Why not?"

"Someone wrote one of the words up there. 'Gullible.' I don't want you cheating on the quiz."

"Yeah, right," Vinnie said, grinning.

"Really, Vinnie." I pointed to the ceiling panel above him. "See?"

The students around Vinnie looked up, combing the ceiling.

"Hey! There it is!" said his neighbor. "See?"

Vinnie looked straight ahead. "You can all stop because I'm not going to look."

Some students from across the room got up to look.

"'Gullible' is up there, Vinnie," said Angie, pointing. "No kidding. It really is."

"I'm not looking and that's that." His face became red. "Are we going to get on with the quiz or not, Mrs. Kies?"

I read the words, and they wrote them down. As they turned them in, I checked. Everyone in the class got the word *gullible* correct, thanks to the ingenious rascal who wrote it on my ceiling in the first place. I wished it had been my idea.

Chapter 9 – Truths and Consequences

Truth is often eclipsed but never extinguished.
Livy, Roman Historian

In the Introduction I explained that architects designed our school with the library, or IMC (Instructional Materials Laboratory), smack in the center of everything. All other rooms fanned out from it in all directions.

In theory, the philosophy behind the model, that all learning revolved around books and information found in the IMC, was a profound concept. In reality, it necessitated that all PHS librarians take on an additional and undesired role: traffic cop. When we began school in the new building in 1969, it didn't take long for me and the other seven hundred ninety-nine students to figure out that using the path through the IMC to get to our next class on the other side saved much valuable energy.

Our librarian, Mrs. Myrtle Velzy, tried to maintain a semblance of order and nip the jaywalking nonsense in the bud. Among ourselves, we high school kids referred to her as Myrt. She was fortyish when I started high school, petite, fashionable...and harried. We'd be studying or reading quietly in the library, and she would jump up, run over to the offenders, and scold: "Stop! What do you think you're doing? You know you can't cut through here! You need to go around!" While she focused on one lawbreaker, three others snuck behind her back and out the door.

Soon she resorted to giving out detentions. We responded by developing stealthier strategies to avoid detection. We might linger among the library's shelves pretending to look at biographies or magazines on the cylindrical spinning display racks, then furtively weave our way across the room. Or, we might wait for her to become distracted by the phone or a question and make a mad dash into the end zone, hoping to remain unrecognized.

An open mezzanine positioned over the center of the library housed several rows of individual study carrels where we listened to foreign language tapes or studied independently. Aesthetically, the loft gave the library an artsy feel. But as teens are prone to do, students soon began performing gravitational science experiments...dropping pencils, paper, and other objects from above.

It was all Myrt could do to supervise the main floor, let alone the balcony. In the years when I was a student and continuing through my teaching years, rumors abounded about students smoking cigarettes and pot and having sex up there. Whether these stories held any scrap of truth, I do not know for, no matter what anyone says, I did not witness or partake in any behavior of this sort.

However, thirty-five years and a few librarians later, while I was teaching, two of my Creative Writing students wrote a script for a horror film. They made a dummy to toss over the loft's railing in a fight scene. It looked so real in the final cut of the movie that I screamed right on cue as the body went headlong over the side to its demise. The balcony was removed in an update to the library. This was probably a good safety decision, but that doesn't stop me from remembering the nostalgia of it.

All the yearbooks of bygone days were stored on a shelf in the back room of the library. One day, one of my students who was on the student yearbook staff brought me one of those old relics and pointed to my cheerleading photo from 1970. Yup, there I was, holding up the right side of a pyramid with one of my peers standing on my knee.

"You were a cheerleader? Where are your glasses?" she asked. "And your hair is so long and pretty. Wow, you were so thin back then."

Being a PHS alumnus and subsequent teacher wasn't always easy. When students found out I went to PHS too they begged to hear stories about my good ol' days. They feigned innocent curiosity, but I knew they were looking for dirt. They'd begin with questions such as, "Did you get good grades? Were you popular? Who was your favorite teacher?" Gradually, they upped the ante: "Did you smoke pot? I heard everybody smoked pot then. What did you do for fun? Did you ever skip school? Were you a goody-two-shoes or did you get in trouble? Come on, tell us! We won't tell anybody else." (Yeah, right. I learned my lesson well by telling my puppy story later to my Creative Writing class.)

Because I went to school with some of their parents, I was discreet with my answers. I fervently hoped their parents would return the favor.

Adolescence is a time of growing and learning, and most of us weren't as smart as we thought we were at the time. Like most teens, I tested limits. When I was a sophomore, I took typing class with Mr. Riess. The clacking of manual typewriters resounded like a forest full of woodpeckers. When the two new electric typewriters arrived, my peers and I rushed to class in hopes of being able to claim them for that hour. They were easier on the fingers and came with built in erasure tape so we could correct our mistakes when practicing our drills.

I enjoyed typing. In fact, on the spring exam I typed the fastest rate of anyone: almost eighty words per minute (WPM). To get that number, Mr. Riess showed us how to take the total number of characters typed and divide it by five. Then, we took that number and divided it by the number of minutes spent typing. We also added up our errors and subtracted them from our score. Mr. Riess was so impressed with my typing exam score that he always mentioned it whenever he saw me, even years later after I became a teacher.

However, I didn't deserve his adulation. Exam days, then and now, were open campus at PHS. Meaning students could go downtown for lunch or home or wherever, as long as they were back on time for their exams. At the end of my sophomore year I was hanging with some newly acquired friends. One was Cindy.

Cindy's parents both worked. On exam day we decided to walk to her house and have tuna fish sandwiches, chips, and orange juice. We had two hours to kill before our next exam. We were dancing, rocking out to Cindy's new Three Dog Night album, when someone suggested mixing some vodka with the orange juice, and, well, pretty soon we were feeling pretty fine.

I floated into Mr. Riess's room, trying to keep my absence of inhibition under wraps. It was difficult not to giggle, especially since he was serious and a stickler for protocol. He gave us the piece of text he wanted us to replicate for the exam, set his stopwatch, and said, "Ready, set, type!" With no anxiety about making mistakes, my fingers flew over the keys like a concert pianist. I had the highest score in the class. Literally.

When the buzz wore off a couple of hours later, it hit me that I could have gotten into big trouble—like being expelled—or grounded forever. I don't know what I was thinking. But that was just it. I wasn't thinking.

Dear Mr. Riess,
Please forgive me for not taking your typing exam
in a sober manner. I did not deserve the
high words per minute score I received.
Your former student,
Sue Leamy (first row, second from the front)

* * *

As a teacher, I always tried to remind myself that, as a teen, I did stupid things too, learned from them, and grew up. One of those I hoped would grow up and blossom into maturity someday was Thomas. Daily, he projected his personality from his seat in the back of the room. He derailed discussions, distributed inane comments, and aggravated me to no end. Academically, he completed his work most of the time and contributed appropriate comments to discussions some of the time. Truthfully, most of his harmless wisecracks added an element of fun and a touch of life to the class. Yes, I liked him.

"Hey, Mrs. Kies. I'm going on vacation in November," Thomas told me one day in late October. "My mom said to let all my teachers know ahead of time."

"Good for your mom. Where are you going?"

"Tahiti. My dad's work is sending him there, and he gets to take a guest."

"And he's taking you?"

"Yup!" The South Pacific sun shone in his eyes.

"Wow. Lucky you! We'll all be in school working, and you'll be sunning yourself on the beach."

"Yeah—ain't it great?"

"*Isn't* it great. How long will you be gone?"

"Two weeks."

I was tempted to deliver a lecture. "When I was your age…" But, I refrained from telling him my parents wouldn't let me stay home for even one day unless I was coughing up blood or breaking out in pus-filled lesions. Let alone take me out of school for a vacation. I didn't *want* to miss school. Mom made me stay in bed or on the couch all day. Where's the fun in that? If offered a trip to Tahiti, I'd have jumped on it too.

"I'm not sure what we'll be doing in class, yet," I said. "Remind me again a week before you go so I can get your work ready for you, okay?"

"So, I have to do all the work?"

"Yes. If you miss the work, you make it up."

"But, this is school, not a job."

"School *is* your job right now, Thomas. You don't want to return and be behind everyone else. And, think of how unhappy your mom will be if you get a bad grade."

In my teaching experience, I have found that parents fall into three broad categories when it comes to their children's education: uninvolved, supportive, and overzealous. Since I attended high school, the first and the third groups have grown to outnumber the middle group. Some parents excused their children because they were tired from participating in a sporting event the previous evening or because they went to a hip-hop concert in Milwaukee the night before. Oh, and maybe they have an emergency haircut or tanning appointment, or the family needed to begin their holiday vacation a few days early because the ten days on the schedule wasn't long enough. Students were excused from class to shop for prom dresses and cars—even to help frost Christmas cookies. And, the best one yet? Missing school to go shopping for school clothes and supplies.

Hey, no problem, I wanted to say. *Take off from school whenever you need to. We are here to serve you, the customer. Go get those important things done first, and, don't worry, I'll reteach all the lessons when you are ready. Are you free on Saturday or Sunday maybe? I can come to your house if that works. After all, I am a civil servant.*

And when they returned to school after being absent, their first words were always —never failing— "Did I miss anything?" *No, of course not. We couldn't go on without you. We all sat twiddling our thumbs until you returned. You ARE that important to us.* A few times I couldn't resist saying, "Yes, we watched movies and ate popcorn while you were away. Glad you're back in time for the punctuation unit on commas."

It is a step in the right direction that schools have become more sensitive to family needs. However...Time was when playing hooky was a guilty pleasure, and kids who dared try it were terrified of being caught. Huck Finn slid down the drain pipe to sneak out on Miss Watson. Ferris Bueller faked a fever and did everything he could do to avoid the wrath of Principal Rooney. That 1986 movie is completely implausible today. Ferris's mother would write a note of excuse to the school, no questions asked. Ferris and his friends would be free to roam downtown Chicago on a school day. No big deal. No consequences. Skipping school has definitely lost its edge. The thrill is gone.

Thomas reminded me about his trip and said that his mother forbade him to go on vacation unless he got all his work from his teachers. *Way to go, Mom*! Thomas's parents were divorced, and Mom, it seemed, was the enforcer.

We decided he would come that day after school or before school the next day so I could give him his work and explain it. I told him we would be reading *The Adventures of Huckleberry Finn*. While the class was working on the next day's assignment, I got a book from the back of the room, put his name in it and recorded the number. I got out my *Huck Finn* folder and pulled out the study guides so I could make copies during my prep time. I also prepared the ten vocabulary words and their meanings for the two weeks so Thomas could study and make up the weekly quizzes when he returned.

After class, Sarah, a blatantly honest soul who always spoke the truth no matter how gritty, approached my desk before leaving for her next class.

"It's none of my business, Mrs. Kies, but why are you wasting your time getting all that ready for Thomas? You know he isn't going to do any of it."

"It's my job to encourage him, Sarah. And, you never know.

He might do it."

Sarah shrugged. "Just sayin'."

Thomas never came in to see me after school that day or before school the next. I got an email from Mom requesting his work. I told her the work was ready and about my arrangements with him. After her call, I thought he'd be in before school on Monday morning. Nope.

Before class that day I read Thomas the riot act about being responsible. I handed him his work. "It might be good to get as much of this done as you can before you leave in a few days, Thomas." His brown wavy hair, freckles, and slight build reminded me of Huck Finn, rapscallions cut from the same cloth. "You know," I said, "Huck Finn went on an adventure down the Mississippi similar to how you are going on an adventure to Tahiti."

"Oh, yeah?" He took the book, folded the work and stuffed it all into his backpack. "Guess what? I talked to Dad last night, and he said we're going to go parasailing and rent jet skis."

Thomas left without turning in any work. He came back in two weeks, refreshed and tanned, and happy as hell. His souvenirs included an array of funky T-shirts, one with Bob Marley smoking a joint, and, following the rules, I made him turn it inside out. He also brought back a passel of adventures that he related with creativity akin to Twain. But, Sarah was right. He didn't do one lick of the work. Zippo. Not only that, he'd lost the whole kit and kaboodle somewhere between the school and Tahiti, including his *Huck Finn* book.

Thomas seemed content that he was going to pass the semester by the skin of his poo-eating grin. However, Mom was not so happy. The day before grades were due she emailed me to see if he could make up the work that had been due three weeks prior so he could bring his D- up to a C. I said he'd had enough chances and needed to take responsibility for himself. She wasn't happy with me, but she took it no further.

* * *

Once upon a time, sharing a truthful story about my childhood gained me a legacy I couldn't extinguish. In the memoir unit for Creative Writing class, we would sample a couple humorous stories from David Sedaris' *Dress Your Family in Corduroy and Denim* about his childhood and siblings. An excerpt from *The Glass Castle* by Jeannette Walls provided us with a dramatic approach, and one from *Dreams from My Father* by Barack Obama emoted more philosophical insight. This variety showed students how each writer approached his or her family's stories in very different ways.

We began by discussing family stories. The kind of stories that relatives tell at reunions or while playing cards at the kitchen table. Those stories that were first whispered over the phone or out of earshot but managed to seep through generational retelling. The kind where not all the details may be reliable because they have evolved into family lore. Those that you love to hear because they are entertaining and human with a fabric of truth. The kind you experienced as a child that deserved to be told, explored, and savored.

"I've heard my mom tell about my uncle who was killed in Vietnam," said Macie, who was usually reticent. "He was only twenty years old. I could write about what I think happened to him over there. There are a few facts, but nobody seems to know a lot of it. Or about how his death affected all of us, even me, though I didn't even know him."

"Wow," I said. "Lots of food for writing there. What about you, John?"

"Apparently, I had an uncle who died in prison. Mom says he was convicted of shooting someone, his girlfriend's new boyfriend or something like that. For years no one talked about him."

"If you write about this, make sure to include how it affected you. Memoirs are about you and your point of view."

Mandy's hand shot up. "My older brother got mad at me for following him and his friends around and locked me in the trunk of the car once when I was five." The class laughed. "At the time I didn't think it was funny. I was scared, crying and screaming. I don't know how long he left me there, but boy did Dad get mad at him when he found out about it."

"It's weird, isn't it?" I said. "Sometimes the worst trauma transforms into humor over time."

"Like when you murdered your puppy?" Jim grinned.

There it was. Again. The puppy story that had taken on a life of its own. The first time I shared this episode of my early life, I didn't realize I was delivering dirt to their doorsteps. Their adolescent brains amplified the tale with *Nightmare on Elm Street* descriptors, often leaving out the vital detail—that I'd been a toddler when it happened.

"You did what?" Caroline asked. Out of context, the comments about the story portrayed me as a monster. We've all seen how a speck of truth can give birth to nine-pound conspiracy theories decked out in decorative half-truths.

"She got mad and threw her puppy out the window to its death," said Mark.

"Mark...you know that's not true," I said.

"Well, then tell us what really happened."

"Okay, but no judgment and no embellishment on your part." They all nodded. I knew better than to believe them, but I'd just as well try to set the record straight.

"One spring day my mom was upstairs washing the windows and screens in our two-story house where I lived until I was ten. Still in diapers at the time, I'm told I was splashing in the bucket of water and following our puppy Scooter around. I was a rambunctious child, Mom said. She'd caught me scaling the shelves in the living room and using the cupboard handles in the kitchen to get to the candy bowl on top of the refrigerator. Anyway, while Mom was preoccupied with cleaning, I reportedly picked up Scooter and threw him out the window, saying, 'Puppy, fly!' I pantomimed the toss with my arms. "Thank heavens I didn't lose my balance and tumble out the window along with Scooter."

The first time I told this tale, the collective gasps and titters emitted from the class surprised me. Now I expected it. It was incomprehensible to them that I, their teacher, could do something as stupid as this as a little kid. That I was a little kid once. That I was human.

"Why would you do that?" Caroline asked.

"I was only two or three. I don't remember doing it—or why I did it. The window looked out into the branches of our apple tree in the backyard. I suppose maybe I saw birds flying around, and my toddler brain figured that if birds could fly, all animals should be able to fly? I don't know."

"So what happened to the puppy?" she asked.

"I don't remember. Mom and Dad told me Scooter ran away. I think they were trying to spare me, though. That's a big fall for a puppy. We got another dog when I was five. His name was Coke. His outside dog house was big enough for both of us, and I would crawl in, talk to him, and pet him. As an adult I've had four dogs that I've treated like family members. I can assure you I'm a responsible pet owner."

One year my student Sarah even made reference to the puppy story in her speech on graduation day in some context or other. My teacher peers and parents asked me about it. I surmised that if students believed I really were a cruel person, they wouldn't tease me about it. I chose to interpret the story as an early sign of my relentless hopefulness. If, as a child, I believed that puppies could fly, I would certainly never give up on my students being able to learn.

> If, as a child, I believed that puppies could fly, I would certainly never give up on my students being able to learn.

Sure enough, the afternoon after I told the story to Mark, Tony, and Caroline's class, Grant entered my classroom for sixth period. "Hey, Mrs. Kies. Have you killed any puppies lately?"

As Kurt Vonnegut writes in *Slaughterhouse Five*, every time someone or something dies, "And so it goes."

Chapter 10 – Pissing Contests and Skunks

*I always say be humble but be firm. Humility and openness
are the key to success without compromising your beliefs.*
George Hickenlooper

In the fall of 1968, my narrow blue locker, number 270, became
my home base for the next four years at PHS. It was located in the
south wing near the English and history classrooms with other
freshmen, alphabetically between Richard Lange and Deanna
Leighty. In the winter I stuffed it with my coat and other winter
garb and leaned on it with my shoulder to get it shut.

Sometime in the early 2000s roomier lockers replaced the
originals. Students routinely complained about not being able to
get the combinations to work. To avoid the hassle of dealing with
an uncooperative locker, many carried their belongings with
them in their backpacks throughout the day. A few graduated
without ever using their lockers. I told them this would result in
shoulder, neck, and back problems down the road, but they paid
no heed. Like me at that age, they were invincible.

In grade school I remember toting my belongings in a
satchel-like bookbag to and from school. Most of us ditched those
upon entering high school. In high school we girls cradled as
many as five books in the crooks of our arms. I don't remember
boys carrying much of anything. How did they manage that?
Stylish backpacks now make it cool for students as well as
teachers to carry their stuff everywhere. A variety of waterproof
fabrics of funky colors and patterns provide handy pockets and
comfortable padded straps for ease of schlepping stuff.

One Thursday morning of my sophomore year I left the

biology room to get to English class on the other side of the school. I had four minutes and needed to make a quick stop at my locker to switch out books so I didn't have to carry them all. Getting there required circumnavigating the library. Myrt the librarian was on guard. I may have chatted with a friend or two along the way, and, yes, admittedly I may have been late once or twice that semester. But, on this particular day my teacher, who was a pretty reasonable person most of the time, had reached her limit. Not at all happy, she turned me away at the door and sent me to the office.

Mrs. Heins, the secretary, directed me down a hall to a conference room and told me to have a seat. "The vice principal will be in shortly to talk to you about being late for class," she said. Her tone was much less amicable than when I'd stopped by that morning to buy my weekly lunch tickets.

Mr. Ratched, we'll call him, our vice principal in charge of discipline, had reportedly come to PHS after leaving a job at a boy's reform school up north. He wore black horn-rimmed glasses and had thick straight brown hair chopped short and parted on the side. Though not imposing in stature, his flashing brown eyes and temper were as notorious as a Mount Vesuvius eruption. He must have been in his late twenties or early thirties, but his face still bore the pockmarks left by adolescent acne. I suspect his resentment toward teenagers resulted from having been scarred by this era of his life.

I waited. And waited. I'm sure Mr. Ratched knew that anticipating his reprimand elicited great fear in his clients. What would he do? What would he say? I thought, succumbing to his tactic. *Why couldn't I just go back to class?* Sweat trickled from my armpits, and my feet began to shake in my penny loafers. Edgar Allan Poe nailed the image of this phenomenon in "The Pit and the Pendulum." The bound victim struggles to maintain composure while lying next to a gaping pit in a dark, dank dungeon. He watches the gradual descent of the scimitar fastened to the end of the pendulum as it swings back and forth. Slowly. Closer. Closer.

I heard footsteps in the hall...and voices... *Was it him? Was he finally here?*

Mr. Ratched opened the door and closed it with a bang. He shot me a belittling glare: "Why were you late for class?"

I don't remember what I told him, but my reply didn't meet his expectations of remorse. He leaned over and positioned his magnified eyes inches from mine. "You disrupt class when you are tardy. Do you realize that? This is very disrespectful and selfish! If everyone were late for class, just think of the turmoil that would cause!"

He paced and stood over me yelling for several minutes while I cowered in my chair. My students often used the word "yell" figuratively when someone showed displeasure with them. "Mr. Thompson yelled at me for being in the hall," or "My mom yelled at me for not doing my homework." But, Ratched, I mean, Mr. Ratched, was really yelling. At one point, droplets of his spittle landed on my cheek. I can still see his finger wagging and hear his hand slamming the table. Maybe his mood was a carry-over from a previous discipline session, but holy crap—if this was standard fare for someone late to class, what happened to delinquents who swore at teachers, or vandalized the bathrooms?

Maya Angelou once said, "They may forget what you said, but they will never forget how you made them feel." Mr. Ratched stirred feelings of anger in me I didn't know existed. Afterward, I imagined punching him square in his pockmarked nose, proud of the large amount of bloodletting. At the time I was so frightened it was all I could do to muster the moxie to hold back my welled-up tears.

After leaving the office, I ducked into the bathroom to gather my countenance before returning to class. I told myself not to take it personally. Even though he'd been close enough to spray my face with his saliva, I doubted he'd recognize me in the hall.

Why did he choose to overreact when he had other options? I've since wondered. He could have said, "You disrupt class when you're late, Susan. I don't want to see you in the office for this again," or "If you are late for class one more time, I'll be calling your parents about this." He could have looked up my middle name on my records and used it like my mother did when my behavior left something to be desired: "Now, Susan Jane, I see you have good grades, but you need to adhere to the rules like everyone else." That would have sufficed. Maybe not for students who got in trouble daily, but it would have nixed my tardiness in the bud, pronto.

When I shared this story with my teaching peers who relished the good ol' days of hardline discipline, they usually smiled and said, "I bet you weren't late for class again." And, they were right. I wasn't. Yes, Mr. Ratched scared the bejesus out of me and made me never want to see his cratered face again. But who wants to be hated like that? Who feels good about themselves at the end of the day after acting like a mad dog?

Today I picture Mr. Ratched as a white-haired, shriveled up man, rightfully concerned that those tending to his needs in the nursing home might have been his former students. After becoming a teacher, I vowed never to treat any student the way he treated me. If a teacher yelled all the time, where could they go from there? I decided I'd rather err on the side of trust than terror. My mentor, Jane, modeled how to stay cool and not let anger take over. I followed her example—most of

103

the time.

Early on in my teaching, my rowdy fourth period class refused to be quiet while I was speaking. A couple of them routinely talked to each other across the classroom. One day, after asking and reasoning and threatening for the umpteenth time, I yelled, "Shut up! Please, shut up!" It was far from my finest moment.

After class, Mr. McKichan from the room next door asked, "Was that you yelling last hour?"

I wanted to crawl under a desk. Mr. McKichan had been my World History teacher when I was a freshman, and I didn't want to be known as *that* teacher who loses it and yells. I consulted a few trusted colleagues on how they handled persistent talkers in their classrooms. Sara, the Spanish teacher, said she stopped her lesson, looked at them without saying a word, and waited. "Stay calm and in control. It makes them uncomfortable, and they quiet down," she said.

The guidance counselor told me that instead of getting louder and talking over them, he lowered his tone so they would have to be quiet to hear him. I adopted both strategies and added a twist. When students became quiet again, I told them they'd wasted valuable instruction and work time. I explained that on most days if they used time more wisely, they could get the assignment finished and not have homework. No one wanted homework, so they began to police each other's behavior.

Policing students was my least favorite aspect of my teaching duties. It required being a psychologist, investigator, and mediator all at the same time. Unfortunately, it was also one of the most necessary duties, not only in my classroom but in the halls and throughout the school. I became more assertive and better at it as time went on.

During my first years of teaching, I was far too trusting. Finding that median between Mr. Ratched and desperate Myrt took some practice. I recall one instance that got me into trouble. Remember back in the early 1990s when computer mice still had balls? Underneath the mouse was a tiny compartment that held a small, hard rubber ball about an inch in diameter. The technical term for it was *trackball*. It rolled around as the user moved the mouse, which in turn propelled the cursor on the screen.

In the computer lab when the supervising teacher wasn't looking, a few mischievous students might remove the balls, hence castrating the mice. They'd pocket their trophies and later roll them down the hallways. The culprits were clandestine, and catching them wasn't easy. As more and more balls disappeared, Mrs. Kittle, the library media specialist at the time, held a faculty meeting to propose a solution. "Before you leave the computer lab with your students, make sure to do a ball check," she told us emphatically.

"Is that legal?" asked the teacher next to me, his inner adolescence playing out. Many of the staff found it hard to keep a straight face during this training. Doing a "ball check" meant requiring each student to turn the mouse over so we could be assured that each mouse still had its organ before students left the computer lab. The administration didn't think missing mouse balls was the least bit funny. The trackballs cost ten dollars each to replace, which sounded rather expensive for a little hard rubber ball. School budgets had little wiggle room for new equipment, though, let alone for replacement parts.

One day, Pat Jonas, the publications advisor, asked if I would supervise her staff of students on Saturday. She had a family commitment and didn't want to cancel the work day because deadlines were looming. It was only for a few hours while they edited articles and completed layout for the newspaper and the yearbook. How hard could this be?

While students worked in the computer lab, I was in and out of the room making brief trips to the copy machine and to my classroom down the hall. They behaved well. Not loud. Not annoying. I wasn't sure how much actual newspaper work was getting done, but they appeared to be making headway. Unfortunately, I learned that even those students who appeared to be model citizens could put on a good game face for the sake of pulling one over on the teacher.

When I arrived at school on Monday morning, I headed down the main hall to the commons. I looked up and saw the principal striding toward me on a mission. His hair was sticking up on the crown of his head. Picture Alfalfa on *The Little Rascals.* We staff had come to recognize this as a sign he was not having a good day. It was always best to steer clear if possible. The hallway was crowded with students getting ready for the first period, so I couldn't do an about-face. I had nowhere to go.

He planted his six-foot frame in my path and spoke through clenched teeth. This was his usual manner of speaking even when he wasn't mad. However, his emphatic tone and raised voice indicated he meant business. "Were you supposed to be supervising students here on Saturday?"

"Um, yes," I said, noticing his word choice, "supposed to be."

"Were you in the lab with them the whole time?"

"I left a couple of times to go to my room and to make copies. But, I was there most of the time." Students and staff passed by us trying not to look. But it was like coming across an accident on the road.

"Mouse balls went missing on Saturday. Ten of them." His voice grew louder. "Did you check to see if the balls were there when you left?"

I wanted to crawl under a floor tile. "No. I forgot."

"Forgot? You know better than that! Those balls are expensive. You were supposed to be supervising." He looked at the floor and shook his head in frustration. "I'll be putting a disciplinary letter in your file about this incident." He turned and stomped toward the commons, rubbing the back of his head with his hand.

Stunned and embarrassed, I avoided eye contact with everyone, rushed to my room, and locked the door. My preparation time was the first period of the day. I had an hour to try to gain composure before facing students. Tears formed, accompanied by their frequent companions, anger and resentment.

Our guidance counselor witnessed the spectacle and knocked on my door. She gave me a hug and encouraged me to confront the principal about his lack of tact. I thought back to my run-in with Mr. Ratched. I needed to learn to stand up to these authoritarian males, or I would continue to be the scapegoat for their agenda.

All day I composed and edited my monologue in my head, and after school I went to his office.

"I need to talk to you about this morning." My voice barely wavered. He looked up from his desk. My heart was thumping as I shut the door. "Your chastising me in the hall in front of students and peers was completely unprofessional. You should have called me into your office and talked to me about the incident privately. This was not the way to handle this situation, and I won't be treated like that again."

Before I went in, I decided if he got mad and started to yell, I would walk out. I wasn't going to stand there and take it. But, he didn't.

"I felt you needed this reprimand. Look, I don't like writing you up, but it was necessary. You were in charge and should have been more diligent."

I was surprised at how calm and composed he was. He avoided the fact that my issue was with *how* he reprimanded me, but I decided not to push it. I'd said what I'd come to say and figured an apology was not a part of his verbal repertoire. He delivered his clenched-teeth smile, and I noticed a glint of respect in his eyes as I left his office. He never did anything like that again. In fact, I felt he had my back at every turn. I guess by standing up to him I'd earned his respect.

When I retired, I asked Mr. Engh, the current principal, if he could check my file to see if the letter of reprimand was there. "I've often wondered what it said about me and the missing mouse balls," I said after telling him the story.

Mr. Engh smiled and wheeled his chair around to the storage cabinet behind him. He retrieved my file and thumbed through it. "Nothing like that in here," he said. Either the letter had never been written or he'd removed it.

He was full of surprises. A year later when I was dealing with my student Nathan's dad, that principal became a sage advisor.

Nathan had gone on vacation with his parents and a few friends. When he left, we were just finishing up reading *To Kill a Mockingbird*. The final test was scheduled to be given during the week while he was gone. He said he'd take the test before he left, but he didn't get around to it. So, he took it during his study hall the week he returned. He scored 85 percent, a solid B. Up to this point, I was not entirely sure he could read. I knew he'd copied his daily study guide answers from Kevin. The wording was exactly the same. And, while Kevin routinely answered questions about the book in class, Nathan didn't. When Nathan came in to ask me what he got on the test, I verbally quizzed him.

"Tell me who Boo Radley is."

"Boo who?" he said. Not because he was being clever. He really didn't know that or anything else I asked. I told him I wanted him to take an alternate test to prove himself and convince me he knew something about the book.

"Are you saying I cheated?"

"How else could you get a B on the test and not be able to tell me about one of the major characters?"

The next afternoon while I was preparing an alternate test during my prep period, Nathan's father called. I took the call on the phone in the teacher's lounge. "Listen, Missy," he said, "my son says you accused him of cheating. Do you have proof? A cheat sheet or something? If you don't, you can't make him retake that test. I'll take this to the principal if I have to."

I told him about Nathan's blatant lack of knowledge about the book, and he said his son may have "done some research" by asking others what was on the test. "That's not cheating," he said. "Everybody does that." I took issue with his interpretation of cheating, but *"Listen, Missy"*? As Huck Finn might have said, "Now, them's fightin' words."

The principal said he'd back me in mandating that Nathan retake that test. "But," he said, "I recommend you take some time and think it over to see if you really want to fight this battle. I dealt with many parents and situations like this when I was teaching. It was usually pretty clear to see where the kid got his attributes. Have you heard the adage about getting into a pissing contest with a skunk? Sometimes it's best to back down and solve the problem without confrontation." Wait a minute. Was this the same guy who hunted me down in the hall to yell at me about missing mouse balls?

Have you heard the adage about getting into a pissing contest with a skunk? Sometimes it's best to back down and solve the problem without confrontation."

Mulling over my options, I thought of my other 133 students, many of whom wanted to learn. And, my family deserved some attention too. I'd already spent too much time fretting over Mr. Pissy Pants and his kid. However, my mother's headstrong German genes I'd inherited wanted me to witness Nathan fail the alternate test and watch his dad eat crow.

After weighing the pros and cons, I reasoned that I wasn't going to change the parent or his kid. In my twenties I'd have taken on that parent at all costs. But I was now in my early forties. Who wants that hassle? Knowing when to hold 'em and when to fold 'em is a valuable life lesson, something that comes with age and experience.

While grading Nathan's remaining assignments for the year, I used unrestrained rigor. The reverberation of the words *Listen, Missy* drove my red pen joyfully and relentlessly across every page.

For the first few years of my teaching career in the early 1990s, I had no room of my own. I was a scholastic nomad known as a cart teacher. Everything I needed for my classes that day had to be packed, stacked, and organized on a little four-wheeled vehicle so I could push it to various rooms and teach during my peers' prep periods. This was a logistical nightmare, especially when trying to navigate the hallways between classes.

On the plus side, this forced me to be organized. During my year of the cart, I was assigned to teach each of my classes in a different peer's room during that teacher's preparation period. Some stayed and did their work while I taught, and others left to work in the teacher workroom.

One veteran teacher whose room I used was very fussy. He never failed to chastise me if a desk was out of place or a scrap of paper was left on the floor when I left his room. Daily, I scrambled to straighten the desks, erase the board, and pick up the room, only to have him come in and glare at me as I headed off to my next classroom. I came to think of him as Mr. Persnickety, and sometimes worse, depending.

When I got my own room in the new part of our school, guess who became my next-door neighbor? Persnickety taught three classes of freshman geography. One of his traditions was to let it slip that school was being let out early because of an incoming snow or ice storm. "But don't tell anyone," he'd add to make sure his students told everyone they saw. Being freshmen, they devoured the entire baited hook. All morning their faces looked as if Santa were coming. This practical joke only worked once per year, but Persnickety thought it good fun and a proper freshmen initiation.

I was a greenhorn when I used his room, not realizing that Persnickety used his poker face for duping rooky faculty as well as students. Once he told a first-year teacher that only veteran teachers went to the Holiday Party.

"Don't believe anything this guy tells you," my colleague Jim told me.

Now he tells me! Okay, I get it, I thought. He respects experience and chutzpah. One day in the teacher's lounge Persnickety was bragging about one of his pranks. In a forthright but joking manner, I said, "You know, sometimes you can be a real jerk." I smiled, and he roared with laughter. He loved that I'd called out his behavior. From then on, I had his respect.

During my prep time, bits of lively discussions drifted into my room from one of his elective classes. The maximum security prison guards from the Wisconsin Secure Program Facility in Boscobel were the guest speakers. I looked into the room, and they were demonstrating the proper use of handcuffs on a student volunteer. Students were captivated and enthralled.

Persnickety's Advanced Placement Government class decorated the room for the holidays using a life-size cardboard soldier, their own political cartoons and politically incorrect Christmas lights draped over everything. And, after studying a particular country in Social Studies, his students prepared and shared dishes of its native cuisine as a cultural culmination. Persnickety always invited me over to sample the leftover food. Something interesting was always going on in his room, and his creativity spurred me to step up my lesson planning game.

Between classes Persnickety routinely manned his post by the fire extinguisher where two halls intersected and formed a T. He monitored traffic and cultivated rapport with students. This was his element, doling out compliments, smart remarks, and one liners all in the same breath as students passed. One day two girls got into a tussle down the hall. When he heard the commotion, he sprinted into action to separate them. In the heat of battle one of the girls jumped on his back. He hurt for a week or two but recuperated. At the end of that school year he had to go to court and testify in the matter.

Then, one day my school neighbor found he had cancer. He underwent grueling chemo sessions. When he returned to school, I struggled with how to let him know how much I'd missed him, how glad I was that he was back. I presented him with a bag of Hershey's Hugs and we hugged. As his hair began to fall out, he accumulated a collection of funky hats, from a red-and-white-striped *Cat in the Hat* top hat to a ten-gallon cowboy hat. Through all those treatments, he modeled a positive attitude and kept his students entertained with snarky comments.

Persnickety's grandson Andy came to his room almost every day after elementary school so they could walk home together. Grandpa, or Pop, as Andy called him, prepared for the following day of classes while Andy worked on homework. Andy often stopped by my room to say "hi" and fill me in on his school day. Sometimes I helped him with his spelling words for that week. Later, after Persnickety retired, Andy became one of my Junior English students and a chip off the old Pop.

Upon retiring cancer free a few years later, Persnickety remarked: "Now, every day will be a snow day, only without the snow."

For fifteen years, we'd watched each other's homerooms and each other's backs, except for that one time in the hall. Before he left, he bestowed upon me a few of his plants, including a ten-foot cactus, as well as his podium. His students made it for him years ago in shop class when he began teaching. Embellished with layers of political stickers from three decades, student autographs, and laden with thirty-plus years of experience and memories, it represented a legacy.

All but one cactus that he gave me perished, and the podium he bestowed upon me no longer wobbles because one of my students fixed it. "I can't trust you with anything, can I?" he chided me when he found out. Just like old times.

After I retired, our paths crossed again. Literally. Persnickety is the Trail Coordinator for our local arboretum trail, and I am a crew leader and volunteer. Every Wednesday he gives everyone on the crew a hard time, every passerby a friendly greeting, and every dog a treat. Technically, he is my boss, and I play along to keep him happy,

Chapter 11 – Cultural Awakenings

People judge things by their own experience,
not knowing of the wide world outside.
Japanese Proverb

In the 1960s, Platteville, like most small Wisconsin towns, was a quaint little homegrown garden patch of tomatoes, potatoes, and cucumbers. If it weren't for the University of Wisconsin-Platteville, we residents wouldn't have seen or experienced exotic vegetables like artichokes or avocados. Throughout my childhood and much of my teaching career, most surnames were of obvious German, Irish, Norwegian, or English descent: McDermott, Mellor, Digman, Pederson, Lange, Tiedemann, Shea, Hying, McIntyre, Buchannan, Brodbeck, Wagner, or Cullen, just to name a few. When I was a senior in high school, out of the eight hundred students in the school, only a handful represented a different culture.

During this era, my dad enjoyed beginning his day with other Plattevillians at the Capitol Cafe, later known as Taylor's Cafe, on Main Street. One morning in 1967, Amadi, a UW-Platteville student, sat down on a stool at the counter next to him. From then on, their coffee time became regular fare a few mornings a week. They visited about the weather, Platteville happenings and their families. Dad was captivated by Amadi's stories about growing up in Nigeria, and he thought maybe my eighth grade St. Mary's classmates would be, as well.

A Prairie du Chien lad, Dad's service during World War II allowed him to meet people from all over the world. His job as an X-ray technician in Hawaii and the Philippines piqued his curiosity of other lands and other cultures. Amadi agreed to come, and our teacher Sister Roseen welcomed the opportunity. Though we had seen Black people around town and on television, this was the first time many of us had ever met an African American person face to face.

A couple of years ago I mentioned this story to my junior class during a discussion about race and culture while reading *The Adventures of Huckleberry Finn.* Peter, a student who had immigrated from Africa with his family, raised his hand. "I understand completely. As a young boy, one day my father took me along with him to the city. I remember seeing a white person for the first time. I was shocked. I wondered what was wrong with their skin."

Peter's story was a revelation. I had never thought of this cultural discovery of a different skin color from a Black person's point of view. And, I imagine, neither had my students. We tend to relate to the world in terms of ourselves and immediate surroundings unless we are confronted with, or make it a point to learn about, other perspectives. Through the literature we studied and stories we shared in class, I hoped my students would realize that finding out about our fellow humans was a necessary life-long activity. If our goal was to exist peacefully in the same world, the more we knew about each other's lives and struggles, the better.

I had no memory of studying other cultures in my high school English classes. That's why, as a teacher, I tried to incorporate them into my curriculum. What better place to start studying American Literature than with the very first Americans? We began with "High Horse's Courting" from *Black Elk Speaks* by John G. Niehardt. The author met Black Elk, a Lakota healer and visionary, on the Pine Ridge Reservation in 1930. Black Elk asked

115

Niehardt to tell his story to the world. In the story, High Horse, a young Lakota, tries to win the heart of a girl he loves. He describes this by saying that her beauty makes him feel "sick in the belly." My students laughed at this, I believe, because they could relate to it.

I also showed the movie *Lakota Woman* (TNT, 1994), which tells the true story of Mary Crow Dog, who took part in the 1973 Native American occupation of a church at Wounded Knee, South Dakota. The rebellion began because a number of Native Americans had been murdered, and their attackers were going unpunished. Also, they believed the elections on the reservation were corrupt. The siege occurred at Wounded Knee because it was the same place that the United States Cavalry shot over three hundred unarmed Natives, including women and children, in 1890, and buried them in a mass grave.

Many students did not know this history. On a trip out west, my husband and I visited Wounded Knee, and I described to my students the haunting silence of the place where the graves lie of both the 1890 massacre and those killed in the 1973 siege.

Teaching *The Adventures of Huckleberry Finn* by Mark Twain elicited some good conversations, but it also presented its share of challenges. One of the most complicated and controversial was Twain's repeated, but accurate for the pre-Civil War setting, use of the n-word in telling the story of Huck and his friend Jim, a slave.

In a Great Books video (Discovery Communications, 1997), various experts debated whether *Huck Finn* should be banned because of the use of the n-word or taught to help students understand the historical context of the era. It was, and continues to be, an ongoing debate, making the book one of the most banned books in classrooms and libraries everywhere. It has also been translated into at least sixty-nine different languages (escholarship.org).

The year I retired from teaching, Caley and Nelda, both bright young Black women, sat near each other in my first-hour class. Based on our discussion about Twain and a TED talk (Technology, Entertainment, Design) about the evolution and contemporary use of the n-word, I assigned the class to write a practice ACT persuasive essay on the topic. Adhering to the standard three-choice ACT essay question format, I assigned students to examine their beliefs: Was it never okay for anyone to use the n-word? Sometimes okay depending on the circumstances? Or, always okay to have the freedom to use it? I instructed them to support their opinion with specific examples and rationalizations from their experiences, studies, and reasoning.

Caley raised her hand. "I'm not going to write about this topic."

"Oh," I said. "Why is that?"

She paused. "I just don't want to."

"Don't you think issues like this should be talked about? I'm interested in your opinion."

She rolled her eyes. Nelda followed suit and didn't want to write about the topic either. Did they believe I was targeting them? Was I? I would have given this assignment no matter who was in the class. Maybe that was it. I wasn't being considerate of their presence.

It may be a cliche, but hindsight really is 20/20, or 20/30, maybe. I should have met with Nelda and Caley privately. Maybe they would have explained their reasons to me without being on display in front of the class. They could have chosen a different topic—or possibly written an essay explaining to me why they did not want to do this assignment.

This reminded me of an incident one summer when my older daughter and I attended a Chris Isaak concert in Milwaukee. The hotel where we were staying offered a shuttle ride to and from the venue. After the performance, we hopped into the front seat of the bus. As people filed in, the driver asked about the show. "It was great," I said. "We really enjoyed it." My daughter concurred. "But the best concert I've ever seen was Lyle Lovett and his Large Band."

"Oh, yeah. He's got it going on, ya know?"

"Cool!" I said. "So you like Lyle Lovett too?"

"What? You don't think a brother like me can like country music?" He sounded upset.

My daughter and I exchanged confused looks. Apparently, he thought I was surprised that a Black person would like country music? I was just happy to meet someone else who knew and enjoyed Lyle Lovett. How did this simple, congenial exchange turn into an uncomfortable one? Had he previously been criticized for being a Black person who enjoyed country music? Where was his defensive attitude coming from? I was adrift as to the root of this agitation.

Josephine Baker, an American-born 1920s dancer, singer, and spy, lived in France. When an interviewer referred to her as a Negro, she said, "What did you say?"

He repeated, "I was referring to your race. As a Negro..."

"There's only one race—the human race," she replied.

How true. If only the answer were that simple.

Dear Teachers and Staff,
It's impossible to know the realm of past experiences students
bring with them to our classroom every day.
We do the best we can, keeping in mind that treating students
equally does not necessarily mean treating them all the same.
Sometimes frustrated,
Caley and Nelda's Teacher

My Homecoming Dance

* * *

My mostly German heritage boasts some Irish roots on Dad's side. Every St. Pat's Day, much to my mother's embarrassment, Dad rummaged through his bureau and closet to create an ensemble of every shade of green imaginable. Socks, pants, shirt, sport coat and tie, none of which matched in color or pattern. Resembling a six feet, one inch leprechaun in garish attire, he headed to Taylor's Cafe for his morning coffee. With little to no encouragement, he'd pull out his harmonica and play "Oh, Danny Boy" and "When Irish Eyes are Smiling." If patrons were receptive, as they usually were, he'd liven it up with an Irish jig or two and a couple of G-rated Pat and Mike jokes between songs.

We didn't know anything factual about our Irish ancestors until my dad's sister did some genealogical digging and found that their great-grandparents Edmund and Johanna (Ormond) Leamy and their seven children emigrated from County Waterford to Apple River, Illinois, in the 1850s. This knowledge only reinforced Dad's public storytelling and harmonica playing.

After reading Frank McCourt's gritty memoir *Angela's Ashes*, I got a realistic historical glimpse of Irish culture. Turns out it included far more than storytelling, songs, and pub going. Like horrendous poverty, suffering, and deadly hunger. To say that I was ecstatic that the Irish memoirist Frank McCourt was going to be the featured speaker at the NCTE (National Council of Teachers of English) convention I'd be attending was gross understatement.

Back when districts had sufficient funding, one of the perks was occasionally attending these state and national conventions for professional development purposes. Our English Department came home invigorated with new lesson plans, a tote or two full of free teacher stuff, and—most valuable of all—a fresh outlook. Meeting and talking with a variety of educators from all over the United States gave us the hopeful perspective we needed: we were not alone in our classroom quests and the inherent problems that come with the job.

At the 1996 convention in Chicago I saw actor Al Pacino and Chicago Tribune movie reviewer Gene Siskel. They were promoting Pacino's *Looking for Richard*, a documentary that followed the creative process from inception through production of his feature film, *Richard III,* a Shakespearean tragedy. I admired Pacino in his portrayals of glib, cool, tough-guy characters on the screen, as in *Dog Day Afternoon, The Godfather* and *Carlito's Way.* After viewing the documentary, the audience members were encouraged to ask questions. Pacino's answers veered and lurched, meandering all over the road and into the ditch. The workings of a creative mind, I suppose? Or, maybe he missed having a script in front of him?

Then in 2000, Frank McCourt graced the stage of the NCTE convention after a showing of the movie that was based on his Pulitzer Prize-winning book. Though steeped in the darkness of his poor Irish childhood, *Angela's Ashes* is chock-full of candid humor, stark honesty, and philosophical musings. All qualities I admire in a book—and an author.

He delivered a wry, spot-on, hour-long monologue of quips and ditties to hundreds of us teachers about his thirty years of teaching English in the New York Public School System. When he answered questions at the end, his responses flowed full-bodied and smooth, as Guinness from the tap of an Irish pub. If there were an Academy Award category for Best Live Performance at an NCTE Convention, McCourt would take home an Oscar. Sorry, Pacino.

After the standing ovation, he signed autographs. English teachers, mostly female, gathered around his table, ogling in admiration as we literature lovers do in the presence of a notable author—any author actually. My heart beat double time as I rehearsed my lines.

My Homecoming Dance

Hello, Mr. McCourt. Would you please sign my name tag? I saw that you included a picture of the Leamy School in Limerick at the beginning of the book. The school you attended when you were young? My maiden name is Leamy, you know? (Smile and point to *Leamy* printed on my nametag.) *I'm a teacher and a writer, too. –You'd like to see some of my work? Sure, I can send something to you. I happen to have a story right here in this folder. –Yes, I'd be delighted if you'd read it and make comments. If you like the story I'd love to have a promotional blurb from you for the cover. Thank you so much, Mr. McCourt. –Call you Frank? Why, I'd be honored...Frank. Thank you.*

"Your name is Leamy? You know those people were pirates, don't ya?" he said, handing back my nametag.

Then it was my turn. I stepped forward and managed to spit out that my maiden name was Leamy—like the school he went to—and how my ancestors were from Ireland. The rest is a blur. That I considered myself a writer never entered the exchange. I handed him my nametag to sign.

"Your name is Leamy? You know those people were pirates, don't ya?" he said, handing back my nametag.

"Pirates? Oh, that figures," I said. My shining Pacino moment. I sensed the other women's wry smiles as I turned and walked away. I could have at least come up with a question or a clever retort. Like, *Pirates? Really? Tell me more.* Or, *Dad said there was a rebellious side of the family.* Something—anything—but *Oh, that figures.* Where had my tongue gone when I needed it?

On July 19, 2009, the news reported that Frank McCourt died at the age of seventy-eight in New York City of metastatic melanoma. Alas, there would be no more of his stories of human struggle laced with a wee bit of fancy. No more taped books read in his melodic Irish brogue. And no more chances to find out the dirt he had on my Leamy pirate ancestors. When I related my embarrassing moment with Frank McCourt to my Creative Writing students, they thought the idea that I had descended from pirates to be hilarious. I am comforted that Frank McCourt, my dad, and anyone of Irish descent would likely agree that humiliating oneself for a laugh is part of the responsibility of being Irish.

Chapter 12 – Happiness Shows in all Languages

We must not only learn to tolerate our differences.
We must welcome them as the richness and diversity
which can lead to true intelligence.
Albert Einstein

Having traveled abroad a few times, the longest being three weeks, I can't fathom being a teenager living far away, alone in an unfamiliar country. What would it be like living in a foreign family's home for almost a year? Who would I hang out with at lunch time? What if I got sick? Would I be able to understand their language? What if I didn't like the food? It would test one's social skills and inner stamina, that's for sure. In my eyes, these adventurous teens participating in study abroad programs were wonders to behold.

Alvarro was one of those foreign exchange students. He came to the United States from Spain. One day he wrote this poem for class, and it was published in our literary magazine and is reprinted here with his permission.

The Day of Snow

In a morning as I got up from my bed
thoughts of school were in my head,
thinking about another boring day
same routine day by day.

I open my door very bored
going to the kitchen looking at the floor
eating my breakfast like never before,

same routine day by day.
But today is a different day,
I look at the window in a different way
the sky is white, wishful and wonderful
will it be the same routine day by day?

White feathery, flakes, falling from the sky
white flakes on the ground are getting high
it will not be the same routine this day
there is too much snow.

So no school for today!

Jenny, one of our Lit Mag artists, sketched snowflakes on it to accentuate the words, making it seasonal and attractive.

Lit Mag was Literary Magazine, a club that I advised which met once per week after school to plan and publish the creative work of high school students. We referred to ourselves as Lit Maggers or Lit Maggots. It was an immensely popular club, and, unfortunately, every year I had to turn people away. Not really. We had several more members than Chess Club, which boasted six.

Alvarro was very proud of his poem. He, and all the foreign exchange students I've had, allowed me and other Plattevillians to learn about their lives, their countries, and their cultures without us having to board an airplane. They were here to learn from us, too. Occasionally, that concerned me.

Anna came to us from Sweden. One day during work time I was helping her with an assignment, and I saw tears in her eyes. She was trembling.

"What's wrong, Anna?"

In pieced together English, she whispered that she missed her family. Anna's host sister was sitting two rows over and privy to this exchange. She made no move to comfort Anna or even acknowledge her. After class, they left the room separately. I surmised there may have been some conflict or problems with Anna's placement. After class, I mentioned this interaction to our guidance counselor.

For several weeks, Anna resembled a goldfish out of water, a puppy without a home, or whatever other cliché best conveys that dismal feeling of not belonging. With some finagling of the bureaucracy that got her here, the placement director was able to arrange Anna's return to Sweden after a month instead of a semester. That must have been the loneliest month of Anna's life.

This problem may have happened no matter where Anna had been assigned to live. I understood that the vetting process of students applying to be exchange students was extensive, and the same goes for host families. Either this wasn't a good match, or Anna was not a good candidate for this endeavor. Still, I wish I'd have investigated her droopy walk and sad eyes sooner.

Aleksei was from Russia, and, unlike Anna, he explored Platteville like a pioneer on a long-awaited journey. He joined the cross country runners and swim team and made numerous friends while attending many school events. In English class, we had just finished reading the book *Fahrenheit 451* by Ray Bradbury, and I assigned students to write and videotape their interpretation of a scene from the book. I observed the groups as they worked and noticed that Aleksei and Jason, his assigned partner, worked well together in planning their script, costumes, and filming locations. The day arrived when we all got to view the productions. Theirs proved to be particularly entertaining.

In one scene, Aleksei appeared in a midi-length dress, scarf and wig, hamming it up as Mildred Montag. Completely in character, Aleksei walked out the door of the Montag home with a suitcase in hand. He turned, jabbing his finger at Jason, his pretend husband, and yelling in a high-pitched voice, "Oh, Guy. I leave you 'cause you like burn booooooks." Alexei then stomped down the steps, looked back, and exclaimed with heightened emotion, "That feeex you, Guy!"

Aleksei loved that he'd made us laugh. Never mind that the interpretation of the scene wasn't quite as Bradbury had intended. Since Russia's attack on Ukraine, I've thought of Aleksei. I imagine he'd be in his thirties now. I wonder, Did he stay in Russia? What career did he choose? Did he have a family? What was he doing now?

The German foreign exchange students we welcomed to Platteville seemed to have a canny ability to adjust quickly and fit in. That could be because many people in Southwest Wisconsin have German heritage. Our diet consists of sausages like bratwurst with sauerkraut washed down with beer on special occasions—any occasion, really. Also, the landscape of rolling hills and forests are reminiscent of the German landscape.

One of the first German students I had in class was Clara. She was a fun-loving teen with a broad smile and freckles. She was bright and did fine academically but could have done better if our American social life hadn't been so enticing. She adored parties and activities such as jet skiing on the Mississippi River—and— did I mention parties? Judging by some of the stories students shared after she left, I'm glad she got back to Germany and her family intact.

Christoph, or Chris, as we came to know him, longed to come to our country to play American football. He said that *bundesliga*, German football, was like what we Americans think of as soccer. Chris was a big guy, tall and muscular, with a physique more fitting of our style of football. He bonded with the coach and the team, worked hard, and became a valuable player. Their season ended with far more wins than losses, as well as a win in the first game of the conference playoffs.

Chris was smart and fun to have in class. He told me he

enjoyed reading John Hersey's nonfiction book *Hiroshima* which recounted first-hand accounts of survivors of the atomic bomb. When this World War II unit culminated with a viewing of *Schindler's List*, Chris added a contemporary German perspective to our discussions. He told of his country's disdain for Hitler and about the mandatory lessons about the Holocaust taught in all German schools.

Chris reluctantly raised his hand one day while we were discussing *Hiroshima*. "Mrs. Kies, I don't want to insult you. I know you are doing the best you can—but I have to tell you because it bothers me." *The class and I took a collective breath. Oh, my gosh. Did I insult him in some way?* "You are badly mispronouncing Father Kleinsorge's name. It's 'Klinesoorga,' not 'Klinesorj.'" (Father Kleinsorge is a German priest who is one of the featured survivors in the nonfiction account in the novel.)

Students snickered. *"Danke schön,"* I replied, hoping I'd said *that* correctly. "I'm glad you told me, Chris." I repeated Chris's pronunciation of the priest's name several times, finally to his satisfaction. Everyone relished hearing their English teacher struggling to pronounce a word correctly. When Father Kleinsorge's name came up in future discussions, I noticed that other students also made the effort to say it properly.

And I could never forget Louis. Like Clara, Louis seemed to make the trip from Germany mostly to study the American social scene—and, of course, to play soccer. He was a dynamic asset, scoring goal after goal, leading the team to the playoffs. This athletic talent, along with his charm, allowed him some advantages. One of them was a steady girlfriend. After he returned to Germany, she visited him and his family.

One day the class was taking a quiz. Louis's gaze blatantly roamed to a peer's paper, his body leaning precipitously across the aisle. I tried to catch his eye to admonish him, but he was too engrossed in copying his neighbor's answers.

"Louis," I said. When he looked up, I scowled and shook my head.

After class he apologized and told me that in Germany cheating was a common and necessary skill, as test scores were of the utmost importance to one's future.

"First of all, you're far from skilled at it, Louis. And, second, you'd better not do it again. This time you get a zero. If there's a next time, I'll send you to the principal who will likely suspend you from the soccer team. You might want to spend a little more time on school work instead of soccer and socializing, okay?"

He nodded and grinned that charming grin. "But, that's not as much fun."

The next year Karl made the trek from Germany. After Louis's exploits, I watched Karl closely for roving eyes. But it was all for naught. He and Louis were as alike as wiener schnitzel and apple strudel. Karl played soccer, but he also tried out for and snagged a role in the musical—and he studied. He earned the highest grade of anyone in his hour's Junior English class—without cheating. All with English as his second language.

It's a good thing Louis wasn't the only foreign exchange student I had from Germany. Like humans sometimes do, I might have stereotyped him and jumped to the silly conclusion that all Germans thought cheating was okay.

Italia sent us Lucia with her wavy dark hair and shining dark eyes. She had not been smiling very much lately, though. Having learned from the situation with Anna, I asked, "How's it going, Lucia?"

"I miss home," she said. "And English is so hard."

"Do you feel comfortable with your host family?"

"Yes, they are very nice. I like them a lot. But people here talk so fast. I not understand and get lost with words."

"That's part of why you're here, right? To learn English?"

She nodded.

"Give it time. You'll get better at English the more you hear it. Ask people to talk more slowly. They'll understand and be happy to help you."

It took a month or so, but Lucia's English improved. Her smile grew large above her tiny frame. In May she attended prom with a group of friends, looking lovely and happy in her Cinderella gown. Later that month, however, Lucia contracted an infection that required her to be hospitalized. When informed of this, her mother, a beekeeper in Italy, made the journey to Platteville to be with her until she recovered. It worked out serendipitously because her mom was able to meet Lucia's American friends and teachers and attend her graduation ceremony from PHS in early June.

A couple of weeks later, Lucia bid us *arrivederci*. Her suitcases bulged with keepsakes, and her mind welled with fluent English and more Wisconsin memories and adventures than you could shake a stick at. (We explained idioms like this to Lucia as best we could.) The following summer, several of Lucia's fellow PHS graduates traveled to Italy to sample the food and the beaches, all with their newfound Italian *amica*.

Then there was Eun Kyung Kim, who came from South Korea to learn with us at PHS. I was baffled as to how to pronounce her name, so I asked her to say it for me. Because she was quiet and shy and looked down at her desk when she said it, I asked her to repeat it once more. I still didn't understand. I moved on so I wouldn't embarrass her on her first day. She seemed to want to remain anonymous while she dipped her toe into her new surroundings.

After a few days, I called on her again. "Please remind me how to pronounce your name. I'm sorry, but I've forgotten."

She spoke a bit louder this time. I repeated it, and the class laughed because I blew it. "You call me Kim," she said, which was her last name.

Later that day I asked Sarah, "Can you help me with your guest sister's name? I can't seem to get it."

"Sure. It's easy: Oon Keeung."

This time I was ready. "Good morning, Eun Kyung." Her entire face smiled back at me.

Daily, Eun Kyung chattered in Chinese with a couple of students whose parents ran a local restaurant. During and after class, she spoke little. This wasn't helping her English. One day I noticed Wendy and her friends talking to Eun Kyung, and she smiled at something they said. *Cool.* It took the first semester for her to get comfortable, but she developed a circle of companions who were supportive and kind. In class, she began to speak up and look people in the eye. The day I saw her laughing, I knew she was making strides.

Later in the year I gave students an assignment to be completed by the end of the class period. I let them work in groups so I could observe the discussions taking place about the topic and chime in with suggestions.

"You can work with us, Eun Kyung," Morris offered, but Eun Kyung did not respond.

Thinking she hadn't heard him, he repeated the offer in a louder voice. She turned to him and politely but firmly replied, "I sorry, Morris, but I not want be in your group. You no do work good or care about grade." Everyone, including Morris, laughed at Eun Kyung's honest assessment. I gave her a high five in celebration of her assertiveness and ability to navigate an American classroom.

Tomás was the only exchange student during my tenure to come to Platteville from Portugal. He genuinely enjoyed people and exuded a warmth that won you over the moment you met him. He made a variety of friends, played soccer as well as chess, and pounced on every opportunity this exchange experience would allow him.

For the final project of my Creative Writing class, Tomás opted to write and perform a stand-up comedy routine. "Are you sure you want to do this?" I asked. His English was fluent and very understandable, but I explained that constructing and communicating humor in a second language might be daunting. My doubts proved to be superfluous, as he delivered his monologue with confidence and poise. It wasn't quite *Saturday Night Live* material, but his observations about adjusting to life in our country were keen, self-deprecating, clever, and made us laugh.

When he left, Tomás gave friends and teachers bracelets he made out of cord using the blue, gold and red colors representing his favorite soccer team back home. He also distributed postcards of his home city and high school on the coast of Portugal. His school was located across the street from a sandy ocean beach. It looked more like a vacation getaway. "And why," I asked, "did you leave that to come to Platteville, Tomás?"

"This has been one of the best experiences of my life," he said. "If I wouldn't have come, I'd have missed out on meeting so many wonderful people and learning so much about America." I've kept up with him. After continuing his education in Portugal, he became an anesthesiologist in his home country. Bravo, Tomás!

As I mentioned earlier with my dad's acquaintance, Amadi, the university added culture to our small city. My student Katie's parents both worked at the University of Wisconsin-Platteville. Katie was second-generation Chinese. I first met her when she came to a Literary Magazine meeting as a freshman. Pretty and tall with short dark hair, quiet and shy, she was a mouse in the corner. But that didn't last long.

Once Katie and her eclectic friends became comfortable in Lit Mag, meetings became a hub of creativity, a hive of ideas.

People began to notice us. That fall for the homecoming parade Lit Mag members piled into a snazzy convertible, the car stereo thumping, dressed in attire to reflect the title of the fall/winter magazine: Thug Wives. I was skeptical about this title, so I checked out the definition of "thug wife" in the Urban Dictionary: "A stay-at-home male who cooks and cleans and or looks after his partner and children while maintaining his manliness and street cred." Okay, I thought, I can live with that. (I have since come to understand that today this title would not be appropriate, as the term thug in today's rap music is akin to "gangsta." Remember how I said hindsight is 20/20?)

The next year, due to safety concerns, the police declared that no one on any homecoming float could throw out candy. Everyone, parade participants and attendees alike, were disappointed. Considering this unpopular change in the rules, Katie and friends decided it would be sufficiently satirical to ride down the street in the back of a pickup truck with bags bursting with candy and eating it with exaggerated relish. The sign on the side of the truck said, "It's too bad you can't have any candy. Yum! It sure tastes good! If you join Lit Mag, we might share!"

Every year I urged Lit Mag students to enter their writing in the Creative Writing Festival for high school students at UW-Whitewater. It was a two and a half-hour-trek, and we left in the early morning darkness to get there by 9 a.m. I drove the school van, and students slept on the way. Once there, we got our schedules and attended workshops that focused on the writing that the students from the tri-state area (Wisconsin, Illinois, and Iowa) had turned in.

Katie had many skills. One of them was art. She designed and drew all of our Lit Mag covers. Another of her strengths was standardized test-taking. With superior scores on the ACT, PSAT, and various AP tests, she eventually became a National Merit Scholar. The National Merit Scholarship Corporation recognizes and honors academically talented US high school scholars with competitive awards to fund their higher education. Who better to write an essay that poked fun at the standardized test-taking process with its weirdly worded, uptight rules, strictly timed segments, and enigmatically worded multiple choice questions. It was hilarious. She read it aloud at the festival and received first place in the humor category.

During Katie's junior year the chosen musical was *Thoroughly Modern Millie.* While participating in the practices, she found the characters to be ridiculously stereotypical, the plot historically inaccurate, and the dialogue offensive. It was supposed to be farcical and funny, but, to her, it wasn't. Written fifty years ago, a different era when it comes to political correctness, the original musical featured characters performing in yellow-face with the names of Ching Ho and Bun Fu. It revolved around a slavery ring that sent white women from New York to China to become sex slaves.

When she could no longer tolerate this offensive material, Katie talked to the musical director. Upon hearing Katie's concerns and giving them due consideration, those in charge of the musical decided to switch to an alternate production. The director didn't want anyone to feel uncomfortable with the chosen musical.

Some participants became frustrated that the musical they had been practicing for weeks had been scrapped. Social media posts and discussions among students roiled into emotional exchanges. Students took sides, and, as happens, parents joined the fray as well. They thought Katie should endure the musical's problematic cultural references, suck it up, and be quiet. "Who hasn't felt offended at some time or other?" they commented.

Those who agreed with the director's decision believed that any production sponsored by the school should not display and promote racial stereotypes. This raised some interesting questions. How should a school deal with literature and art that offends people? What if it reflects the once historically accepted but presently inappropriate cultural norms? Should we modify these works to make them less offensive? Should we present them with an explanation of the period in which it was written? Indeed, a live performance where these offensive epithets are pronounced aloud over and over was much different from reading them quietly to oneself as my students did with *The Adventures of Huckleberry Finn.*

Yet, a few years before the *Thoroughly Modern Millie* controversy, PHS put on the musical *Big River*, which was the story of Huck Finn and a runaway slave named Jim taken from Twain's novel. The n-word was removed, and a white person portrayed Jim, not in blackface, of course. This production was not without its critics, and steps were taken to modify the musical so as not to be offensive but still entertaining.

Before this debate about the musical, Katie shared with me that her parents' friends in China witnessed the massacre in Tiananmen Square in June of 1989. This is when the Chinese military opened fire with assault rifles and tanks, killing and wounding thousands of pro-democracy protesters and bystanders. Katie's parents decided to move to the United States. They first settled in a large Eastern city where they endured racist comments and hateful acts directed toward them in their neighborhood. They hoped, by moving to Platteville, they'd find reprieve from this discrimination. If not for people like her who find the courage to speak up, slavery would still exist, women wouldn't be able to vote, and young children would still be working in factories.

> If not for people like her who find the courage to speak up, slavery would still exist, women wouldn't be able to vote, and young children would still be working in factories.

134

During her senior year, Katie illustrated a children's book I wrote called *Saving Sadie* for the opening of our new Platteville Public Library building. And the following year she left Platteville to study at Harvard after being accepted at Yale as well. She was a leader, a kind person, and an activist in the best sense of the word.

Chapter 13 – Bringing Japan Home

A nation's culture resides in the hearts
and in the souls of its people.
Mahatma Gandhi

When I was eight, I received a black lacquerware jewelry box for Christmas. I remember opening it, and a white plastic ballerina popped up and twirled around in a pink tutu to the tune of the Viennese Waltz. What a cultural mishmash of modern marketing! The element that captivated me most was the glittery snow-capped rendition of Mt. Fuji on the top. I traced the peak with my finger, wondering what this exotic place might be like. I could never have imagined that forty-two years later, I would visit Japan and get a first-hand view of that faraway, majestic mountain.

It all happened when our PHS Gifted and Talented Coordinator, encouraged me to fill out the extensive forms for the FMF (Fulbright Memorial Fund) teacher exchange to Japan. She had done this five years prior and thought I might be interested in the experience. Thus, I became one of two hundred American teachers from all over the United States chosen to fly to Tokyo to absorb and observe Japanese culture for three weeks. After the visit, I was expected to incorporate what I learned into an informative unit for my students. Does teaching get any better than this?

All participants first met in San Francisco. There, FMF representatives briefed us on our itinerary as well as important elements of Japanese culture and customs. The next day we boarded the flight to Tokyo. For the first several days I felt I was talking in a tin can due to flying thirteen hours at a high altitude.

Being sick, I spent my first night in the hotel getting to know my first Japanese friend—the techno toilet. I explored the buttons. It not only had a heated seat but also the capability to play music and wash my bottom with several different levels of water pressure. This was in stark contrast to the toilet I used a few days later at the baseball game we attended. That toilet accommodation amounted to little more than a hole in the floor. Always intrigued by bodily functions, my students were completely enthralled when I shared the pictures and descriptions of these contrasting bathroom accommodations with them in a photo presentation when I returned.

I was truly initiated on the third night in Tokyo, at 11:45 p.m., when my body leapt several inches from the bed. My first thought was to get my hands on the joker who had entered my room and was shaking my mattress. I looked around, and no one was there. When I stood up, the sensation was that of standing on a floating pier. At the window, I expected to see a huge crack buckling the roadways and swallowing buildings, including the New Otani Hotel and me. But, traffic flowed. Everything looked ordinary. I peeked into the hallway, and not a creature was stirring. My room was on the twenty-seventh floor, so it didn't seem wise to use the stairs or elevator. I returned to bed and resigned myself to the fact that if the building fell, I'd be going with it.

If an earthquake hadn't been enough of a shake up, on Saturday a typhoon blew in. Back home, we practiced tornado drills, but I had no clue what to do in an earthquake or a typhoon. However, this was second nature to Tokyoites. The hotel staff advised patrons to be inside by four p.m. that day, and most heeded their suggestion. The wind hurled raindrops against my hotel window. The seal around the glass made a freaky sucking sound, likely relieving the pressure so it wouldn't blow in. The next day the headlines of *The Japan Times* read: "Typhoon kills

17, leaves trail of havoc." The bullet trains closed due to the influx of water and mud, causing our long-awaited trip to historic Kyoto to be canceled.

When I told my students about these weather phenomena, many who had never traveled further than a couple of hundred miles from home looked at me in wonder that I had survived to tell about them.

After spending five days exploring the temples, shrines, and the Tsukiji Fish Market in Tokyo, the FMF planners divided our large group into smaller groups so we could investigate other prefectures (states). My destination—Kofu City, a mountain municipality tucked between the Japanese Alps on one side—and none other than Mt. Fuji on the other. We ascended into the mountains on the train, and I looked down on the bright green rice fields in the valleys below, while keeping a watchful eye to the sky for my first glimpse of her.

That moment happened at the end of our train ride when we visited the Yamanashi Prefectural Museum of Art. Before we entered the building, figuring we might not notice her amidst the clouds, our guide pointed into the distance. There, amid a foggy mist of white, I saw her. An outline of her, anyway. Even enshrouded and barely visible, she ruled the sky.

On Saturday I got a closer look. Yumie and Shouzou, my host family, and their neighbors who hosted Debbie, another Fulbrighter, led us to the top of Panorama Mountain. Through the trees, in the midst of wispy clouds known as her veils, Fuji-san stood boldly, lovely and proud, in the distance. Our hosts said that, according to Japanese lore, Fuji is a jealous mountain. Long ago when a nearby peak threatened her in stature and beauty, she erupted and lashed out at her rival, slicing at her and leaving her with an unattractive flat top.

* * *

Seeing Fuji was a long-awaited highlight, but that week we also visited Kokubo Elementary, Yamanashigakuin Junior High School, a technical high school, and Yamanashi University. At last we'd be able to see Japanese education up close. We were surprised that the children at the elementary school thought of all Americans as rock stars and asked us to sign autographs and pose for photos. In a third grade classroom, I introduced myself in Japanese, then in English. Students politely applauded and asked a few questions. I took a seat at a table in the back of the room to watch the teacher present a lesson. Soon, I felt a gentle tug on my hair. I turned to find that one of the young boys from this sea of raven-haired youngsters was inspecting my conspicuous blond locks firsthand.

At the junior high school, though students were required to wear uniforms, one young man stood out. He'd dyed his shoes pink and wore his hair in funky mohawk. One way or another, he was going to make a statement. He jumped at the chance to be in a photo with his peers, and we teachers noted how kids of that age group craved the limelight. Students there began English classes in elementary school, so by the time they were in junior high, they could converse with us. I ate lunch with a group who asked me questions about school lunches in America.

On our last night in Kofu City, we feasted on sukiyaki, smoked fish, tempura, and warm sake at a ryokan, a traditional Japanese inn. After dinner, the women and men went to separate *onsens*, spring-fed communal mineral baths. As with the showers in physical education class, I, like most of my peers, was not comfortable with disrobing and bathing in front of others. But, when in Japan... One young woman in our group was doing her best to be modest while sitting on the tiny stool provided and rinsing off her body. Still wrapped in her towel, she accidentally tipped backward on the stool, her legs shooting into the air. So much for modesty.

The next day before we boarded the train back to Tokyo. In the subway station, Sharon, a teacher from Minnesota, accidentally caught a finger in her necklace, sending beads skittering across the tiled floor like jumping beans. Immediately, the Japanese commuters around us stooped to retrieve the beads and placed them in her hands. She tried to tell them it wasn't necessary, but they persisted until every bead in sight was retrieved.

I'd become pleasantly accustomed to the bowing and courtesy of the Japanese people. While preparing to depart from Narita Airport, baggage attendants asked about our stay, wished us a safe flight, and invited us to come back to visit. When I passed through the metal detector at Chicago O'Hare, my belt buckle set off the alarm. "That's funny," I said, "it didn't do that in Tokyo."

The burly woman attendant shot back: "Well, Hon, you ain't in Tokyo no more, so take off your belt and move it, will ya? You're slowin' down the line."

This trip turned out to be a wonderland of learning. Like Alice, sometimes I felt overwhelmed with the many splendors and unexpected drama of each situation. My mind reeled with ways to share my experiences with my students. Besides my photos and stories, I chose to teach the book *Hiroshima* by John Hersey. It went beyond the history books and told the true stories of six people who experienced the dropping of the atomic bomb. I told students how, when in Tokyo, we Fulbright teachers listened to a ninety-five-year-old survivor relate his memory of that day. He was in his home when he saw the big flash of light. Miraculously, he and his baby son survived. However, his wife died of radiation poisoning the following year.

"Wasn't he—weren't all—the Japanese mad at us Americans for doing that?" asked a student.

"I was concerned about that when I went there too," I told her. "But when someone asked him that question, he said that the people of Japan did not blame the people of the United States. The Japanese government had done terrible things as well, like bombing Pearl Harbor and torturing American prisoners. He explained that *regular people* in any country just want to live their lives in peace and freedom, raise their kids, and do their jobs."

The slideshow of photos from my trip portrayed *regular, everyday people.* The crowd at the baseball game in Tokyo, buying snack food, laughing at the mascot, and the two young boys grinning because they'd just nabbed an errant foul ball. My hostess Yumie smiling in her living room with her dog Belle perched on her lap. The interested faces of teens gathered around a computer screen in the high school. Two middle school girls in gym class holding basketballs and flashing smiles and peace signs. The concentrated faces of the elementary school choir while singing "Take Me Home Country Roads" in our honor. A young wait staff standing by the buffet table loaded with a splendid array of scrumptious dishes. The Yamanashi University parking lot overflowing with hundreds of bicycles of its students.

To culminate the unit about Japan, we read the true story of *Sadako and the Thousand Paper Cranes.* Sadako, a young girl from Hiroshima, loved to run fast. When Sadako fell ill, her doctor diagnosed her with leukemia, caused by the fallout from the atomic bomb dropped in 1945 when she was two. According to an old Japanese legend, anyone who folded a thousand origami cranes would get their wish. Sadako wished to be well. Though she reached her goal of folding a thousand cranes, sadly, she died at age twelve. In her honor, her friends and family erected a statue of Sadako lifting a large paper crane into the air. The inscription at the foot of the statue in Hiroshima Peace Memorial Park reads, "This is our cry. This is our prayer. Peace in the world."

It would be fun to make paper cranes in honor of Sadako

after reading the story, I thought. But would juniors dismiss it as infantile elementary school stuff? I took that chance and passed out brightly colored origami paper and put on a YouTube video of crane-making instructions. We paused often to get each fold correct, so the crane would come out looking like a crane and not a stomped on crumple of paper.

"You've just got to put this fold here. —See? —There, you have it. —Just one more step."

"I don't get it, either."

"Here, I'll help you. Look at mine."

Those who understood how to make a crane helped those who didn't. Talk about an exercise in fine motor skill development, following technical directions, and demonstrating cooperation and patience. I repeated this activity every year after that, amazed at how my juniors enjoyed this process of making cranes. Some stayed after class to finish. Others wanted to know if they could make another. And another.

Some took the cranes with them and some left them for me to string up from the ceiling. Suspended from thread at varying heights, they swirled and spun, propelled by students walking by or air circulating in the room. They looked like peace in motion.

Dear Educators,

Please model cultural curiosity in your classroom.
Take in every opportunity to learn more about the world
and its people to share with your students.
Signed,
Still Learning

* * *

One morning during my first class period I wrote a quote by Henry David Thoreau on the board. While waiting for the bell to ring, someone translated the quote into Spanish underneath the original quote. By the end of the day, others had followed suit, and the quote graced my board in seven other languages besides English. French and Spanish by the students of those languages in our school; German, Chinese, and Norwegian as per the foreign exchange students; and Hindi and Farsi by my second-generation students of Indian and Iranian descent. Platteville had certainly become more diverse since I had been a student.

My students constructed a cultural wonder. (Mind you, this was before the invention of Google translate.) All those languages looked different, yet expressed the same sentiment. You know John Lennon's lyric from his song "Beautiful Boy": "Life is what happens when you're making other plans"? Well, sometimes learning is what happens when you're teaching other lessons.

Sometimes learning is what happens when you're teaching other lessons.

PART III – THE WEIGHT
OF IT ALL

Chapter 14 – In the Name of Sports

If you win through bad sportsmanship,
that is no real victory.
Babe Didrikson Zaharias

My student Sadie tore into my room, papers flapping.

"I have something for Lit Mag. Please read it, Mrs. Kies," she said. "I think it's good. I hope you like it!"

Tall and independent, Sadie was a self-described band geek. I looked over her essay entitled "My Two Cents on Sports" she hoped to publish in the student literary magazine, the after-school club I advised. It was candid and clever, and the last line made me laugh: "So, fear the band!"

The essay lauded band members as valuable, capable, and skilled athletes because they often "march in thick uniforms designed for cold weather when it's eighty degrees out, while carrying a heavy instrument," and marching and playing an instrument can be "like holding your breath underwater as the swimmers do, or like sprinting for runners." It was forward thinking, funny, and candid. She maintained that marching band members implemented physical and mental skills as much as athletes, but that this fact often went unnoticed.

In the movie *Dead Poets Society* that I showed every year during the transcendentalism unit, Mr. Keating, the prep school teacher played by Robin Williams, takes his English class to the soccer field for a vigorous workout. He tells them, "For me, sport is actually a chance for us to have other human beings push us to excel."

If only sports in our society, and our school, embodied that sentiment.

At PHS, like other high schools, many parents live vicariously through their kids when it comes to sports, cheering on their child or their child's team to dominate others. This ideology probably goes back to the first ancient Greek sporting contests or maybe even to caveman times. Understandably, physical prowess in the form of being able to win in battle or slay the beast was valued as necessary for survival.

I loved to play sports when I was young. My father, an avid Green Bay Packer fan, taught me the rudiments of football, along with softball, basketball, and ice skating. One summer we attended a summer Packer practice in Green Bay. "Everyone gets autographs," I told my cousin Jan. "That's lame." So, instead of standing in line, I approached then quarterback Bart Starr from behind and brushed the toe of my tennis shoe against the heel of his. "Ha! I just touched Bart Starr's tennis shoe," I whispered, and my cousin laughed. It's a wonder someone didn't apprehend me. And, I see now that getting his autograph would have been far more lasting and lucrative.

My friends, neighbors, or cousins and I routinely played unsupervised games of baseball or football, kickball or kick the can. We learned teamwork and strategy, and how to work out disagreements among ourselves. It also gave our growing bodies a good workout rather than sitting in front of the TV. Today, screens tempt kids at every turn to watch the action instead of take part in it. A couple of my students were chronically absent from school because they became addicted to video games and stayed up all night playing in competitions.

When I entered school and found that only boys participated in organized sports, I felt deflated. We girls played our role as their cheerleaders. Five of us did, anyway. Not willing to sit still in the stands, I tried out and became a cheerleader in seventh grade and continued into high school. In 1972, the year I graduated from high school, President Richard Nixon enacted

Title IX of the Education Amendments, which outlawed discrimination by sex in any educational program or activity receiving any type of federal financial aid. Finally! Many high school girls today do not realize how this law and other equal rights legislation changed the course of their lives.

In my years at PHS both as a student and as a teacher, one aspect of sports remained constant: parents often schmoozed coaches to enhance the chances of their kid being noticed and becoming a starter on the team. You know, the squeaky wheel? No money exchanged hands that I'm aware of, but if it had I wouldn't be surprised. Sometimes parents coached their own kids in city leagues. Occasionally, this situation worked out well, but more often than not, the parent was either extra tough on their kid so as not to be seen as favoring him or her—or the parent favored their kid to the point where all the other team members became frustrated with the coach and the child. The poor kid couldn't win for losing.

A parent who regularly hurled criticisms and obscenities at the referees during his kids' basketball games was ejected from the gymnasium and eventually banned from attending any school competitions. When I was in high school and cheering at a basketball game in a neighboring town, the referee issued several warnings and technical fouls to parents exhibiting poor sportsmanship. Fed up, he stopped the game and booted an entire section of parents and fans from the gym. Just a few weeks earlier in a town nearby, the police were called to a youth soccer game because the parents got into a scuffle over a disagreement about the game. And, of course, there is the University of Wisconsin-Madison student section that is notorious for their obscene, insulting chants directed at the opposing team and fans. This has become a sport unto itself.

It's easy to get caught up in the competition of the moment. At a three-on-three basketball tournament for my youngest daughter, I am ashamed to say I expressed my displeasure with the ref about an errant call. That ref absolutely needed to make an appointment with her optometrist to have her eyes checked. I was sure of it and told her so.

Sports can teach kids many things, both good and bad, depending.

I'm sure at this moment some readers are upset with my criticisms. Angry even. Sports are ingrained in our culture as all important and divine. A sort of religion. I have had students who could name every NFL quarterback, every Big Ten point guard, and all MLB home run stats but couldn't tell you the name of the current governor of our state—and, in some cases, the president.

In high school I was not only a cheerleader but a band member and majorette. As I said, there were no women's sports, so the male athletes got all the press and community attention. Marching band and pep band entertained at freezing football games and in the stuffy gym at basketball games. Few people gave us a hoot or holler, except maybe our parents.

For me, band class provided a respite from sitting, listening, and taking notes. Like a team, we all played our parts in an attempt to create something beautiful together. Our instructor, Mr. Ron Thompson, was strict and expected nothing but the best from us. He was our coach. We competed in concert and marching competitions, usually taking home a first place award. I met my future husband in the band room as a sophomore clarinetist. He was a senior and first chair trumpet player. His well-developed embouchure was a definite asset when it came to making out.

The Lit Mag staff and I published Sadie's essay on marching band being a sport in the winter issue. We figured some students in sports might not agree with it, but, oh well. Boy, were we wrong! The negative response descended upon us like the thundering of the PHS marching drumline. On the day the publication debuted in January, students appeared at my door every hour between classes requesting copies of Lit Mag. In the fifteen years I had been the advisor, this had never happened. I once mentioned Lit Mag to one of my classes, and many said they had never heard of it—even though copies were overtly displayed in my classroom.

"How dare Sadie say that band is harder than sports," said Tammy, a member of Lit Mag. Tammy hadn't known about the article because she'd been attending swim practice every day after school that fall. "I've been in both, and playing sports is much harder than band. How could you put that article in Lit Mag, Mrs. Kies? It's an insult to PHS sports!"

"Try not to get so defensive, Tammy. Look at it as a satirical piece saying, 'Hey, don't forget about the band members, the unsung heroes at sporting events.'"

"No, it's not. It's insulting and demeaning. Can I write a rebuttal?"

Bad feelings between the band members and the sports teams swelled, and those who participated in both were pressured into taking sides. I never thought one essay could energize the student population to this proportion. I liked that it created dialogue among students, but I wasn't keen on the rancor that accompanied it. Worst of all, it entrenched the students more firmly in their cliques.

Tammy's counter article answered the challenge and came out in the spring issue. "Take the NFL championship game, for instance," she wrote. "It is one of the most televised events across the nation. It raked in around 111.3 million viewers this past year [2012] according to sportsillustrated.cnn.com. I'd like to see the Grammys do that." This pacified those in sports, and she ended with a gentle jab: "Sports and band are simply different things, with neither better than the other. Sports are just as challenging, if not more so, than band. So, fear the band? No thank you, I'd rather play a sport."

Her response helped pacify those in sports, but I was relieved to see summer come to give everyone a chance to exhale and breathe into a fresh start the next year. I wished they would come to see how sports and music have always gone together. That's why we have school songs, workout and warmup playlists, and therapeutic tunes to relax to. Both camps deserved their due.

I learned three things from this experience: One, I needed to do a better job teaching my students about satire. Two, nothing promotes awareness like controversy, and, three—sports in our school and our culture was *very serious* business.

Dear Parents and Coaches of Athletes,
Sports should be fun and teach kids how to be better people,
physically, mentally, socially, and emotionally.
If that's not happening, there's something wrong.
Signed,
A Good Sport Enthusiast

Chapter 15 – The Ladies Doth Protest

She had not known the weight until she felt the freedom.
Nathaniel Hawthorne, *The Scarlet Letter*

Miss Clark, my freshman English teacher, was in her early thirties, unmarried, and attractive. She wore a bright red lipstick that paired well with her olive-colored skin but didn't always coordinate with her outfits. Back then, she was considered an "old maid," a social term of the time used to label such a woman as "ill fated." A better phrase to use might have been "purposefully independent."

In 1907 Miss Clark's grandfather, George Wedige, built the historic building on Second Street, known then and now for its drinking establishments. Miss Clark spent time during the summer, on weekends, and evenings helping her mother, who inherited the bar, tend to the endless duties of running a business. Early on, a couple of school board members were not happy that one of the district's teachers moonlighted in such a place. But she heeded them not. If she could manage us freshmen, she could certainly hold her own with the school board.

Miss Clark was not unlike future English teachers I would encounter in high school and college. Eclectic and quirky, she occasionally let loose a smile or chuckle about the text we were studying for reasons that escaped us, her students. Because she expected respect, she got it, and was by no means an easy A.

Her class awakened my intellectuality. The nuns at St. Mary's, though skilled at teaching the diagramming of sentences and proper grammar, made no attempt to interpret literature. We knew the basic narratives of the Bible but rarely discussed its foundations or implications. To the Franciscans, all stories were black and white, much like their habits. There were protagonists and antagonists, good and bad, right and wrong, and not a lot in between.

Miss Clark's passion for her subject matter emanated from her like cool water from a spring. I remember discussing Nathaniel Hawthorne's *The Scarlet Letter* and Willa Cather's *My Antonia* in our first period class, both novels featuring strong, independent women. Hester Prynne, an adulteress, thrived and grew as a person despite hateful Puritan scrutiny. And there was Antonia Shimerda who endured hardships and discrimination after her family immigrated to Nebraska from Bohemia. It was clear Miss Clark admired these women and their emotional fortitude to stand up to societal scrutiny.

The large window of her classroom looked out on the front parking lot, which gave us a front row seat to late students making a mad dash to the entrance or, on rare occasions, the arrival of a police car. In the fall of 1968 we were discussing homework before school when we noticed a commotion and congregated at the window.

My classmate Valerie pointed. "Look, there's Larry."

"And John, and Sarah, and...Terry," I said.

Most of the students *we* recognized didn't know *us* from Eve or Adam. They were seniors. We were freshmen, nonentities in their world. That is the way of high school.

I leaned forward to get a better look, the grooves of the radiator vent pressing into my palms. A squad car pulled into the parking lot, and two officers got out of the vehicle. They waved their hands toward the entrance as they indicated the students should get up and get to class. Sit-ins on the nightly news were common fare. But right outside our classroom window?

"This is so cool," said Ted, one of our student council representatives. "Why should they be forced to fight or die in a war they don't believe in?" Outside, Ted's brother Joe stood with his buddy Steve, hoisting a cardboard peace sign above their heads.

Two years before this, when I was in seventh grade, our class attended a funeral on a school day. My classmate Kay and her family received word that her brother Bill had been killed by a sniper while on guard duty in Vietnam. When a casualty of war hits close to home, the war becomes real. People's emotions magnify and their opinions gradually settle into concrete. It was 1967, three years into the war, and those opposed to the conflict said things like, "So sad—another senseless death of a young person. We never should have been there in the first place." Others praised Bill's bravery, proudly proclaiming him "a hero who died for his country."

Neither view brought him back to Kay and her family.

At the time, though befuddled by the politics behind the war, I was adamant that the resulting deaths were senseless. Why couldn't the leaders of the countries all sit down and talk about it like we students were supposed to do when we disagreed? Night after night on the evening news, we viewed limbless, injured soldiers and body bags being unloaded from helicopters. It was the first war to be televised, and after four or five years, people numbed, either out of necessity to maintain sanity or the ability to disassociate from it and carry on with their lives.

When the United States instituted the draft, effective on December 1, 1969, all young men between the ages of eighteen and twenty-six were required to register and adhere to the results of the lottery. Joining the military was no longer a career option but a possible requirement. Hence, protests erupted among young people across the country.

During my sophomore year, my friend Dianne and I went to the Army Surplus Store on the corner of Main and Second and bought green Army flak jackets for ten dollars each. On the back of the coat I painted my boyfriend's name inside a big red heart

153

with an arrow through it. It was my "make love not war" statement. My dad offered to buy me any jacket I wanted for any price in lieu of seeing me wearing "that disgraceful thing." We never talked about *why* he hated that coat, but as a World War II veteran, he may have interpreted it as an offense to the country and those who served it. Kind of like wearing the US flag.

For some reason, he gave in. Maybe it was a parental "choose your battles" moment for him. Maybe he was confused by how he felt about the war. Maybe he decided that it was best to let me start making my own decisions about my attire. Or, maybe he knew I'd wear it anyway. I usually respected his wishes, but that coat represented the first sentence of my independent voice. And I wasn't going to relinquish it.

In February, 2011, forty-two years after witnessing that sit-in from Miss Clark's window, I became a protestor for the first time in my life. Now, *I* was an English teacher at Platteville High School. Three of my teacher peers and I requested a personal day to protest Governor Walker's proposed Act 10[1] legislation (official wording: "An Act relating to: state finances, collective bargaining for public employees, compensation and fringe benefits of public employees, the state civil service system, the Medical Assistance program."), which, among other things, would halt collective bargaining by public unions.

AN ACT relating to: state finances, collective bargaining for public employees, compensation and fringe benefits of public employees, the state civil service system, the Medical Assistance program.

According to the NEA (National Education Association), "Collective bargaining is an exchange of ideas between unions

---

[1] The entire document and ammendments can be found here: https://docs.legis.wisconsin.gov/2011/related/acts/10

and management who must negotiate in good faith over the terms and conditions of employment such as salary, benefits, and working conditions. Collective bargaining can also be used to secure student-centered demands like a full-time nurse in every school, recess, or fewer standardized tests." It benefits not only those at the bargaining table, but the community as well.

Our local union representatives had bargained so we could have two days per school year for personal and family business. What better way to use a personal day, we reasoned, than to rally to keep them? Our conversation in the car that day on the way to Madison bolstered our feelings of camaraderie for one another and concern for the future of our profession.

"If this legislation passes, we're really going to take a hit," my colleague said as we headed north on Highway 151. Her husband also taught in the district. "With my husband and me having to pay more toward our insurance and retirement, our yearly income will shrink by at least $14,000. I'm not sure we can manage. Our son's in college and our daughter, well, she wants to go, too."

"I hear you. I feel like I've been sucker-punched," said Jane, now a thirty-three year veteran. (Jane was my friend and colleague, the special education teacher who passed away ten years after this conversation.) "The money hit is bad enough, but with collective bargaining gone, we'll have no input on class size, curriculum, or work expectations. Can you imagine the chaos I could be dealing with?"

Our discussion expanded to concern for our community and our state. With the public school system and the university being the primary employers in Platteville, it was understood that this cut in income would affect local businesses. Those who worked as nurses and firefighters would likewise be affected by this legislation. It was far-reaching, and we wondered, though the bill was intended to cut the deficit, how much these cuts to public services would end up costing society in the long run.

Upon reaching Madison, we pulled into the WEAC (Wisconsin Education Association Council) parking lot just off the beltline. Here, we were among the many teachers and other public workers to board a shuttle to the Capitol building. An organizer addressed us before we left: "I know you are all passionate about this cause, and that's good. I completely understand. However, be aware that there are paid and primed agitators in the crowd who will say and do anything to try to get a rise out of you," she said. "Make sure to stay calm and peaceful, okay?"

We all nodded and cheered, our hands producing a muffled but spirited assent. Accustomed to frigid Wisconsin weather, we'd layered sweaters under our parkas and protected our extremities with boots, hats, and gloves.

The bus dropped us off in front of the Capitol. The four wings of Wisconsin's capitol building support the majestic dome, on which perches the female statue of "Wisconsin." She represents the state motto, Forward. That day, under her outstretched arm, thousands upon thousands of people filled the blocked-off streets around the square. People toted signs, people chanted, people pumped fists, people held hands, marched, sang, beat drums, and rang cowbells. Validation swelled in my heart, and hope took flight.

Then an Act 10 supporter drove by and yelled, "Why don't all of you shut the hell up and get back to work where you belong?"

We'd heard Governor Walker on the newscasts railing that public workers had far better benefits than the private sector. He said that wasn't fair and that it was only right that state workers pay more toward their health and retirement benefits. Well, hell hath no fury like people who believe they are paying taxes for other people to live better than they do. No one seemed to consider that teachers paid taxes too.

In a YouTube video clip by documentary filmmaker Brad Lichtenstein, Walker told billionaire Diane Hendricks of Beloit that the first step to making Wisconsin a completely red state was to break the public worker unions. "Divide and conquer," he told her. And that's exactly what Walker did.

Once the fire was lit and outrage fanned, Walker's Act 10 supporters remained blissfully deaf to any dialogue. *They* were angry. What they didn't know or want to hear was that for many years teachers had negotiated for better benefits in lieu of higher salaries because it was more affordable for the districts where they worked. Teachers had already compromised, but they didn't care a lick about that. And this made *us* angry.

From teachers' perspectives, being villainized and made out to be greedy because we received benefits like health care, personal days, and retirement seemed counterproductive. Why didn't people see that it would be far more beneficial for them to urge their employers to improve their own benefits instead of getting angry at public workers. The workers who provided them with necessary public services? This did not have to be an "us or them" situation, but that's how Walker portrayed it. And many believed him.

Righteousness and passion ran high on both sides.

When my husband and I farmed on shares with the farm's owner in the eighties, banks charged upward of twenty percent interest for farm operating loans. I returned to college to become a teacher to help with income and insurance benefits. After feeding calves in the mornings and getting four of our five children off on the school bus, I attended classes at UW-Platteville three days a week. My mother babysat our youngest who was almost two. During the summer I took correspondence courses through the University of Wisconsin system. Five years later, I graduated in the spring of 1991 with my degree to find that there were 250 to 300 applicants for every teaching job.

After subbing and working as a teacher's aide at PHS, I finally attained a position a couple of years later for $21,000 per year. According to the National Association of College and Employment Journal, the engineers who graduated in 1991 were offered an average of $49,000 (Koncz, Andrea, 8/2/2016). Supply and demand, right? Now that there are not enough teachers to go around, shouldn't their salaries be skyrocketing?

A band played on a stage by the south entrance to the Capitol. We joined protesters bouncing around to the music and waving signs to keep warm. When we entered the doors to use the restroom, security guards told us to deposit any signs mounted on sticks in the large pile. We'd worked too hard on them to relinquish those signs. So, we removed the sticks and took the signs with us. In the restroom, women were using yarn to tie two signs together so they could drape them over their bodies, sandwich-board style. It helped insulate against the cold too.

"Hey, that's creative," I said.

"Act 10 is like a slushie in the face, you know?" one woman from northern Wisconsin said, making reference to the ultimate put-down on *Glee*. "We've *gotta* get creative."

"Yup," another said. "Here, help yourself to some yarn. I brought it so I could knit if I got bored. That's not going to happen." She chuckled.

In the center of the first floor, a man with a megaphone led the crowd in singing "This Land is My Land" and "We Shall Overcome." We climbed the steps to the mezzanine, our voices congregating high in the belly of the rotunda. Outside, the throng of people moved clockwise around the square. "This is what democracy looks like!" Those with drums led the chants: "Hey, hey! Ho, ho! Scott Walker has got to go!" "Whose house? Our house!"

After lunch and hot cocoa at Noodles and Co. on State Street, we proceeded to the main rally which would begin at one p.m.

Sunshine lit up the cold sky as the Madison Firefighters' Bagpipe Band snaked through the crowd in support of the cause. People clapped and high-fived free hands as they passed. Several union representatives spoke on behalf of the American Civil Liberties Union; United Auto Workers; National Education Association; American Federation of State, County and Municipal Employees; Service Employees International Union; and Wisconsin Education Association. Each speaker elicited a roar that surpassed that of a Packer touchdown at Lambeau Field.

We drove home that day, no longer kicked puppies but scrappy Badgers. The demonstrations continued for nearly a month, attracting more than 100,000 people in one day (*Milwaukee Journal Sentinel*). Protesters camped out in the Capitol and future rallies included visits by Wisconsin native and actor Bradley Whitford, movie maker Michael Moore, and the Reverends Jesse Jackson and Al Sharpton. Some of us drove up after school was out for the day to offer support, and one night MSNBC's Ed Schultz broadcasted his show live from the rotunda. News cameras multiplied like bunnies. I had often heard the term media circus. Now I was witnessing one.

On April 16, Sarah Palin set up camp on the north side of the Capitol where a couple of thousand Tea Partiers gathered and yelled to counter anti-Walker protesters. My friend Kay's eighty-five-year-old dad worried about her because Fox News aired a film clip of a riot with pushing and punching between police and protestors. In the background, palm trees waved in the wind. Palm trees in Wisconsin? In February, no less?

During the six times I went to Madison to protest, I witnessed only one tremor that could have resulted in violence. On the day of Palin's visit, a single-file regiment of pro-Walker Tea Partiers pierced the en masse movement of the protesters by marching opposite the flow of the crowd. One young Tea Party woman led the procession that passed in front of me. Chin in the air, she wore the countenance of a soldier headed for battle. She held the stick of our American flag with both hands, thrusting it up and down, her elbows jutting out at right angles, jabbing anyone challenging her route. Those who followed her did the same. The crowd parted to let them pass, recognizing it as an attempt to instigate violence. This group agitating the crowd while bearing our United States flag later reminded me of the perpetrators of the January 6, 2021 insurrection.

One damp, blustery day, my husband and I sipped coffee, shuffling our feet to keep them warm, on grounds outside the Madison Capitol. Officers in SWAT gear patrolled the crowd from atop the buildings. It looked and felt like an action movie set, until I noticed the young mother behind us. She had her baby tucked into her coat to nurse as she chanted in favor of workers' rights that had existed in Wisconsin for the past fifty years.

Locally, every morning before school as students were arriving between seven and seven thirty, about fifteen of us staff members grabbed our signs that said, "We (heart) your kids." We waved and smiled, hoping parents would support us and understand that we were upset because Act 10 negated our ability to negotiate for better educational conditions for their children. Standing in the parking lot with my sign, I was reminded of the sit-in I'd witnessed in that same parking lot in 1968. This time I was an informed protestor, not a curious onlooker.

On Fridays after school we met at the Badger Bar, now owned by my former teacher, Diane Clark. Her mother and aunt had passed away, making her the sole proprietor. By then she had long retired from teaching. A mix of antique signs, photos, and knickknacks of the kitschy sort gave the place the aura of a local museum. The mosaic design in the tile floor mimicked that in the tin ceiling, and a jungle of plants filled the west-facing windows.

Miss Clark was a hospitable host to our informal meetings. In 1945 the Platteville Veterans of Foreign Wars group rallied here, as did the area Democrats in 2006. We discussed the political happenings of the week and planned a local protest of Act 10, beginning with a rally at City Hall and culminating in a walk down Main onto Water Street.

In our small community, as I'm sure it probably did all over the state, and even all over the country, Act 10 made for some uncomfortable conversations between relatives, friends, and coworkers. A few members of our staff did not support the protests and said our governor was only doing his job and trying to balance the budget. We wondered why it was necessary to attack teachers and public workers to do so.

The fact that teachers and support staff were required to pay union dues was also an issue of contention. The Fair Share clause of the contract required nonunion members to pay a fee because, according to the NEA (National Education Association), "this arrangement was justified on the grounds that the union was obligated to represent all employees faithfully." All benefitted, so all should pay.

On occasion, tempers heated up, and the pot boiled. Just what Walker intended.

The passing of Act 10 demonized, belittled, and demoralized the teaching profession. Similar legislation enacted across our nation resulted in droves of retirements and resignations. Today, few new teachers enlist in college training programs, and substitute teachers are on the endangered species list. According to a podcast on November 8, 2023, EdSurge with Jeffrey R. Young, "...since 2010 the number of students enrolled in teacher prep programs at colleges has fallen by more than a third, from about 900,000 students in 2010-11 to only 600,000 in the 2018-19 academic year (American Association of Colleges for Teacher Education). COVID-19 only made these statistics worse. In the fall of 2020-21, 20 percent of college teaching programs reported another drop of 11 percent.

In a March 17, 2023 article for *The Badger Herald,* Jeremiah Frodl followed up on the resulting fallout of Act 10: "By passing Act 10, we put a small dent in our budget deficit and put a massive issue in our education system." He reported that, now, "Wisconsin is fifth in the nation when it comes to teaching vacancies, only losing to Georgia, Florida, Alabama, and Mississippi. Adjusting for population moves us to third ("Twelve Years Later, School Districts Still Paying Price for Act 10.")

The Badger Bar continues to be a meeting place for PHS retired teachers and staff on Friday afternoons. We reminisce with colleagues about past students, lessons, and the good 'ol days before Act 10. Sadly, Diane Clark passed away at the age of seventy-seven in 2015, but her independent spirit lives on. Her friend and former student, Kevin, now fills orders for customer libations. Platteville High School teachers continue to have retirement celebrations in the establishment, toasting those who've served, and continue to serve, the students in our district.

On the first Friday of every month, PHS retirees host current teachers and staff for a Pour it Forward celebration, offering them a free drink and door prizes. It keeps us abreast of educational policies and trends. We dole out encouraging pats on the back and thank Platteville teachers for the work they do. And we hope that will help to see them through another week, another month, another year.

Dear Teachers and Staff,
You ARE rock stars and deserve to be in the
Educational Hall of Fame, and don't you forget it!
Thank you for all you do for our kids,
Much Gratitude,
The Retired Ranks

Chapter 16 – The Men Doth Protest Too

Fiction is to the grown man what play is to the child; it is there that he changes the atmosphere and tenor of his life.
Robert Louis Stevenson

"How come we don't ever have a men's literature unit?" my student Aaron asked me during third period Junior English one day.

"You've had a men's unit in school ever since you've been old enough to read, Aaron. How many books have you read by women authors?"

"I don't know. I don't read books." He was one of *them.* It was obvious his claim was a sham. His intelligence and good vocabulary gave him away. Maybe not an imbiber of school-assigned reading, Aaron *was* a reader, no doubt about it.

Most books in my young reading years were written by men, and most of the books were *about* men and boys. Take, for example, *The Adventures of Tom Sawyer* and *The Adventures of Huckleberry Finn* by Mark Twain, both wonderful books that I enjoyed. However, the few female characters were a letdown, grossly undeveloped and stereotypical. John Steinbeck, Ernest Hemingway, F. Scott Fitzgerald, and Edgar Allan Poe rounded out the list of American authors, with a brief nod to the poetry of Emily Dickinson. For the Brits, William Shakespeare, Charles Dickens, George Orwell, and Thomas Hardy led the pack. Jane Austen's *Emma* and *Pride and Prejudice* did receive some recognition, but were often looked down upon as "chick reads."

On my own I read Nancy Drew and Beverly Cleary books. I don't recall reading anything assigned in school by a woman until Miss Clark's Freshman English class, and then not again until I attended college and took an eye-opening survey course in

Women's Literature. Reading about different cultures was also rare. "Rikki-Tikki-Tavi" by Kipling was the extent of any ethnic literary exploration. And again, it was a male author. Women and girls, over half the population, had been reading and studying literature about and by men for years. How would we ever learn about women then and now if we didn't read their stories?

A few years into my teaching career, I developed a Women's Literature Unit in an attempt to bring awareness to women's historical struggles to be taken seriously. I chose writers and pieces that exemplified the hills women climbed, and still climb, not only to become writers—but to become themselves.

To personalize this unit, I often shared that my grandfather told my mother when she was in eighth grade that there was no need for her to go to high school. She'd just get married and have kids anyway, and no one needed an education for that. My mother, however, insisted on continuing her education. Because at that time travel was more difficult and their farm was thirteen miles from the nearest high school, her parents arranged for her to board with a couple in town during the week. In this way, she paved the way for her two younger sisters and brother.

This anecdote surprised my students, but it wasn't until I threw down my ace that I really got their attention: "Did you know that when I began high school, right here at PHS in 1968, there were no women's sports? No volleyball or basketball or track, gymnastics, softball—nothing. Only boys could compete in school sports."

"Girls had no sports?" a female student asked. "Really?" This revelation created a chatter of disbelief. From there, I segued into women and literature. "It was a man's world. Literally. All the publishing house owners and editors were male until the late 19th century. And, their customers were male, as women had little or no income or education."

I explained that when women became so bold as to write,

they often kept it secret, like Jane Austen who hid her work underneath the mending in her sewing basket. Many disguised their identity by using a male pseudonym, like George Sand, George Elliot and the Bronte sisters. It was not happenstance that contemporary writers like J.K. Rowling (*Harry Potter*) and S.E. Hinton (*The Outsiders*) masked their sex by using their initials.

Choosing literature for this unit was like unearthing buried treasure. I tried to incorporate variety in style, subject matter, and culture. Chitra Divakaruni's short story "The Bats" portrayed a woman in Calcutta, India who repeatedly returned to her abusive husband maintaining hope that he would change. Also, Charlotte Perkins Gilman's "The Yellow Wallpaper" depicted a woman with postpartum depression whose doctor husband did not take her feelings seriously, driving her insane. And then there is the story "Old Woman Magoun" by Mary E. Wilkins Freeman. In this shocking tale, a grandmother allowed her young teen granddaughter to eat poison berries rather than allow the child's father to pay off a gambling debt by offering the thirteen-year-old in marriage to an older man.

My favorite of this unit was *Trifles*, a one-act play written by Iowa writer Susan Glaspell. It addressed the "Missy" syndrome of condescension. Based on a real-life incident, the story's main character was in jail and accused of strangling her husband. The county attorney, the sheriff, and a neighboring farmer visit the rural house to try to determine a motive. The men do the official investigating while the sheriff's wife and neighbor's wife piece together the crime while waiting in the kitchen of the accused. Because of their compassion for their peer's situation, they conspired to hide evidence to protect her from prosecution.

Students planned a mock trial based on the evidence from the play. They performed the roles of judge, prosecution, and defense attorneys and staff, and character witnesses. On the day of the trial, study hall students came in to determine a verdict based on the trial. A bailiff, set and costume designer, and videographer helped bring the production all together. To aid students in becoming knowledgeable of the court procedures, I gave them copies of the *National High School Mock Trial Rules for Competition.*

This activity proved to be worthwhile and fun, but it came with challenges. The study hall jurors showed favoritism and sided with the attorneys they knew as friends or from sports or other activities. When I chastised them, a student pointed out that this was similar to what the two women did to help out their peer, Mrs. Wright. Touché. After a few years of holding the trial, the study hall jurists became familiar with the play through word of mouth. This tended to skew the verdict. I suppose an English teacher could have worse problems than students discussing in detail a piece of literature they hadn't even been assigned to read.

One day, as he came into the room, I noticed Aaron whispering to classmates. When I asked what was going on, he said, "Oh, nothing." So, of course, I knew there was something.

A couple of weeks later, Aaron strolled to the front of the class, bearing a huge grin and a yellow T-shirt. "I, well, actually the whole class, got something for you, Mrs. Kies," he said, handing me the article of clothing. I held the T-shirt up for inspection as the class let loose with laughter.

Students chided me. "Put it on! Put it on!"

"No," I said. "Why would I wear this?"

Word got around, and students stopped in my room to see the shirt. On the last day of the unit, I chose to humor them and wear the yellow T-shirt. On the front was a 1950s woman in a skirt, heels, and apron. She stood at the stove stirring food in a frying pan. Underneath the picture, in bold black letters, it said: "I belong in the kitchen."

"Just remember," I said after the laughter subsided. "The only reason this is funny is because it *isn't* funny."

A few days later, my sixty juniors turned in their essays they composed for the Women's Lit Unit. The very next day, I heard a litany of requests: "Mrs. Kies, are we going to get our papers back today?" "Do you have mine done? What did I get?" "Are they in the grade book, yet?"

Like most writing assignments, once I got in my groove the first twenty-five or so flew by pretty easily. I learned a lot about my students through their writing. However, after the fiftieth one, the torture became akin to that bestowed on the narrator in Poe's "The Pit and the Pendulum." The walls began closing in, and I felt trapped, sure I'd crack any minute due to the psychological pressure.

"Hey, I'm not a machine. I've got a life, you know," I told them after being asked when I would have them done...yet again.

> "Hey, I'm not a machine. I've got a life, you know," I told them after being asked when I would have them done...yet again.

"Like what?" Sam asked.

I should have viewed this as rhetorical. I made the mistake of answering. "Well, last night I went to yoga, then my book club meeting and..."

Laughter tittered throughout the room.

"What?" I asked as the chuckles continued.

"Book club and yoga? I suppose you sat around and talked about—books," Amanda said.

"Shouldn't you really take a break from all that?" David added.

On the day I handed back their papers, students were most concerned with their grade and that's it. Not the comments I'd spent hours writing. Not how they could do better the next time. I appreciated the few who seemed to be looking over them carefully so they could improve.

"What are you doing, Aaron?" I asked as he approached the

front of the room.

"I'm stapling my paper. I know it's late, but at least I got it done."

"I'm glad you did. One staple will do, okay?" I said and gave him *the look.*

"Hey, don't worry. I didn't touch your precious automatic stapler. You said not to, and I didn't."

He handed me the paper and I counted. "Really, Aaron? Twenty-three staples? Really?"

Dear Aaron,

You challenged my lessons and made me a more
thoughtful teacher. I hope I did the same for
you as my student. Thanks for the T-shirt.

Not!

Regards,

Mrs. Kies

Chapter 17 – Hi-Ho, Hi-Ho! It's Off to Work We Go!

This above all: to thine own self be true.
William Shakespeare's *Hamlet*

One day in the middle of the third quarter of the school year when I was yet a half-time teacher, Donna, the sophomore English teacher, came into the lounge laden with a large box.

"Wow, what's that?"

"This," she said, plopping the box onto the table, "is at least forty-two hours of grading."

The following summer I remember standing behind Donna at the public library as she checked out a stack of books about investing and retirement planning. At the end of the following year, Donna announced her retirement, leaving me her legacy—a full-time teaching position—and that damned Career Research Paper writing assignment. How ironic the career unit played a primary role in Donna leaving her teaching career, and the beginning of my full-time contract.

When preparing to become an English teacher, I knew I'd be reading papers. Lots of papers. My advisors and professors prepared me for that. However, I'd naively envisioned varied literary analyses, moving personal revelations, or persuasive essays on vital current topics. But, careers? How much can you read about becoming a CPA—or auto mechanic or doctor or hairdresser or whatever—until you want to become one just to escape the job of reading about them?

I could see how this assignment helped students explore their futures, yet I didn't want this assignment to cause burnout. So, I tried to exorcize the evil thing.

"Wouldn't the freshmen benefit more as they planned their high school classes?" I proposed at one of our English Department meetings. But the freshmen teacher said her students already did speeches on careers. Writing a paper would be redundant. And, the junior and senior teachers were savvy, too. Their students arranged college visits and job shadows, wrote resumes and job application letters and performed mock interviews. "The Career Research Paper has always been a sophomore expectation," they told me.

The unit began with Charlie Clark the guidance counselor visiting my classes. Charlie had a Dad-joke sense of humor and a penchant for relating every possible topic in any conversation to a song. One year, for his *anticipatory set*, as educational guru Madeline Hunter called the *hook* of the lesson, he played "Que Sera, Sera."

"Okay," he said. "If any of you can name the artist of the song or the movie in which it was featured, Mrs. Kies will give you a couple of points extra credit."

It was a good idea, except few teens are connoisseurs of old movies. But that doesn't mean they didn't try: "It's Madonna!" "Real funny, Dude—it's somebody old—like Marie Osmond." "No, Dummy. The movie is Disney, um, Cinderella maybe?"

When Charlie told them it was from the film *The Man Who Knew Too Much* with Jimmy Stewart and Doris Day, who sang the song, they shrugged in befuddlement.

"Is your career choice anything like the message in the lyrics to the song, 'What will be, will be?'" Charlie continued. And students piped up, pretty much as he had hoped.

"No, we choose classes and work toward the career we want," said Mandy, astute as always.

"Yeah. It doesn't just happen. Nothing just happens," added Michael.

Then, from Jeremy, who considered schooling beyond high

school akin to a prison sentence,"I have an uncle who never went to college. He runs his own company and has new cars every year and loads of money."

Charlie doled out pamphlets about four-year and two-year colleges, their various degrees and costs. A discussion of educational choices ensued as they shared some of their individual career interests. By the time Charlie finished his spiel about the differences between in-state and out-of-state, private and public institutions, and financial aid applications, their eyes had glazed over. On information overload, their minds craved after-school plans, not college plans.

The next year Charlie dressed up as Carmac the Magnificent, an old Johnny Carson *Tonight Show* persona. But students didn't recognize that allusion either. Charlie, decked out in cape and turban, told the student volunteers' futures in a crystal ball: "You are going to be a garage mechanic and make lots of money..." And to the next one: "Oh, look, Bob! I see you changing diapers in a day care center!" or, "Just a minute now...it's coming into focus...wait...here it is. Yes! There you are, Sarah. You're wearing a red wig, a big red nose, and look at those huge shoes."

His point, again, was that careers didn't come to them out of thin air. To illustrate, he shared his own evolution from seminarian, to wannabe rock star, and from shoe salesman in the family business to accountant.

"I stand before you today as a guidance counselor and weekend disc jockey. Careers are paths," he told them, "not destinations. One veers into another, a process of growth and change. People used to choose a career and stick with it their entire lives, getting a gold watch when they retired after forty years. Statistics show that you'll probably change jobs an average of twelve times in the course of your adult lives."

On the second day, each student filled out an inventory of questions about their personal interests. This was an attempt to indicate where their aptitudes were in respect to specific occupations. For example, were they primarily a social, technical, investigative, or artistic person? A combination? The results of this self-reflection introduced them to lists of possible careers. Some, they hadn't heard of before, like stevedore, brewmaster, or phlebotomist. Close to home, careers leaned toward the standard variety, such as teacher, farmer, accountant, lawyer, nurse, police officer, beautician, bartender, etc. This career exploration helped students see beyond the cornfields that landlocked us, or insulated us, depending on one's perspective.

Once Charlie abandoned me, the Career Research Paper Unit became several weeks of eating liver, minus the onions. First, students chose a career to research. At fifteen, most humans have no idea what they want to do to sustain themselves for the rest of their lives. As when I was young, television and the media affected student's career interests. When *CSI* became popular, the number of students who wanted to become crime scene investigators boomed. Just a few years before, students didn't know this career existed. *Grey's Anatomy* spawned doctor and hospital worker wannabes. The most recent career fad among my students involved a different media: the internet. They dreamed of becoming a fabulously popular YouTuber and earning big money from ads.

After students chose a career to research, they found an address where they could send for more information about it using a reference called the *Occupational Outlook Handbook*. I taught them to compose and format a business letter of request for information and to address an envelope. I didn't realize I needed to teach the latter until that first year when I collected the letters to put in the mail. Addresses were inverted, illegible, and improperly punctuated. Most were undeliverable. Handwritten snail mail thank-you notes or letters to Grandma and Grandpa that my mother taught me to do were as obsolete as landlines or pantyhose.

While waiting for the career information they requested to arrive, we researched other sources in the library and online, taking notes and outlining. I dangled ten points extra credit in front of them for conducting an interview with a person who worked in their career of choice. All of a sudden, everyone wanted to research whatever work their parents did for an easy interview.

I gave detailed instruction in formatting a bibliography and citing sources, as well as stringent warnings about paraphrasing to avoid plagiarism. They did peer edits, made revisions, and turned in the final product. It was a day of doom for me. Like my predecessor Donna, I would serve my sentence by reading and grading seventy-five papers. *Hail Mary, full of grace...*I thought praying I would make it to retirement too.

Though, as I said, most students had no clue about what future career they wanted to explore, there were always a couple who knew from an early age what they wanted to be. I remember my student Sandra, for example. She passionately wanted to become a marine biologist. Ever since she could remember, she'd loved animals, science, and water. For her, it was marine biology or bust. The nearest ocean was over a thousand miles away, so Platteville was not exactly a hub for marine biology exploration or education. The Mississippi River wound through the valley only twenty-three miles down the road, but Sandra wanted to work with and study dolphins and whales, not clams, catfish, or carp. We talked about the possibility of working in a zoo or moving to one of the coasts to attend college. This didn't daunt her, and she researched, wrote, and turned in an exemplary paper.

I remember thinking, *Wow, this girl knows what she wants!*

She graduated, and we lost touch. Then, when she was twenty-one or so, I saw Sandra at a graduation party. She was eight months pregnant and married to a local farmer. She was indeed caring for lots of animals—just not the marine type. I saw her again last spring, and she has added two more healthy, lively kids to her brood. She seemed content to have followed the path of a nurturer, a tweaked version of her original passion. Que sera sera!

When I was in third grade, my friend Joanie and I walked our usual route home from school on the south side of Main Street past the stately homes of the college professors. From a pile of leaves, I picked up a striking green and orange oak leaf tinged in pink for my science project.

"What do you want to be when you grow up?" I asked.

"I don't know. Maybe a teacher, or a mom. What do you want to be?"

I was dying for her to ask. I'd been thinking about it since watching Phyllis Diller on *The Ed Sullivan Show* on Sunday night. "A comedian," I said.

Joanie's blond bob flopped over her face as she doubled over in laughter. I was off to a good start, I thought. In a gaudy dress and ratted hair, Phyllis Diller delivered punchlines as sharp and witty as any male comedian: "We spend the first twelve months of our children's lives teaching them to walk and talk," she'd said, "and the next twelve years teaching them to sit down and shut up."

Unfettered laughter filled our living room. *Could there be any better occupation than making people laugh?* If there was, I couldn't imagine it.

Like my student Sandra, my first choice career plan didn't pan out. My plans took the scenic route when I married my high school beau and became a mom. For thirteen years we worked on his parents' farm, then moved to a home near Platteville. My husband labored for a neighboring farmer, while I tried my hand in the fast-food industry at a famous chain. This was far from being a comedian, but having a sense of humor was never more important.

Sharon, an acquaintance from high school, interviewed me and gave me the fast-food job. After watching a few hours of (excuse my yawn) training videos, Sharon and the other managers tutored me in the art of washing trays, dumping fries in the fryer and perfecting the ideal ice cream cone complete with a perfect curlicue on top, though mine had a tendency to lean to one side.

A manager's position looked like something I could aspire to. I hadn't worked off the farm or outside the home before, except for a couple of brief jobs, one in a clothing store and another giving baton twirling lessons. Lacking a substantial resume, on applications I euphemistically described myself as a "household engineer."

"Sorry, but I need to go home," I told Sharon one day. She was standing at the front counter supervising and assisting the order takers. "My husband ran out of milk," I said, rolling my eyes in desperation, hoping she would catch on. She was busy with a customer, and I didn't want to expand on the details. "You know, breast milk for the baby," I whispered. "Apparently, there's no more in the freezer, and she's hungry and screaming."

The customer politely looked the other way, and Sharon said I could go home. What else could she do?

A few days later, I was mopping the floor under the front tables after the noon rush. Carol, the assistant manager on duty, instructed me in the physics of mopping: "Push the mop forward and back so you can apply enough pressure to remove those stubborn spots." She demonstrated and then passed me the mop handle. "Put some elbow grease into it. Good!" she said after watching me and returned to her duties.

Wearing my rust and yellow polyester outfit, complete with designer cap, all reeking of rank fryer fat, I operated that mop like a good mate swabbing the deck. I worked my way to the back of the store near the bathrooms, scrubbing just as Carol showed me. Delores, another assistant manager, punched in and approached me with a disapproving look on her face.

"Sue, let me show you a more efficient way to mop the floor, okay?"

Before I could say anything, she snatched the mop from my grip. "If you swish the mop in broad sweeps from side to side like this, you can cover way more floor in a lot less time. See?"

For the next week, I mopped the floor according to the wishes of the manager on duty. The following week, I quit.

A few months later our family settled into a rural home in Glen Haven, Wisconsin, where we farmed with a well-established land owner. Once the chore routine became established, with me feeding the baby Holstein calves morning and evening, I took my college placement tests, got an advisor, and signed up for two classes at the University of Wisconsin-Platteville, thirty miles away.

Dear Fast-food Industry:
Thank you for motivating me to return to college.
I cannot express enough appreciation
for your inspiration. If not for you, I might
never have become a teacher.
Signed,
Your Most Skilled Floor Mopper Ever

I racked up class after class on my transcript, taking correspondence courses in the summer. Three years later, in 1988, I was scheduled to pre-student teach at PHS with Mrs. Kingeter, my former Junior English teacher. This class included observing the teacher for a minimum of forty hours, helping out with routine tasks, and teaching at least one lesson. I was excited, but scared. What if I didn't measure up to my former teacher's expectations? What if I didn't measure up to my own expectations? What if the students hated me? What if I wasn't cut out to be a teacher?

After finding a parking spot in the visitor's area, I checked in with the secretary in the main office. She buzzed Mrs. Kingeter's room and announced my arrival on the intercom. "Good, send her down to my room. She knows where it is."

Walking down the familiar hall, I realized I was right back where I started from. I felt out of place. I was in my thirties, far removed from being a student. I didn't really feel like a teacher, yet, either. I passed the door of the girls' bathroom where my girlfriends and I chatted and primped between classes. Then the bell rang. Teenage bodies burst into the halls like torpedoes launching in different directions. Self-consciously, I hugged the wall. Most students zipped by me like I wasn't there, while others gave me a brief but curious glance.

Mrs. Kingeter shook my hand. "How nice to see you again," she said. "So, you're going to be an English teacher." She showed me to a desk in the front of the first row. Her desk now occupied the far side of the five-sided room instead of the front, and the student desks faced the opposite way. It felt smaller than I remembered. "During my prep time we'll have time to chat and discuss the week's activities."

Students filed in and took their seats, eyeing me with curiosity. This was a lower-level junior class, which was called English B to attempt to disguise that fact. Later in the week, I heard them refer to it as "the dummy class" amongst themselves. As they entered, I smiled, saying an occasional hello, wondering if I had the moxie to fend them off from gobbling me up. Let alone teach them something.

"Here, you can correct these so you don't get bored," Mrs. Kingeter said, handing me a stack of vocabulary tests from the day before.

Mrs. Kingeter's short blond bob sported a bit of gray now, but her smile, buried amid fleshy cheeks and chin, remained the same. She was a square-shouldered woman whose brisk steps meant business. Her eyes always sparkled, even when she was mildly perturbed. When truly provoked, though, the smile vanished, and her eyes bore holes in the perpetrator.

When I was a junior, Mrs. Kingeter taught us lessons about grammar and writing, as well as American literature. One day we were discussing the two chapters we were supposed to have read of *The Great Gatsby*. Gary, a longtime classmate since the elementary grades who had not liked being in school for nary one day of all that time, was being disruptive—again.

"This discussion would be more interesting to you if you had read the assigned pages, Gary," Mrs. Kingeter said, trying to get him to pay attention.

"I did read," Gary said, grinning. The class chuckled.

Mrs. Kingeter went on with her lesson. A few minutes later Gary flicked a folded-up wad of paper across the room. Mrs. Kingeter stopped talking. She glared at her disruptor. "You've had your last warning, Gary. Go to the office. I don't want to see you in this room again until you can conduct yourself respectfully."

She pushed the intercom button to let the office know he was coming. Gary sat there, arms crossed. Mrs. Kingeter took a couple of steps toward him and calmly pointed toward the door. It was a showdown. None of us moved a pinky. Finally, Gary got up and left, kicking the leg of a desk and mumbling as he exited the room and punctuated his exit with the slam of the door.

Could I do that without cracking? I wondered. I was not as imposing as Mrs. Kingeter in voice or countenance.

Consumed with grading quizzes, I looked up now and then

to be attentive to her lesson on the friendship between George and Lennie in Steinbeck's *Of Mice and Men*. I felt like a student in her class again trying to prove myself. Only this time it was not just a grade on the line but my future as a teacher. Would I have the moxie to pass this test?

She finished the lesson and gave the students about twenty minutes to complete the study guide for the next two chapters of the book. Now I can concentrate on grading these quizzes, I thought. Most students opened their books and began to work. I was correcting away—

"Jesse!" Mrs. Kingeter called out suddenly. "Open your book and get to work!" My body leapt a couple of inches from my chair. I hoped no one noticed.

Soon it was lunch time. When I was a student, the teachers' lounge was a mysterious place and strictly off limits. I recall our teachers emerging from its bowels, trailed by wafting smoke clouds. Every day after teaching us a new concept on points, planes, or angles, our geometry teacher Mr. Johnson gave us our homework and then left for half an hour to visit the lounge. When he returned, he jovially asked, "How are you doing? Are there any questions?" We quickly learned not to engage him. His combined coffee and cigarette breath was lethal.

Mrs. Kingeter bought my lunch in the cafeteria, and I followed her into this taboo territory. I scanned the room. Student art work from years past graced the wall, while soda and snack machines stood guard in one corner. Two long tables surrounded by chairs took up the middle. Couches and some end tables lined the outside wall. It's so small, I thought. *What a disappointment. Where are the pool tables and dart boards?*

"This is Sue Kies, everyone," Mrs. Kingeter said. "She will be observing in my room for the next week."

"You've come back to us," said Mr. McKichan, my freshman social studies teacher. "Welcome!"

180

On Thursday that week I taught my lesson on poetry. Mrs. Kingeter and I had talked about it on Tuesday. I showed her my lesson plans, and she gave me the go-ahead, with a disclaimer: "I think this exposure to poetry will be good for them. But be prepared and don't be disappointed if they resist or act disinterested."

Oh, great.

My lesson required them to write a "work" poem. We talked about what poetry is and read poems as examples. One was called "Short Order Cook" by Mike Daniels about a guy who worked in a fast-food place. Another was one of mine, called "Watching Ashley," a poem I wrote about observing my youngest daughter at play. I pointed out examples of alliteration, the repetition of sounds at the start of words in the lines of each, as well as onomatopoeic words that sounded like the word they represented. Their job was to write a poem about a job they liked or were proud of. It had to be at least ten lines and contain at least one example of alliteration and onomatopoeia.

"When all the poems are finished, I will type, print and assemble them into a booklet so each one of you can have one. Now, let's get started. What are some jobs you could write about?"

"Hauling manure?" Sam said.

"Good. What else?"

"Cutting grass?" Tom said.

"Wonderful. What about you, Sarah?"

"I don't know. I don't have a job."

"But, you do things, right? It doesn't have to be something you get paid for."

"How about washing dishes?" Tina asked.

"Fine. So, I want you all to have this done by tomorrow, and I'll collect them and give suggestions. Only suggestions, though, because this is your creative work, not mine."

"How much is it worth?"

"Two points per line, and five points for using alliteration and onomatopoeia correctly."

Jesse, the lad Mrs. Kingeter admonished, was small and wiry with pierced earlobes and a red bandana tied around his head. One day I glanced in his direction and he mouthed some unintelligible comment and winked at me. He did this several times in the course of my observations of the class. Mrs. Kingeter did not see these antics, and I didn't mention them to her. Not knowing what else to do, I simply ignored them.

Most students turned in the poems, though a few were a day or two late. The following Monday they took turns reading them to the class, and I was pleasantly surprised. Especially by Jesse. He wrote about going out in the quiet of the morning and starting the tractor. He described the moment as "shattering the still." I've always been tempted to steal that line in one of my own poems.

Years later after I'd been teaching for a number of years, Jesse returned to speak at an all-school assembly in connection with our HOSA (Health Occupations Students of America) club. They were sponsoring a community-wide awareness campaign about the dangers of drunk driving. Jesse, in his thirties and substantially heavier, was the featured speaker. Had I not recognized his name, I wouldn't have recognized him.

He told us the story of how he had been driving while intoxicated and crashed. After coming out of a coma, he underwent years of rehabilitation. Though he learned to walk and talk again, he was not able to hold a job or live on his own because of the brain injuries caused by the accident. His family was there to support him that day. Jesse's message to students was blunt.

"This could happen to you. Don't be stupid like I was and think that it can't. If you want any kind of a future, don't take the chance—don't drink and drive."

Chapter 18 – Technobesity

We don't ride the railroad. The railroad rides upon us.
Henry David Thoreau, *Walden*

Technology, though a wonderful teaching tool, has always had its glitches. The clacking of reel-to-reel film projectors and the beeping of filmstrip projectors signaling the user to click on to the next frame used to be common sounds for us students in my days at PHS. While student teaching in the spring of 1991, I remember one little—uh—shall we say stinker—stuck his pencil in the reel and broke the projector as I was showing a film.

In my first few years of teaching I utilized a filmstrip featuring Edgar Allan Poe's short story, "The Pit and the Pendulum." When the filmstrip broke, I began using just the audio tape. I turned down the lights and gave each student a piece of paper to draw their interpretation of the images presented in the story. Some turned out pretty artistic and scary, and I hung them up in the room at Halloween time.

Back then, we recorded attendance on sheets of paper, filling in the dots with a No. 2 pencil next to the names of those students who were absent or tardy. Volunteers from study hall collected them from a hook outside the classroom doors and took them to the office. Cunning students who had friends performing this duty might talk them into erasing the dot by their names so they could skip class without detection. After a few of these instances, the secretary checked for suspicious erasure marks before running the sheets through the Scantron machine.

Somewhere at the start of the twenty-first century, we began using computers to report attendance, as well as grades, health concerns, announcements, progress reports, etc. Districts developed websites that report everything you would ever want to know about a school, including the size, district philosophy, subjects, teachers, curriculum, community, school board, and the number and types of toilets. Parents and students can log in at any time to check grades. I often stayed at school on Friday afternoons to make sure grades were up to date. That way parents could check to see whether their kid had all their assignments turned in.

I remember walking into the lounge during my first year teaching as a coworker expressed dissatisfaction with the previous Apple II user who'd left a zillion tabs open, slowing down the processing. This was 1991.

"Yeah, I hate it when that happens," I said, though I was the one who had not known how to close the tabs.

This bulky, beige Apple II computer occupied a cart in the PHS teachers' lounge. Teachers who embraced technology used this resource as a word processor to type up handouts, worksheets, tests and quizzes to print out, copy, and use in the classroom. It was a handy innovation because it allowed us to save our work and edit it for other classes or from year to year rather than typing new copies every time we wanted to make changes.

We first saved our work on 5.25-inch floppy disks, which evolved to 3.25-inch disks, then to CDs. This seemed so handy, and I had a drawer full of these various media. The internet already existed somewhere out there but did not find its way to us in Southwest Wisconsin until the late 1990s. If we sought information, we used dictionaries, encyclopedias, reference books (including phone books), and librarians.

Soon, more computers took up residence in a corner of the library, and not long after that twenty-five machines became available in a lab. Teachers needed to reserve the room on an online sign-up calendar two or more weeks ahead of time to have any hope of using it.

"Did you get the wrong day again, Mrs. Kies?" a student moaned as we walked back to my room after finding another class there.

When email first became available, students snuck into the lab between classes and during lunch to check and send messages until we teachers chased them out again. That was the start of media mania.

By the late 1990s, PHS had three computer labs: PCs in the business area, formerly the typing room; Macs in the technical education area; and more Macs across the hall from the library. When I retired in 2019, the district provided MacBook Air laptops for teachers and Chromebooks for students in middle and high school, and almost every individual, students and staff, had their own smartphone. Many teachers were equipped with interactive smart boards and projectors, and some used YouTube videos for classroom instruction. In twenty-seven years, we'd come a long way, baby!

Sometimes I wondered what my dad would think about today's technology. He passed away in 1981 before personal computers and mobile phones. Employed by the Retail Credit Company, which eventually became Equifax Services, Dad gathered information about clients seeking insurance coverage or making claims. He then typed that data into the appropriate forms, one by one. He kept this confidential information on five by seven inch cards stored alphabetically by the client's name in filing cabinets in his office.

Two days a week he drove to towns in the surrounding area, interviewing people face to face. The other three days he tapped away at the keys of his manual Royal typewriter. Today, his job would be done entirely on a computer, the files stored somewhere in the cloud. I don't think he would have liked this upgrade, as his favorite part of his duties was getting out on the road and talking to people, honing his jokes and stories at every stop. On my days off school I occasionally accompanied him on his route, observing his congenial banter firsthand.

"Hey, if it isn't Earl the Squirrel," said Ding, the Belmont grocer who bestowed nicknames on everyone. "And you've got Small Fry with you today, I see."

I remember Dad marveling over a *60 Minutes* episode about futuristic communication. "Geez. What next? Someday we'll be able to see the person we're talking to on the phone?" he said, amazed.

When automatic windows and power steering came into fashion, Dad pooh-poohed them. "Anyone who can't roll down their own window or steer their own car without help shouldn't be driving." Yet, he took pride in gifting Mom a snazzy automatic mixer one year for Christmas and a trendy hooded salon style hair dryer the next. And, the first time we watched a Packer game on our new color TV, he would never turn that vibrant green and gold back to black and white.

Love/hate relationships with technology existed long before computers when automation entered the workplace to replace humans. The good and bad of technology grow together in our lives, and whether a particular invention is viewed as a weed or a flower lies in the eye of the beholder.

Before computers and cell phones, down time during the last few minutes of class was dicey. Anxious for the bell to ring, students became louder and louder, eventually rising from their seats to scuffle, gossip, or line up at the door several minutes ahead of the bell.

"They're like cows lined up to get out the barn door," said the Spanish teacher at lunch one day. While they're standing at the door, I 'moo!' at them." When cell phones became available, they could quell boredom anytime, anywhere. Making no sound and expelling little to no exertion, they "chatted" with friends,

Tweeted, Instagrammed—often with students sitting right next to them.

It was both hilarious and bothersome when students impulsively slid their phones from their sweatshirt or pants pockets just far enough to look down and peek at the screen every few seconds. I was astounded at how adept they were. Their fingers blindly punched out messages from inside the front pouch of their hoodies. The guilty, glazed look on their faces and the ever-so-slight movement of their forearms gave them away.

"How did you know I was texting?" they'd say, then add, "it's my Mom, so you can't yell at me."

Yeah, right, I thought, then realized it probably *was* their mom. Adults had phone addiction problems of their own.

Knowing I sounded like my grandpa when he began with, 'Back in my day…' I lectured them: "You know, there used to be one pay phone in the Commons for the entire student population of 800 students. If I wanted a ride, I called home and let it ring. Mom and Dad knew if there was no answer on the other end, it was me needing a ride home from school. I saved a lot of change that way." I mistook the confused look on their faces to mean they didn't believe me. Until my student Sonja asked, "Pay phone? What's that?"

Many teachers placed a box in the front of the room where students deposited their silenced phones before class. Phones became a routine discussion at faculty meetings. Each teacher brought their own opinion. Some wanted to completely outlaw phones and confiscate them on sight. Others thought it best to only let students use them between classes and at lunch. The other option was to let them have their phones and police them as needed in class. This debate took place regularly, with various strategies and rules winning out. None of them satisfied everyone.

As school budgets dwindled, technology took top priority. If

I wanted to order markers and construction paper, I made sure to write, "These items are necessary to make storyboards for video projects." Or, "Students need this origami paper to make paper cranes for their Power Point presentations."

Video cameras and computer software aided our different disciplines and took us into the twenty-first century. Ceiling mounted projectors in every room replaced the aging array of televisions on squeaky wheeled carts. However, I often found myself wishing that human capital could be seen as valuable as technology. With some exceptions, most schools, for budget purposes, continued to stretch employees to the limit, understaffing or laying off the music, art, and foreign language teachers. Good teachers and staff are a school's most valuable assets. It seemed as if the new staff coming in was being hired for the purpose of enhancing technology instead of the other way around.

Out of necessity to help staff adjust, the district conducted technology workshops during inservice and work days. The Platteville School District employed two knowledgeable tech guys and a savvy librarian at each school. And this was good. But any teacher knows that the fastest way to solve any technology problem is to ask a student. That's why the current PHS media specialist (librarian), established a Tech Squad. These students helped teachers and other students deal with any technological questions or glitches.

One day my creative writing class went to the computer lab to work on their personal essays. The capabilities of the computer in front of them was an amusement park of distractions. Like many writers, they procrastinated by checking email and surfing the internet before getting around to their actual writing.

"Creativity usually doesn't bubble to the surface like crude oil," I coached them. "It's work, and you've got to put in the time.

So, get that document open and let's write!"

Most of them tapped away on the keys and appeared to be busy. I was correcting papers at a table behind Jaiden where I could casually see his computer screen. Jaiden should have been nominated for Best Actor for his performances in the ongoing documentary "The Art of Procrastination." Shame on the Academy for snubbing him.

On that particular day he had the computer camera on and was recording himself, making faces and goofing around, not one typed word in sight.

"Jaiden, get to work and stop messing with the camera," I said. "Time's wasting, and your personal essay is due tomorrow."

"That was soooo perfect, Mrs. Kies," he said, chuckling. I was on the verge of reaching my limit with him—a month ago. Correcting a quiz or two, I gave him time to comply. When I looked up again a couple of minutes later, he was still not typing.

"I mean it, Jaiden. Get writing or—(Okay, think fast to come up with an enforceable consequential consequence.) I'll take your computer privileges away and you can write your essay by hand."

He hunkered down and laughed again. "Oh, my God. This is tooooo good."

I smacked down my red pen on the table and approached him. "Okay, what *are* you doing?"

He angled the computer screen upward.

"I don't want to watch your silly video, Jaiden. I want you to get busy with your essay. Right now!"

"Oh, I think you'll want to see it." He hit "play" and turned up the sound. As if narrating a golf tournament, Jaiden could be heard whispering into the computer microphone: "Well, I'm sitting here bored, trying to have fun recording myself and pass the time and be creative somehow, but I know that any minute now my teacher, Mrs. Kies—see her in the background there?—is going to look up and yell at me. She's mad because I'm not doing what I'm supposed to be doing—and she's going to say, "Get to work, Jaiden!" (His mimicry of me was totally off. Totally.)

As if on cue—the video showed me saying just that. He laughed. Soon the rest of the class was gathered around the computer to watch.

The narration continued: "Okay, she's correcting stuff, and I'm still not doing my work, so it's just about time for her to yell at me again. Oh, yes." He laughed. "There she is…and…wait…she's even getting up and coming over to tell me to stop or she'll take away my computer privileges. This is sooo perfect," he says, cracking up.

The timing was good. And it was sorta clever. But, I'd never tell him that. "Hey, wait! I've got an idea," Jaiden said. With the touch of a few keys, he added special effects to the video. My voice dropped an octave or two and slowed down like Darth Vader then raised in pitch and sped up like the Chipmunks.

"You sound like you're on crack," Jenna said, unable to stop laughing.

Jaiden posted his masterpiece on YouTube. I lost track of how many views it got. Creativity abounded that day. Just not the kind I had planned.

One year I decided to update the *Our Town* unit using technology. It had been a part of my teaching repertoire for about two years and began with my juniors reading the play by Thornton Wilder. Students found it surprising that Wilder had roots in Madison, Wisconsin. His father, Amos Parker Wilder, was editor and part owner of the *Wisconsin State Journal* from 1862 to 1936 before becoming a United States consul to China.

I assigned students parts to read in front of the class. The Gibbs family pulled up chairs on one side of the classroom and their neighbors, the Webb family, on the other. Set in the early 1900s in the fictional town of Grover's Corners, New Hampshire, some of the vocabulary was understandably dated. Students never failed to react to the word *queer* and the idiom *beat about the bush* being used in their common early twentieth century context. However, the play's relevance lay in its timeless universal themes. Its three acts portrayed distinct themes: growing up, love and marriage, and death.

That year I had two classes of juniors, first and fifth periods. Because the script required sounds to be simulated, I assigned Jason to be our sound effects person in the morning class. He often demonstrated a talent for making noise at the most inopportune times on a daily basis, so I decided to capitalize on his talents.

"You'll need to make the sound of a train whistle, a factory whistle, a horse's whinny, milk bottles rattling, and a rooster crowing. Do you think you can handle that, Jason?"

"Of course," he said, with overt confidence. The actors read their parts, and when it was time for the factory whistle to sound—nothing. "Jason? You're on," I reminded him. "Jason?" After a lengthy silence followed by giggling, I filled in for him. It's a common and puzzling phenomena. Often, the verbal kid from the back of the class freezes and folds under the pressure of having sanctioned access to center stage.

When we finished reading the play in class after a few days, we moved on to the follow-up project. This involved students using their creativity to relate the play to their own lives and times by writing and acting out their version of *Our Town Today.*

"I want you to portray what people in the future should know about the present culture of Platteville, Wisconsin. You know, your common, everyday life events that wouldn't make it into the history books. The things that make life, life."

"Won't that be boring?" Sonya asked.

"That's what Wilder is saying in the play. Through the ages, most of our everyday life is repetitive and boring—and that's what makes these activities precious. Only occasionally does something of huge consequence happen in our lives. The most comforting activities in our lives are routine, inconsequential and, therefore, often overlooked."

Both the morning and afternoon classes chose names for the cast of characters and divided into three groups, one to represent each of the three acts. Group One wrote scenes of dialogue that captured their everyday lives, like getting up, going to school, work, and home life. Group Two did the same using love and marriage as a theme, where two characters meet, date, and fall in love. And, Group Three tackled the theme of death, thinking of a contemporary way for the main character to pass away as Emily Webb does in the play.

When the scripts were finished, they practiced their roles then went to the auditorium to perform their creations on stage. Both the morning and afternoon classes did their own projects. They repeatedly asked me who had done the better job. Each class was positive they'd outdone the other. I dodged answering the question. A little healthy competition could spur the most reluctant students to perform better. Jason suggested we videotape their final performances so they could watch both and judge for themselves. "Good idea," I said.

Before digital cameras and digital editing became available, teachers and students could check out the big, clunky cameras which held a VHS tape. I assigned Marcus to do the taping for fifth period. Marcus loved making movies. He and a classmate filmed a stellar rendition of the ending scene of *Of Mice and Men* when they were sophomores. They'd filmed it by a stream in a clearing, with Marcus playing Lennie. His performance would have given John Malkovich a run for his money. Marcus's mother's camera work, however, was a bit shaky as she struggled to keep her balance while negotiating the rocks in and around the stream where they were filming.

A big, strapping lad with red curly hair, Marcus went the extra mile when it came to theatrics. He sometimes wore white contact lenses to school, giving him a creepy, zombie look. For high-profile activities like an award's day, pep assembly or homecoming week, he sported a Scottish kilt, white shirt, and knee socks. His Gene Simmons' makeup for Halloween, complete with a painted black tongue, became tradition by the time he was a junior.

To discourage any shenanigans, I made sure to observe as Marcus taped each group for his class. Students knew their lines and worked hard at capturing their parts. Other than some extended giggling, everything seemed to go as planned. But, as with mice and men, you know what they say about the best-laid plans.

On Monday morning I popped the tape into the VCR. It was always nice to ease into the week without having to think too hard about lesson plans. After watching their video, students couldn't wait to watch fifth period's to compare performances. A few minutes into the viewing, students exchanged looks. Then titters circulated and swelled into tentative laughter. I didn't know what to do. Was it just one scene? Would there be more? We kept watching.

It seemed Marcus had forsaken the universal themes of the play and found his own. Focused on Mrs. Gibbs as she spoke, the camera gradually drifted over her chest. Then, as Mrs. Webb exited the stage, the camera slunk down for a view of her butt. Marcus's camera work tainted the overall work his class's three groups had put in. How could anyone who was watching concentrate on the dialogue when the camera drifted from their faces in the middle of a line? I told students how disgusted I was with the video.

That was only the beginning of the problem. Now, what would I do with fifth period? After first period watched fifth period's video, fifth period would want to see it, too. It *was* their video after all. In between classes, I heard my first period student Cathy call out to a classmate down the hall, "Can't wait to watch our porno, can you?"

Oh, dear! Before fifth period began, I talked to the female students featured in the video and asked if they wanted to watch it in private or in front of the class. "It's our video. We should watch it together as a class," said Tilda. "It can't be that bad." They all nodded in agreement.

I motioned Marcus into the hall and educated him on sexual harassment and how he hadn't treated his classmates respectfully in the video. "I'll be talking to your parents, Marcus," I said, "and you'll be getting an F for your part in the project." He didn't say anything. He knew there'd be consequences. He apologized to the class, and we watched the video. They reacted with laughter much like first period, except that this time there was no surprise.

I thought the horrific episode was behind me. Then at parent/teacher conferences one of the fathers of the fifth period girls asked about the incident. I explained what had happened.

"You mean you showed the video—twice? Why?" he asked.

He was right. In retrospect, I'd made the wrong decision. I should have turned the video off as soon as I saw what Marcus had done. I should have explained to the girls and both classes that showing the video was not okay. Sexual harassment presented in this type of benign manner had plagued women for years and continued to do so. Growing up in the fifties and sixties I'd witnessed the misogynistic jokes on popular television shows and the uncomfortable sexual portrayal of women in beer commercials and other ads firsthand. Those objectifications of women stick with us, causing body shaming and insecurity. And, it is never okay. I wish I'd told the girls that.

A year or so after this incident I read in the news about a

teacher from Minnesota who put in a video and left the room to run an errand. A neighboring teacher investigated after hearing the raucous laughter and squeals coming from the room. It seems the teacher grabbed the video from his VCR at home, thinking it was a program he had taped about the Civil War. Little did he know, the video he brought from home was not what he intended.

Dear Classroom Teachers,
Always preview your videos. Always! No exceptions.
Signed,
Learned From Experience

After juniors read excerpts from *Walden,* we discussed Thoreau's belief that technology only *appeared* to simplify our lives. In his view, new inventions made our work easier, not so we would have more free time, but so we could do even more work. Technology, he claimed, *added* duties and stress. He set forth the analogy of overworked humans to mean little ants who are so focused getting work done that they bite whatever or whoever gets in their way. He also believed technology often removed us from our first-hand touch with nature and/or, thus— our human nature—which would never lead to a good end.

When I began teaching, I recorded grades in a handwritten grade book. If a student wanted to know his or her grade, I used my handheld calculator, or a paper and pencil, to add it up and divide it by the total number of points possible. Time did not allow for figuring grades every day, so students got reports mid quarter and then at the end of the quarter and then again at the end of the semester. Students did the best they could and hoped their performances would add up to attain the grade they desired. When computers and electronic gradebooks entered the scene, students relied on "insta-grades" to calculate how hard they needed to work, or not work, in order to get the grade they wanted. This resulted in more emphasis on grades and less emphasis on effort and the learning process.

"Our inventions are wont to be pretty toys, which distract our attention from serious things. They are but improved means to an unimproved end," said Thoreau.

Chapter 19 – Techno-fun!

No great discovery was ever made without a bold guess.
Sir Isaac Newton

One of my colleagues, Leslie, and her small son moved to Platteville from Door County in August of 1998. She taught at PHS for one year. Oh, what a fun year that was!

One day Leslie told me with a chuckle, "Boy, I fooled them, didn't I?" She was commenting on securing the freshman/sophomore English teaching position and was referring to her attire, not her qualifications. To the interview, she'd worn a tailored navy blue suit, white blouse and low heels; however, her daily teaching wardrobe consisted of, among other attractive but eclectic outfits, a pair of Shakespearean bloomer-type pants and a variety of flowered hippie-style maxi skirts paired with boots or sandals.

After an inservice meeting at the start of the year, I helped Leslie move her wooden desk from her home into her classroom which was right around the corner from mine. Sitting in my truck in the school parking lot, we discovered we shared identities as "daddy's girls." Our fathers doted on us, their only daughters, doling out attention and affection as plentiful and sweet as candy on Halloween. Our eyes welled up as we shared stories of losing them, our most beloved supporters; coincidentally, both of sudden heart attacks while we were still in our twenties.

Leslie had majored in art and minored in English. Her arrival sparked new life into the curriculum I'd been teaching for seven years. She touted basics like grammar, yet thrived on thinking outside of any shape, not just the box. If students seemed lethargic in class, she'd ask them to stand up and lead them in some basic yoga poses and stretches to get the blood flowing.

According to the Language Arts Common Core Standards we adhered to at the time, Sophomore English needed to include an introduction to "media elements." My *Fahrenheit 451* unit I'd been teaching for about five years checked all the boxes. After reading the novel, students worked in groups to write and produce a scene or two from the book. They explored the importance of perspective in telling a story and used a variety of camera shots and angles to portray their chosen scene visually.

Ray Bradbury wrote *Fahrenheit 451* to forewarn readers about the dangers of censorship. Written in 1953, students noted how accurately he predicted the common use of wall-sized televisions, tiny earbuds, drug dependence, helpful robots, artificial intelligence, and the widespread manipulation of public information we see today on social media." In this dystopian society, fire departments didn't put out fires but doused the homes of book owners with kerosene and burned them to the ground. Authorities didn't want people becoming confused with all those different ideas and causing problems for society. Bradbury was indeed ahead of his time.

Before they began to prepare their videos and enthusiasm mounted, every year I warned them: "You'll get an F if you do something dangerous or cause harm to anyone or anything. Parental permission is a must for anything questionable. And before you begin filming, I need to see your script, along with a storyboard of your camera shots."

I told Leslie how a student from a couple of years before set some rotting hay bales on fire in a rock quarry on their property in the country. After getting his parents' permission, Todd neglected to tell the neighbors what was happening. From the hillside, his group filmed the flames jumping high in the evening air to represent the scene in the book where Fire Chief Beatty burns an old lady's house down. When they heard blaring sirens and saw two fire trucks pull into the quarry, they were simultaneously shocked and thrilled.

"We got my parents' permission, Mrs. Kies. Really we did!" Todd said that Monday, much like I'm sure he told the fire department that day. "We won't get an F, will we?" The group was stoked about the unexpected touch of realism the fire trucks added to their video. The Fire Department, not so much.

Then there was Jeff's group who talked him into dressing up in a skirt and stockings, woman's wig and makeup to portray Mildred Montag. They filmed him talking to Mike who portrayed Fire Chief Beatty in the middle of Platteville's Main Street. The looks of passersby in their video ranged from quizzical grins to angry glares. At least they didn't set anything on fire.

Another concern with students creating anything on video was their tendency to stoop to inane silliness. Self-conscious students often giggled their way through their lines, and the hams of the group used the opportunity to endlessly muck it up for the camera. This resulted in ten minutes of wasted tape that they showed as outtakes at the end of their two-minute video.

Leslie had two classes of sophomores, and I had three. We met regularly to discuss lesson plans, and one day we came up with the coup de grace for the *Fahrenheit 451* video project. We hoped it would add incentive to make these videos more polished and fun to watch for students and us—the bestowers of grades. Thus, the First Annual PHS *Fahrenheit 451 Video Awards* were born. After viewing all the films, we would choose Best Actor and Actress, Best Supporting Actor and Actress, Best Soundtrack, Best Cinematography, Best Director, and, lastly, Best Film.

"Everyone will dress up for the ceremony when we hand out the awards," Leslie told her students, as did I.

"Can we have a red carpet?" Ginny asked.

"Maybe," I said. "But remember, if you win, you'll have to give a short acceptance speech to thank everyone who helped with the video."

Leslie and I were as excited as our students. If we were going to have an Oscars ceremony, we had to have Oscars. We went to K-Mart after school and bought little plastic people in the toy aisle and miniature flower pots in the crafts section. We glued the people onto the upside down flower pots. After those had set, we spread newspapers in my driveway and sprayed the five inch high miniature statues with metallic gold paint. We wrote the names of the awards on each with black Sharpie. When we were finished, we stood back to evaluate our awards, wondering if students would like them—or laugh at them. You never know with teenagers. Either way, we'd had a blast making them.

Our effort was not in vain. Students put phenomenal work and creativity into these projects. One of Leslie's groups fastened a video camera onto a remote control car to portray the mechanical hound searching for the fugitive Montag. As the car raced down the street, viewers witnessed the chase scene filmed in black and white through the mechanical hound's eyes. A group in one of my classes dressed up the family dog in aluminum foil and had it sniffing for Montag's scent, then running him down in hot pursuit.

After the ceremony, students carried their awards around like real Oscars.

"What a marvelous idea," the French teacher told us at lunch. "The students are so proud of them."

At parent/teacher conferences that quarter, one mother said, "Amy's Best Actress Award is still on her dresser amidst her sports trophies."

The next summer Leslie returned to Door County and invited me to visit her for a few days. Together, we attended both a Shakespeare play and a concert. She sold her home there and moved to Chicago to take a teaching job, then to Rochester, New York, for another position. She was now teaching her first love—

Art—at college level.

"I'm going to present a paper at Oxford," she wrote in a Christmas card. "I can bring a guest. Would you be interested in going?"

Does it snow in Alaska? Leslie and I traveled to England in the summer of 2007. In London we attended a play, rode the double decker buses, and did a pub tour that ended in the well-preserved area of 1930s London, the setting for Dickens' *Oliver Twist.* Then we visited Mandy, a fellow songwriter Leslie had met online, a young woman from a town near Windsor. Did I mention that Leslie wrote and sang songs? I sipped ale as her friend, then Leslie, performed to an enthusiastic crowd on a pub patio during open mic night.

Then it was on to the main event at Oxford University where we stayed in the dormitory at Manchester College. The narrow hallways with cozy fireplaces in every room resembled the setting for Harry Potter. Leslie and other teachers took turns presenting their papers every morning over the next few days, which freed our afternoons to tour Oxford. We saw the Bodleian Library, the Bridge of Sighs, the Museum of Natural History, and Bill Clinton's former dorm and favorite hangout. At Christ Church College a painting of Alice Liddell, the dean's daughter and inspiration for *Alice in Wonderland,* hung above the entrance to the great hall. Our guide gave us the rest of the story, letting us in on Lewis Carroll's affinity for children, especially for photographing little girls. Some of them nude.

Evenings included Pimm's on the Lawn[2] and delectable dinners made by an award-winning British chef. After our meal one night, some attendees provided entertainment, and Leslie

---

[2] Pimms on the lawn = 1 cup Pimms Liqueur, 2 cups lemonade, 1 slice Apple, 1 slice Cucumber, 1 slice Lemon, 1 sprig fresh Mint, 1 slice Orange, 1 Strawberry, Ice.

performed a few songs. I chatted it up with an art director and play producer, and a writer from Chicago who knew Norman Mclean of *A River Runs Through It* fame.

Our dads would have been proud of us, and not the least bit surprised. Here were their beloved daughters attending Oxford, even if it was only for a few days.

In 1999, the year after Leslie left PHS, I began the new challenge of teaching AP (Advanced Placement) Language and Composition at the junior level. This is comparable to a freshman level college English class. The University of Wisconsin-Madison offered summer seminars to train AP teachers, and I attended along with many other English teachers from Wisconsin.

To be in this AP class at Platteville High School, students had to meet two of three criteria: a cumulative grade point average of at least 3.5, an above average score on the language arts portion of their standardized sophomore test, and/or their sophomore English teacher's recommendation. Over the summer after completing their sophomore year, AP students read one required book and one nonfiction book of their choice. They wrote a paper on each and turned them in during the first week of school in September. If they didn't turn them in or got less than a C on the papers, they would be transferred to the regular Junior English.

AP classes did not exist when I was in high school, and, even if they had, I wouldn't have been a candidate for such a rigorous curriculum. During the summer I was immersed in camping and traveling with my family, going to the pool and goofing around with friends. I enjoyed reading, but writing papers in the summer? Wasn't gonna happen. As a teacher of AP, I wondered if I would be able to keep ahead of my students.

During the school year, AP Language and Composition juniors made it through most of the regular junior American Literature curriculum, plus more than half again as much of world literature and nonfiction reading and writing. In the spring, students took the two-and-a-half-hour-long test which consisted of killer multiple choice questions and three written essays. If they passed the test, they could receive college credit for an English class, depending on the college they decided to attend.

The best part of teaching AP was that students chose to be in the class, and most of them loved to read and write. They did what I assigned and their participation in substance-filled discussions made "The View," the daytime talk show about current events originally hosted by Barbara Walters, seem like a preschool class. It could be intimidating. Some students had IQs far beyond mine, but I viewed myself as their coach. A coach didn't necessarily have to be able to actually *do* what she coached. She just had to know how to get her enlistees as far as they could go. They had the smarts already. It was my job to introduce them to mind-expanding literature and advanced writing techniques. I learned so much from them and our conversations. Sometimes I had to remind myself that they were still teenagers.

Sierra was one of those students. One week during my second year of teaching AP, Sierra missed several days of school due to illness.

"I was on the couch, feeling like crap, watching Oprah," she told the class and me when she returned. "And, guess what? She announced the new book for her book club...*One Hundred Years of Solitude*. Wouldn't it be cool if we read it in this class?"

"Why would we want to do that?" Brent asked. "And, why were you wasting time watching Oprah on a day off school?"

"Let's hear her out, okay?"

"Thank you, Mrs. Kies. I'm getting to the fun part. Oprah said that after your group reads the book, you can make a video and send it in to her show. If your video is chosen, Oprah comes to your town, and they tape the show there."

"Oh my God! Oprah? In Platteville?" said Ellie. "Let's do it!"

"Wait a minute," said Connor, always the pragmatist. "Would

this be an extra book to read, or would it be replacing one already in the curriculum?"

"Who cares? It'll be fun," said Kim. "Especially if it means we take fewer of these boring practice tests."

"I'll look into it," I said.

In a *New York Times* book review, author William Kennedy wrote, *"One Hundred Years of Solitude* is the first piece of literature since the Book of Genesis that should be required reading for the entire human race... Mr. Garcia Marquez has done nothing less than to create in the reader a sense of all that is profound, meaningful, and meaningless in life."

In my research I also found that Gabriel Garcia Marquez won the 1982 Nobel Prize in Literature for this novel. Written in the genre of magical realism, the story combined the real and imaginary in everyday life in generation after generation of the Buendia family in Colombia, South America. This was different from all other works in my curriculum and would definitely be a challenge for my AP class and for me.

I requested the books from the Gifted and Talented Coordinator, and they arrived in about a week. Brent groaned when he discovered that it was over 500 pages long. Several others shared his sentiment but agreed to take it on.

Using Oprah's online reading guides, we divided the reading into four sections and video-taped class and group discussions. Students filmed classmates reading on the treadmills in the weight room, at the city bowling alley during physical education class, and in the crowded hallways of PHS. Even Henry Hillmen, the school's mascot, got in on the discussions. For the climax, the class acted out a scene from the novel. We followed a trail of blood (bits of red paper) to the auditorium to find the lifeless body of Brent. Blood, (red yarn) trickling from his head.

"If only he'd have read the book," I said on camera. Dramatic music followed. The class shook their heads in despair and understanding as we looked upon Brent with sorrow.

For the grand finale, we filmed outside of Platteville at a location known as the Big M or Platteville Mound, the largest M in the world: 241 feet high and 241 feet wide. On October 16, 1937, the UW-Platteville mining engineering students placed whitewashed stones on the hillside forming the M in honor of themselves and their Homecoming. It has remained ever since, and once a year the UW Pioneers outline it with smudge pots and light them in celebration. How could this huge small town idiosyncrasy fail to gain Oprah's attention?

On that very windy day, Sierra stood at the base of the "M" and narrated: "Could this M stand for Macondo (the Colombian town in the book), or Marquez (Gabriel Garcia, the author). No, it must be for Melquiades (the gypsy magician), for he put it there so we all could ponder the lonely meaning of life."

The camera raised from Sierra's face with the M in the background and zoomed in on the class and me. We were sitting and reading on the climbing steps alongside the M. Our hair blowing over our smiling sunlit faces, we looked up and waved: "Hi, Oprah!" we yelled.

Chandler and I edited the video, dubbing in recordings of the PHS band playing the theme from "Mission Impossible" at the start and "Tequila" at the end. We became immersed in the project, and our hopes soared.

We sent it in and waited. When we didn't hear anything for a long time, we surmised we didn't win. We all but forgot about the video until Sierra found out when the Book Club program was going to air. Our curiosity about the video that *did* win peaked. I asked Mrs. Kittle, the media specialist, to tape the program for us. With a classroom of critical eyes, we watched and wondered, Who could have outdone our video masterpiece?

We were thrilled to see two short clips—very short—in fact, one-second clips of our video made it into the introduction to the show. They were sandwiched between a dozen other miniscule snippets as a compilation of sample entries. When it registered that we'd just seen ourselves on Oprah, we clapped and cheered, rewound it, and played it again.

It turned out that the winning video was submitted by a group of women from San Diego. Most of them, we agreed, appeared to be a gaggle of giggly stay-at-home moms. If it sounds like we were a tad judgmental—we were. They swung from trapezes in a circus acts school and surfed in the ocean, all while reading *One Hundred Years of Solitude*. When Oprah's Book Club van came to visit them, the women wined and dined her with newly purchased dishes in a large suburban house. One of the women's husbands, referred to as "Margarita Man," served Oprah his special recipe in a huge glass.

"We shouldn't feel bad," Sierra said. "There's no way we could compete with that."

"Yeah," I said. "I don't think our principal would have looked kindly on us serving margaritas in school—no matter if it *was* for Oprah."

Even Brent piped up in our defense: "Our discussions about the book had much more substance than theirs!"

"*Our* discussions, Brent?" Sierra said. "Well, at least we can say we've been on the Oprah show."

Just recently, my friend Dona, a former classmate and fellow retired teacher, was substituting in a grade school classroom. The absent teacher had left instructions to project material from the computer onto the screen in front of the class. But, wouldn't you know it, the internet was down.

Dona wondered what she could do and looked through the storage closet where she found her solution.

"What is that?" students asked as they entered the room. "Mrs. Clancy never uses that."

"This," Dona said, sweeping her hand over it like Vanna White over a newly revealed letter, "is an overhead projector."

"A what? What does it do, anyway?" asked one of her students.

She flipped the switch and students "oohed" and "aahed."

Remember those hollow, glass-topped blocks of metal with a periscope arm shooting straight up? Before Smart Boards and Google Slides, every classroom had one sitting on a cart, including mine. All I had to do was flip on the switch, and voila—the information from the transparency, the clear sheet of mylar, appeared on the screen for the entire class to see. I chose my favorite color of erasable Vis a Vis marker to write text or underline a word or an idea. Interestingly, *vis a vis* means *face to face* in French. Unlike the chalkboard or white board, I could face the class without worry of a spit wad hitting me in the back or a student poking another with a pencil. It worked stupendously when correcting awkward or ungrammatical sentences with the class. In its day, it was a remarkable teaching innovation.

About midway through my teaching years, Stan, one of my students, came up with an even more creative use for the overhead projector.

I loved movie days at the end of a unit as much as the students. This meant I could get caught up with grading, updating the gradebook, or planning the upcoming unit. Over the years, I've memorized most of the dialogue and music to these films I showed four to five times a day for the umpteenth time.

On this particular day, we were viewing the new *Great Gatsby* film, the one with Toby McGuire as Stan and Leonardo DiCaprio as Gatsby. It hadn't been out long on DVD, and most students had not seen it, yet. First period watched the first forty-five minutes of the movie and looked forward to continuing the next day. I spent my second period prep time running errands and taking a much needed bathroom break. Students filed in third period and took their seats while I rolled the TV/VCR to the front of the class.

I pushed the rewind button and heard no spinning sound, so I pushed the eject button. The flap opened, but nothing popped out. No video. *Damn!* Thinking I'd misplaced it, I looked on my desk, in my desk drawers, the shelves behind my desk, and the storage cabinet in my room. Students were getting restless and concerned they wouldn't get to watch the movie.

"I don't get it. We watched it first period," I said, looking under a stack of tests I'd been grading and all around my desk.

"Maybe somebody pranked you," Joe said.

Immediately, I looked at Tristan who was smiling as smug as a Cheshire Cat.

"Okay, Tristan, where is it?"

"Hey, I didn't take it, Mrs. Kies. Honestly I didn't!"

Students continued to look behind books on the two rows of shelves in the back of the room and on top of the cupboard. My room looked like it had gone through a police shake down.

"If you know something, Tristan, spit it out. We all wanna watch the movie," said Joe. "It's not funny anymore, okay?"

In a situation like this, there's nothing a teacher likes better than peer pressure. Finally, Tristan cracked. He said he'd heard Nick, from my first period class, bragging about taking it. It made sense. Nick could be a rascal, to put it mildly. He liked to give me a hard time and make under-his-breath smart-aleck comments to make others laugh. He loved attention. Knowing this, I tried to give it to him before he asked for it. When making the seating chart, I put him front and center.

One day, a student who had long legs and was seated behind him, poked him in the back with his knee. "Ouch!" Nick yelped. "Be careful of my kidney."

"Don't worry, Nick," I said. "You've got another one."

This was my attempt at humor when kids complained about

bumping their arm or leg, or anything else they had two of. It usually got a laugh and we moved on. This time the class began looking at each other like I'd just stepped in a pile of dog doo.

After a moment of awkwardness, Jolene said, "He doesn't have two, Mrs. Kies. He only has one."

Nick affirmed that he'd had one kidney removed a year or so ago because it hadn't been functioning properly. I apologized profusely. Nick enjoyed every second of my eating a huge mouthful of crow.

That day, however, the question was, What would my lesson plans be for the rest of the day if I couldn't track down the video? I looked up Nick's schedule on my computer. Thankfully, he was in my neighborhood. I stomped down the hall on a mission and knocked on the door of the French room. "Excuse me, Madame. Is Nick·here?"

My tone of voice and agitated body language prompted the French students to respond before Madame: "Oooooohhhhhh, Nick. You're in trouble now!"

Nick looked surprised and a bit sheepish that I'd take him out of class. Not so much, though, that he couldn't manage a smirk.

"Okay, where is it, Nick? What did you do with it?"

"Do with what?"

"I know you took the *Gatsby* video. Is it in your locker? Your backpack? You need to give it to me now. I need it for my classes today!" I'd forgotten one of the main rules of teacher/student interaction: Don't let them see you sweat.

"I didn't take it. Really."

"Tristan said you did."

"Tristan? He's just trying to get me in trouble." That damned smirk again.

"I know you took it, Nick, and if you don't get it back to me, you're going to have to...buy me a new one." (There's that

209

consequential consequence again. Teachers have to get really good at those.)

The high school library had a copy of the 1972 version of *Gatsby* with Robert Redford, Bruce Dern, and Mia Farrow. Far more accurate of the times and classically beautiful, the movie satisfied me just fine. The students? Not so much. They viewed it as boring and old-fashioned. Maybe this would pressure Nick to return it. Every day, I chided him about returning it or buying me a new one.

A few weeks later after my angst about the missing video had abated, Nick came to see me during my prep time.

"Did you find the video, yet, Mrs. Kies?"

I looked at him. "Ha, ha, Nick. Did you buy me a new one, yet?"

"You'll be happy to know that someone told me where they hid it," he said, not skipping a beat, only the slightest crack of a smile showing. "You won't believe it." He walked over to the overhead projector and raised the top. He reached into its belly where the light bulb is located and pulled out my *Gatsby* video. "What a good hiding place, huh?"

Sheesh! It had been right under my nose the whole time.

"I don't suppose you'd want to tell me who put the video in there." It was my turn to smirk.

"Nah. It's not nice to rat on other people."

But sometimes people did rat, like when my students and other teachers told me about Cassie and her boyfriend spending lots of time together in the darkroom.

Back in the mid-1990s I was assigned to be the photography advisor for the school's newspaper and the yearbook because my minor in journalism provided some basic knowledge of black and white photography. Since this was before digital cameras, I was able to help students with the photo developing and finishing process if needed. Before becoming a photographer for the publications, students took a technical education class teaching them the basics. My main duties were to assign photos, enforce deadlines, and supervise the darkroom.

Often, students would wait until the last minute to take the photos. If something went wrong with the film in the camera or the developing process, the photos often didn't get done in time for the story or layout. The yearbook and newspaper writers would tell me about it, and it was up to me to stress the importance of deadlines to the photographers. On occasion, I would take and develop the photos because my crew didn't follow through.

"You can't have Bobby in the darkroom with you," I told Cassie, one of my photographers. Other teachers told me they'd seen the two of them entering and leaving together. "He's not a photographer, and, well—you know—people talk."

"He helped me finish up some photos, that's all."

I hope that's all they were finishing up, I thought. I recalled the time my boyfriend, now husband, walked me to math class. We were just having a short smooch when my teacher appeared. "Ha! Caught ya! No more of that, now," she said, holding the door open for me. "Class is starting."

Now, I was the teacher: "He's not a photographer. Okay?"

Cassie nodded and gave me a pouty look.

Dear Teachers and Staff,

We were all young once, and some things never change.

Fondly remembering,

The Author

PART IV – RELEASE

Chapter 20 – Requiem

In paradisum deducant te Angeli.
(May the angels lead you into paradise.)
Gregorian Chant

During my freshman and sophomore year at PHS, I took Latin with Mrs. Trudy Pankow. My dad had attended Campion, a Catholic high school in Prairie du Chien, where Latin was a required course, so he was able to help me with the vocabulary. In class we conjugated verbs and worked on translating the *Iliad* to English. Mrs. Pankow was a competent teacher, and I thoroughly enjoyed this study of language, albeit a dead one. In my second year, I served as president of the Latin Club.

Two years of a foreign language was suggested for those who planned on going to college. I had no burning desire to take Latin, but Spanish and French had overflowing rosters. St. Mary's students like me were the last to register, thus the guidance counselors "highly recommended" we take Latin. Later, as a teacher, I came to understand that instructors of elective classes like art, technical education, family and consumer education, business classes, or foreign language vied for students. If numbers became too low in certain classes, teachers of said courses could face a reduction in their contract or even receive a pink slip. I'm sure Mrs. Pankow was relieved that the guidance counselors had her back.

Most people who *chose* to take Latin planned on going into health-related fields because medical and pharmacological terms are rooted in it. I knew already that a health career was not in my future. I was not a fan of hospitals, doctor's offices, or blood. However, there I was in Latin class—and liking it! It was enlightening to gain some understanding of what the priests had been saying at Mass for those ten years before they switched to English in 1965, thanks to the Second Vatican Council.

The study of Latin also helped me better understand English grammar and vocabulary. I discovered *ambulare* meant "to walk," which helped me see where amble and ambulatory hailed from. Without realizing it, I was becoming familiar with etymology, the study of the history of words. *Bene* meant good in Latin, lending its root to benefactor, beneficial, benevolence, etc. I liked to point out to my students that Benvolio in *Romeo and Juliet* was the quintessential good guy, which couldn't have been a coincidence on Shakespeare's part. This study of Latin set the stage for my becoming an English teacher twenty years later.

I've always thought that authors who conveniently dropped foreign phrases into their writing sound intelligent, culturally aware, and well-traveled. As a reader, knowing these words makes me feel like I'm in on a private joke. When I don't understand them, the authors come off as snooty or condescending. I'm hoping to do the former by calling this chapter "Requiem." In Latin this means "a mass in honor of the dead," and this chapter attempts to do just that—give the departed their due.

Death stomped its big, ugly feet in my path many times during my teaching years: students, past students, and colleagues, as well as my mom—and my twenty-five-year-old son. Upon learning of the death of Sammy, my colleague's son in 2009, my blog entry read: *It's been a tough few days. A beautiful boy left us, and his mother is bereft; no, knocked down flat— whammied. He was artistic and sensitive, and, probably, the world became too much. It can do that sometimes.*

The deaths of people we hold dear bookmark our lives. We recall where we were and what we were doing when we found out. Our routines interrupted, we pause to contemplate our loss as well as our own inevitable fate. Death is devastating and mystifying for all—but particularly for young people. When they experience it for the first time as an adolescent, grief, compassion, hurt, confusion, and anger whirl into dust devils of emotion.

One day while I was teaching, a student I'd had the previous hour came by my room. In a panicked voice, he told the class and me that the New York Trade Center Twin Towers had been attacked. What? *Oh, come on.* The urgency in his eyes told me he was serious. The bell rang, and many of us scurried to the library. There, on every TV screen tuned to a different news channel, movie-like horror scenes played over and over. I was among twenty or so teachers and students watching. No one commented, other than the few who mumbled, "Oh, my God."

Death seems to numb us first. Then it awakens the stark awareness of the gift of life. We become accustomed to people when they are here. Their presence is a given, their words and movements expected. When they leave us, we comb through our minds to examine every little thing. That's what happened when we lost my sophomore student, Krystal.

Playing with different room configurations kept my life interesting and kids guessing. Every year, and sometimes mid-year, I changed the layout of my classroom. Occasionally, I lined students' desks in rows diagonally, from one corner of the room to the other, which formed a big triangle. Or, I arranged them auditorium-style, in rows five or six deep with an easy arc facing toward the center of the room. My favorite and most often used was a U-shape, which created a performance area in the middle.

The year I had Krystal as a student, the students' desks were positioned in the shape of an L, with my desk in the corner of the room facing them. The rows were only about four seats deep, so I could see everyone and they could easily see me.

Krystal sat two seats from the front near the intersection of the arms of the L. A shy, petite young teen with shiny blond locks, she paid attention and did her work. She had a ready smile and was well-liked. In high school terms, she was popular. She'd known most of her classmates since elementary school, which is common in a school our size. Classes as a whole take on personalities, depending on their leaders, and I recall Krystal's class as congenial, if a bit goofy at times. Many enjoyed good fun and frequent laughs, but none were mean or malicious.

I didn't know Krystal very long or very well. We'd only been in school a couple of months when she became confident enough to raise her hand and contribute to discussions. And then it happened.

We found out the details at a faculty meeting before school on Monday, though many of us had heard about the accident over the weekend. The principal said one car passed the other car on a rural road outside Platteville. The car being passed went out of control, flipped, rolled into the ditch and landed in a field. Krystal was ejected from the vehicle. All involved in the accident were friends and classmates. All survived, except for Krystal.

I'm sure her parents thought, Why did it have to be Krystal? I know. I thought similarly when our son passed away. It's not that you want it to happen to someone else—you just don't want it to be *your* child. When death occurs to a young person or anyone really, it's common to rack one's brain with all the "what-if" scenarios of prevention. Even though it will do no good. Other parents were likely thinking Oh, my God. Poor Krystal. Poor Krystal's family, as they poured out compassion and sympathy. I'm sure they were also thanking God it wasn't their kid sitting in the car where Krystal had been sitting.

At the wake, family, friends, students, and faculty formed an endless line that snaked out the door and around the block of the funeral home. They were there to offer condolences and convince themselves this was real. No one knew what to say, but, as difficult as it was, they knew they had to be there for Krystal, her family, and themselves. Throughout the evening, her friends and classmates congregated in clumps, sobbing, hugging, and remembering. Remembering and sobbing. I walked by the casket, then offered helpless sympathy to her parents. Her body bore little resemblance to the beautiful fifteen-year-old girl we'd all known.

During the following week, our two PHS counselors offered support to students. Guidance staff from neighboring schools also came to help students cope. With no answers, they listened. How do you attempt to explain or justify the death of a young person? It makes no sense. It should not exist in this world.

Some of these teens grasped their sorrow like a life jacket, the grief keeping them afloat. They hung on to each other and arranged a shrine of memorabilia by Krystal's locker: pictures, flowers, notes, sentimental objects and trinkets. Some students offered to help the family in any way they could. Others avoided the topic and remained stoic, showing no outward feeling, tucking it away for later, a personal and private conference.

No one sat in Krystal's desk for the rest of that quarter. It was as if we were all waiting for her return.

At the start of the second quarter I rearranged my room. Students did not comment on the change, but I sensed the silent sighs of relief. Even though her empty desk was no longer prominent, she was not forgotten. She never will be. Krystal's grave is near my parents' plot. When I visit them, I can look over at her resting place and recall her smile and the beautiful life that was snatched from our midst in several ugly seconds of time we all wished we could reverse.

Just before Thanksgiving somewhere in the middle of my teaching years, my third period juniors were studying transcendentalism, the Emerson and Thoreau philosophy of trusting your natural inclinations, your sense beyond your

217

senses. It was my favorite unit. I hyped it up by dangling the juicy carrot we would consume at the end: the movie *Dead Poets Society* starring Robin Williams.

"How come all the stories and poems we read in English class are about death?" I remember my student Conrad asking that day. I was passing out copies of the poem "Thanatopsis" written in 1817 by William Cullen Bryant.

"Yeah, can't we read something about real, live, modern people?" James said from the back row.

"Didn't I hear you talking about a movie you'd seen over the weekend where lots of people and things were blown up?" I asked. "'It was so awesome,' I believe you said?"

"Yeah. But that was fake. That's different," said Damien, coming to his friend's defense.

Damien had a point. Death, the fake kind, was much more palatable.

In my Anticipatory Set, as education guru Madeline Hunter called the introduction to a lesson, I explained that the word "thanatopsis" was the Greek word for a meditation on death. Written in the eighteenth century, the poem represented a literary period called Romanticism.

"Romantics look positively at everything, even death," I assured my students. "Even though it is old and about dying, the poem is not morbid and surprisingly uplifting and hopeful."

My encouragement was met with disbelieving looks, but I forged on.

They broke into small groups and read the poem stanza by stanza to decipher Bryant's wordy text and write down their interpretations. I strolled among them. Struggling with the old-style syntax, one group managed to extract Bryant's belief that when we die our bodies decompose and change form to feed other living things, like oak trees.

"It's like the 'Circle of Life' in *The Lion King*," Mindy said to group members. Kudos to Disney for revamping and marketing classic ideas to the masses, I thought.

"Good connection, Mindy," I said, moving to the next group.

They were wading through the part where Bryant advises the acceptance of death as something everyone experiences: *Thou shalt lie down/With patriarchs of the infant world—with kings, The powerful of the earth—the wise, the good, Fair forms, and hoary seers of ages past, All in one mighty sepulchre.*

"Death makes us equal. Doesn't matter if you're rich or poor," said Sally. "We all die."

The group went on to the next line: *All that tread the globe are but a handful to the tribes that slumber in its bosom.*

"He's saying there are more dead people than living people," Jeff said. "We are in the minority."

"I wonder if that's still true today?" Tom asked. I gave him permission to Google it on his phone. "On this site put out by the BBC, it says there are fifteen dead people for every living one."

As a class, we discussed the closing line: *By an unfaltering trust, approach thy grave, Like one who wraps the drapery of his couch, About him, and lies down to pleasant dreams.*

"I think he's trying to comfort us," Jake said. "Death is natural and we shouldn't fear it."

Many shook their heads in agreement. Then Sarah piped up, "How many people do you know who die by 'lying down to pleasant dreams'?"

"Yeah, that's true," Jared added. "There's cancer and car accidents—or being blown up by a bomb in Iraq."

"And sometimes babies die," Hazel said. "They don't need rest. They haven't even had a chance to live yet."

"All valid points," I said. "Death isn't always peaceful and serene." I told them about my grandpa who went to bed one night covered in the blankets of his own bed. He never woke up. He was seventy-five. In my mind, too young, but no pain. No suffering.

The transcendental way to go. We all agreed that this was rare.

Students took turns sharing personal stories about death. Karissa told of an aunt who was murdered by her husband and Sally about a young cousin who perished by suffocating in a corn bin. Then we discussed a *60 Minutes* segment about the many old people in hospital beds waiting and wanting to die, but kept alive by machines for months on end.

"People should be allowed to die if they want to," said Steven.

"That's euthanasia, a whole other topic," I said. "And a very controversial one."

Then, Calvin raised his hand. "I can't wait to die," he said.

All air and sound was vacuumed from the room.

"Don't worry," he said, after a moment. "I'm not saying I'm going to—you know—do anything. But just think. Death is that moment when we finally find out what comes next—if anything. People have wondered about what comes after death for as long as they've existed. Think how cool that moment will be."

On that candid thought, the bell rang. Every year after that, Calvin's proclamation returned to me when we studied that poem.

Dear Calvin,

I hope you're still waiting to find out what happens.

I hope you will be waiting for a long, long time.

When it does happen, I hope it's more beautiful and moving than you ever imagined.

Glad you were my student,

Mrs. Kies

Chapter 21 – Also Close to Home

*How lucky I am to have something
that makes saying goodbye so hard.*
Winnie the Pooh

As I said, Platteville is a smallish city. You know, everyone knows what everyone else is doing? Well, my student Tyler's family lived kitty-corner to my mother. When Mom sat in her chair near the picture window to watch TV, she could also see their home across the street.

"The neighbor kids are adorable!" Mom said one day. This was before I had Tyler as a student. "They get along so well, and they're always dressed so cute." Both items scored big points in my mother's book.

I shared this anecdote with Tyler one day after class when he was a junior. He threw his head back in laughter.

"We sure fooled her." He smiled. He said when he was in middle school, he accidentally set off an explosion in the family garage while conducting a science experiment. "My parents had to call the fire department and were really upset with me. I'm glad your mom didn't see that one."

During class discussions Tyler liked to sit atop his desk to better interject his opinions and get a more encompassing view of the interactions in the room. To his parents' dismay, he didn't get too caught up in grades, but he thrived on learning. He absorbed everything around him and was a pleasure to teach.

One day his usual exuberance transformed into a veil of cheerlessness that continued throughout the week. Later that day, the guidance counselor informed teachers that the family wanted us to know that Tyler's mother had been diagnosed with cancer and was undergoing aggressive treatment for it. A few days later, I asked Tyler privately how his mother was doing. I wanted him to know I was aware of the situation and understood if he needed more time to complete his work. His aunt had moved in with the family, he said, in order to help keep house, prepare meals, and see to the wellbeing of Tyler and his siblings. He said his mom had some good days in the midst of mostly bad.

The year progressed, but Tyler's mom didn't. The day after the funeral he came to school. "I know I don't have to be here," he told me, "but my mother would want me to."

"I'm so sorry, Tyler." We were alone in the hall after other students moved on to the computer lab.

"I'm okay. I'm relieved she's not suffering anymore."

I nodded.

We were walking to the computer lab, when suddenly, his face lit up. "I found a way to always keep her close to me." He stopped, lifted his pant legs, and revealed a pair of loud patterned socks that shouted hues of blue, red, yellow, and green to the world. "These were her favorite."

Tyler was the oldest of his three siblings. Eventually, I taught the others, all as intelligent, talented, and decent as the next, but in different ways. William Cullen Bryant forgot to address one other aspect of death in his poem "Thanatopsis." Even after parents are gone, a part of them lives on in their children.

Platteville, like other school districts, is not immune to teen suicides and the painful reverberations that follow for those who are left to go on. Zachery was in eighth grade but had many friends at the high school. He was outgoing and participated in rodeo competitions with many high school FFAers (Future Farmers of America). Completely unexpected, Zach's suicide left family, friends, and middle school teachers reviewing the previous days' happenings and conversations for clues. No one could piece together the puzzle of his feelings that brought on his will to stop living.

Kyle was one of my students at the time and a dear friend of Zach's. If there was trouble to be had anywhere in the school, Kyle was usually in on it. I met him his freshman year, the only year I ever had lunch duty. (Our choir teacher deserves a medal and a gift-laden appreciation ceremony for performing this thankless assignment year after year.) After observing Kyle repeatedly throwing grapes across the lunchroom at unsuspecting victims, I sent him to the office. The vice principal sentenced him to a week of lunchtime detention in the office away from his friends. He was not happy with me, but when he became my student his sophomore year, Kyle and I got along well. He knew I wasn't going to put up with his shenanigans.

When Zach died, Kyle was devastated. On the day of the funeral, Zach's high school friends wore cowboy hats and rode their tractors to school. Big, tough Kyle wrote an elegy for him which was published in our literary magazine that spring. The summer after Kyle graduated, I saw him at the local truck stop. He proudly lifted up the sleeve of his T-shirt to show me a raw section of his arm displaying his hour-old tattoo in honor of Zach.

Not a big fan of body ink, I couldn't say it was nice looking, but I told him, "Zach would be honored, Kyle."

Then there was Jennifer. She was in my daughter's class. Stunningly pretty and kind to boot, she, like Zach, loved the outdoors, particularly horses and participating in rodeos and riding competitions. I chatted with her on a school bus one time while on a field trip. The thing I remember about our brief conversation was her maturity, her ability to easily converse with me, a teacher.

I hadn't realized she'd been battling depression. As is often the case, no one did. One night, overwhelmed with her pain and feelings of the moment, Jennifer ended her life. As Don MacLean wrote in his song "Vincent" for the artist Van Gogh, "This world was never meant for one as beautiful as you." However true, these words do nothing to help her parents and younger sibling who were left to continue on with her beauty and grace no longer in their lives.

Miss Rebecca Lewis taught band at Platteville Middle School when my kids went to school there. She ran her marching band class like a boot camp, and I doubt she ever took anything less than first place in any competition her students entered. She was a teensy, feisty woman with dark hair and big, beautiful eyes fringed with long lashes. She reminded me of pictures I had seen of Anne Frank. Though she was *Tough* with an uppercase T, she tempered it with fairness and compassion.

Her success came from hard work. Students showed up for practice at 6:30 every weekday morning for several weeks before a parade. They wouldn't dream of being late or missing practice because they would have to then explain it to Miss Lewis, and nobody wanted to do that. Mainly because they didn't want to let her down. Her passion, drive, and pride were contagious, and students played and marched their hearts out to please her.

Miss Lewis choreographed intricate marching steps and motions that complemented the music the students had memorized. She made it fun to be good. She chose snappy, popular songs that got the crowd clapping and singing along. When my middle son and daughter were in the marching band, they played "I Will Follow Him" from the movie *Sister Act*. Students held their heads high, looked straight ahead and kept in step every inch of the way. And, when they were finished performing, they remained in full uniform until they had the chance to completely change out of it. She allowed no untucked or unbuttoned shirts, as it gave a sloppy representation of the band. Miss Lewis taught them more than how to march and play an instrument. She taught them to have pride in themselves and their work.

One time at a solo and ensemble competition, my son was talking and goofing around when he wasn't supposed to be. Miss Lewis gave him "the look." He came home and told me about it straight away before Miss Lewis would have the chance. He said, "It was like she shot daggers at me with her eyes." I laughed, wishing I could master that level of teacher look.

When the Platteville High School band director position opened, Miss Lewis moved her energy and work ethic from middle school to high school. Her football halftime shows were productions to behold. People came to the football games just to watch the band.

One summer in 2003 Becky was entertaining her niece for a few weeks. They had a great day of horseback riding and fun at a nearby state park and were headed home. A drunk driver crossed the center line and hit them head on. Her niece was injured, but Becky didn't make it. Her students, past and present, as well as the entire community, went into mourning.

In my mind's eye, I can still see her bounding up the street with her black labs in tow, her ponytail and the dogs' tails bouncing in stride. One of our staff members once recalled going to have lunch with her. When Becky opened her purse, she let out a yelp. "Aaaahhh!"

"What's wrong?"

"Oh my gosh! My aunt's ashes were in this bag in my purse." She held up the empty bag. "I've got to go wash my hands!"

The year Jesse was my student, I recall using the paragraph booklet project to teach the importance of recognizing and mastering the various types of writing. Most students enjoyed completing it, and it was one of the few assignments that I enjoyed correcting. Unlike the dry and fact-based Career Research Paper, the paragraph booklets were creative, short, and fun to read!

The first task of the project involved choosing a topic that they loved. A topic they would enjoy writing about. A passion, a joy. The popular fare tended to be sports: volleyball, football, cross country, swimming. Every once in a while, though, an original (and sometimes bizarre) idea surfaced, like chocolate, *The Simpsons*—and even toilets and slugs. Somebody has to be interested in plumbing or limacology, right?

The first of four paragraphs they would compose was the *expository* paragraph. Students were to look up and report facts or a set of instructions related to their topic. For example, the future plumber might explain the science behind what happens when we flush a toilet. Next, they completed a *descriptive* paragraph that employed the senses to describe an aspect of the topic, like the different styles of toilets, sizes, and shapes. The *narrative* paragraph told a story, like the time the future plumber's family purchased a new toilet. And the last one, the *persuasive paragraph,* convinced their audience about some aspect of their topic, like what is the best type of toilet seat to buy and why. The goal was to recognize and gain practice in these basic modes of writing and understand that any one topic could be approached in very different ways. Really good writing, I told them, combined all four of these modes because this gave a good picture of the topic as a whole.

We reviewed the basics of paragraph writing: topic sentences, supporting sentences, transitions, and details. They wrote each paragraph and edited it. When they finished the final drafts of all four, they arranged them in a booklet with pictures, either drawn, cut from magazines, or legally downloaded and printed from the internet. They also designed a cover that included a clever title and their name.

Jesse loved motorcycles. He wrote about how to start a motorcycle and how it felt to ride one, including the wind, the roar, the exhaust. His narrative paragraph was about how and where he bought his motorcycle, and his persuasive paragraph convinced readers of the best bike to buy.

His red cover bore a big, sporty bike with lots of chrome. I was thrilled. Not with the subject matter, but with Jesse's enthusiastic response to his topic. Numerous pictures of various makes and models of shiny bikes filled the booklet. I could be wrong, but it seemed Jesse, whose favorite class was not English, came mighty close to liking this assignment.

I hadn't seen Jesse on his motorcycle, but from his writing I could picture him: his hair tousled by the wind, the sparkle of thrill in his eyes, his girlfriend's arms hugging his torso. That's probably how he looked on that day, the year after he graduated, before the accident. His girlfriend survived. Jesse didn't.

Jesse's dad and I had graduated from PHS together. His mom was a few years younger, and I couldn't imagine their grief and pain. And I didn't ever want to. At the wake, after searching my brain what to say, I remember telling them, "I'm so sorry. No one should have to go through what you're going through." In retrospect, I know this didn't help at all. Just because it was true, it didn't change that they were indeed having to "go through it." There's nothing one can say at a time like this. Nothing that helps, nothing that comes close, nothing that can possibly ease the pain of losing a child. Nothing. My husband and I would find this out firsthand a few years later.

These deaths of my students sent my thoughts back in time to my classmate, Tim. Tim sat toward the front of the room in Miss Clark's freshman English class. One day, we were reading "The Rime of the Ancient Mariner" by Samuel Taylor Coleridge. It was hard to concentrate, and I'm sure I wasn't alone. My eyes kept wandering to the empty desk on the far left side of the room, third from the front in the first row. Tim was small and wiry with a toothy grin and eyes curtained by long dark lashes. He was very cute. Because he was quiet and well behaved, the fact that he was not there was not impactful. It was *why* he wasn't there that caused the albatross of doom to befall on the room, the halls, the school.

The previous weekend, Tim and some of his buddies had been returning from a day of hunting in the woods. One of the guns accidentally went off, killing Tim. Everyone—family, friends, classmates, and townspeople—reeled in disbelief. Our class members were given the option to attend Tim's funeral. Instead of school bells ringing that day, church bells tolled down Main Street in Tim's honor. I sat in the balcony with friends and remember watching his family follow the casket up the center aisle in a slow procession to the front pews. Some bore their pain with loud sobs, while others dabbed at tears with a tissue. Others sat in a hushed stupor in the gaping hole his death created.

My grandma and my great-uncle died, both unexpectedly, but they'd been older. They had experienced life. Tim's death was unprecedented in my world at that time, that age. It hadn't occurred to me that a classmate would die. Could die. When you are fourteen, you can't fathom death. You're still getting accustomed to living.

Fourteen is gut-wrenchingly young, but twenty-five is too young, too. That's how old our son Kelly was. Kelly Phillip was born on Wednesday morning, April 9, 1980, a few weeks premature, weighing six pounds, one ounce. He was long and skinny and healthy—but yellow. We had to place his bassinet in the window so the natural sunshine could help his jaundice. His two older brothers, ages seven and eight, bragged about their little mite of a bro to anyone who would listen.

Flash forward twenty-five years of love, laughter, and life. On Wednesday, July 6, 2005, at 10:30 p.m., the ring of our bedside phone startled us. An Appleton police officer identified herself: "Your son collapsed in his apartment and the EMTs are taking him to the hospital. We suggest you come as soon as possible."

In a stupor of panic we arrived at the hospital where we were met by Kelly's girlfriend, her parents, his boss and his wife. On the way to see Kelly, the attendant handed me my son's billfold and driver's license in the hallway. I remember wondering why they were giving these things to me? The rest is a blur.

There are worse things than death, people often say. I've come to understand that this is very true. For three weeks we hoped and prayed for his recovery, which did not come. Because of an episode of cardiac arrhythmia, his brain had been without oxygen too long. We transferred him from Appleton to UW-Madison Hospital for a second opinion. The doctors all agreed. The Kelly we knew and loved would never return to us. How could this be? Through experience I had learned firsthand that death could happen to young people, like my classmate Tim and my student Jesse. To other people. Not us.

Jane came to visit us at UW-Hospital in Madison where Kelly was under hospice care. (Yes, this is none other than Jane, my mentor who snored during inservice and held the recruiters at bay.) We were out for a much-needed walk that day on a nature path behind the hospital. When we returned to the room, we found this note:

Hi, Sue and Dave and Family—

1:00 Tues.

Forgive my stationery. I stole it out of "The Hunchback." (A novel left randomly lying in the room.) I just can't get your family off my mind. I've even been dreaming of you. I've been sitting with Kelly for a little while. He is very calm. In fact, the atmosphere in the room feels calm. Kelly is very lucky to have been born to you. You're great parents and siblings. I am sorry to have missed hugging you today, but I am happy that you were able to be away

for a bit. Of course you know I'm available absolutely any time.
My heart is with you.
Love and peace,
Jane

Kelly died the next morning on Wednesday, August 3, 2005.

After his death, Debbie, a former PHS English teaching peer and Kelly's former teacher, sent me Mary Oliver's poem from *In Blackwater Woods.* If you live longer than a loved one, you may find comfort in this poem that explains the three things necessary to exist in the world: to love what is mortal, embrace it and know how much you rely on it, and when its time comes..."to let it go."

How could our family possibly go on without him? How could I go back to teaching in a few weeks? Stilled by grief, I didn't want to go anywhere, see anyone—or do anything. My hands kept shaking, my stomach kept churning, and my eyes kept crying. How could I return to teaching?

Somehow, I managed to show up. On my first day back, Dean Isaacson, our superintendent at the time, visited my room and sat down next to me at my desk. He offered condolences and support. It would have been easier for him to do nothing—or just send a card or note. I realize that people don't know what to say. One can't go wrong by acknowledging what happened and offering compassion. School became the only place where, at least part of the day, I *had* to think about something other than losing Kelly. And, there was comfort in being needed. And in my peers.

That year was my turn in the teacher evaluation cycle. In May, Vice Principal Lisa Finnegan and I reviewed the goals I had set that fall at the beginning of the school year. I had no recollection of ever doing this. She handed me what I'd written for my main goal: "To make it through the year."

The summer was horrific, a torturous litany of firsts and anniversaries of the previous year's tragedy. Before Kelly's death, summer was my favorite season. Long days, pleasant temperatures with plenty of outdoor activities and time to recharge my brain. Not that summer. The next year was hard, too. All the coming days, months and years would be. Life would never be the same, and I had to learn to live with that.

I had a repertoire of stories about my children I often told students when it related to what we were studying in class. For example, when we studied Ralph Waldo Emerson's essay "Gifts," I liked to relate the one about our oldest daughter humorously christening a vase my husband gave me for Christmas as the "Leg Vase." You know, in relation to the "Leg Lamp" in the movie *A Christmas Story*? And during the Career Unit, I often mentioned our oldest son's winding path to find his career in electronic, robotics, and computers.

The second year after Kelly's passing, I'd just told yet another of these stories when Tabitha commented, "Geez, Mrs. Kies, how many kids do you have, anyway?"

The class laughed at her candor. But, I stood there, stunned, and then began to cry. The class was at a loss. Here was their teacher sitting on a stool before them, sobbing. Stacy, a polite, sensitive girl in the front row, calmly got up from her desk and put her arms around me while I continued to weep.

After I composed myself, I thanked her and explained that this was the first time I'd been asked how many children I had since our son Kelly passed away. This question caught me off guard because I didn't know whether to still count him or not. Did I still have five kids—or four?

Stacy, again, came to the rescue. "He's still your kid, right? You should count him." I became very human to that class. Probably more human than any student in the room wanted me to be. I've no idea where Stacy's mature sense of compassion came from. It may have been instinctive—or learned. I don't know. Even as I retell it, the memory of that hug and that

231

affirmation brings comfort to me.

Dear parents who have lost children,
I totally get your grief.
But I truly wish I didn't.
Compassionately,
The Author

Chapter 22 – Stepford Schools

Moving forward, the focus should be on promoting authentic assessments that reflect the broad range of students' learning and skills including creativity, leadership, critical thinking, and collaboration.
John Rosales and Tim Walker, NEA Today, 03/20/2021

About ten years into my teaching career, a group of parents challenged the teaching of Maya Angelou's autobiographical book *I Know Why the Caged Bird Sings*. The parents' main objection to the book was the scene in Chapter 12 where Angelou describes being molested by her mother's boyfriend when she was seven and a half years old. These parents believed this scene was too mature for fourteen-year-olds to read in freshman English class.

Our policy in the English Department at Platteville High School for as long as I taught there was to offer a different book with a similar theme if a parent or their teen found the curricular material objectionable. During class discussions, the student or students doing the alternate reading worked on it in the library independently. This happened a handful of times in my experience and seemed to work well for everyone involved. In this instance, however, this policy did not satisfy the parents. They believed that this option singled out their children. Because of this and because of their concerns about the book, they didn't think any of the freshmen class should read it.

As the debate picked up steam, lots of people began reading the book: parents, school board members, administrators, and many of the students. Years ago, this ironical quirk of book-banning wasn't lost on Mark Twain. When the Concord, Massachusetts, Public Library removed *The Adventures of*

Huckleberry Finn from its shelves in 1885, Twain remarked, "This will sell us another twenty-five thousand copies."

Miss Cheryl Schober, the Freshman English teacher, developed this unit for *I Know Why the Caged Bird Sings* when she began teaching at PHS. Angelou's work became part of the curriculum because of its expert prose, compelling nonfiction narrative, and contemporary themes. During the first few years of my career, I taught the book to several freshmen classes using her materials. No one objected, and I enjoyed teaching it as much as students enjoyed reading it.

During this period of controversy, one of my sophomore students asked, "Why should a few parents get to choose what we read in English class just because they believe it isn't right for *their* kids?" Several of her classmates echoed her concerns.

At the designated school board meeting, many teachers, students, and parents rallied to retain Angelou's autobiography. They emphasized that the topics of rape, police brutality toward Blacks, and economic inequality prevalent in the story set in the 1930s and 40s continued to be relevant in present-day society. There were strong feelings on both sides.

The School Board decided to remove the book from the freshman curriculum but conceded that it would be appropriate at junior or senior level. Disappointed with the outcome, the freshmen teacher requested that I work it into my junior level American Literature curriculum for the following year. The problem was that my juniors were already reading four novels, one per quarter. What book would I drop to make room for this one?

After much deliberation, I decided not to drop any of the novels. Instead, I offered students the option of reading either *I Know Why the Caged Bird Sings* or *The Adventures of Huckleberry Finn*. Racism was a main theme in both coming-of-age works, but that was about as far as the similarities went. The differences in time period, style, tone, and genres are as wide as the Mississippi River. Twain wrote the fictional *Huckleberry Finn* comedic characters to poke fun at society's rules and norms just after the Civil War, whereas Angelou's *Caged Bird* related her true story using dramatic vignettes about the people who affected her young life, both positively and negatively, while growing up in the Depression Era.

Nevertheless, I tried to make it work. Half the class discussed *Huck Finn* one day, while the other half read *I Know Why the Caged Bird* to themselves. And, vice versa the next day. Having discussions of two very different major books going on in class on alternate days became overwhelming for me and distracting for students. It wasn't like I could send half the class to the library to read and study on their own as I had done when one or two students chose an alternate book. This approach didn't give either book its just due.

The next year I offered *Caged Bird* to sophomores as one of the book options for the Novel Choice Unit in the spring of the year. For that unit, students chose a title off the list and discussed it in a group with others reading the same book. To satisfy the School Board's decision, I required students who read Angelou's autobiography to return a signed consent form from their parents. This worked much better, and Cheryl and I were glad the book was still being offered.

In the course of my career, a few students confided in me that they had been raped or sexually abused. I made sure the school counselor and social worker knew. Reporting this is mandatory. We adults often do not want to believe that young teens experience bad things, especially when it comes to sexual abuse. Sometimes school is the only place teens feel safe telling someone about it.

A mature discussion about Angelou's molestation, as well as the five years she remained mute as a result of the circumstances surrounding the abuse, might be life-saving for young teens who experienced their own traumatic ordeals. Those who thankfully had not experienced abuse could develop empathy, awareness, and understanding for those like Angelou who had.

A letter to the editor in the Sunday, December 3, 2023, *Wisconsin State Journal* made a poignant statement. A woman wrote about a sexual assault threat in middle school by a prominent member of the community. Fortunately, nothing came of it, and the writer never told anyone until years later when she confided in a family member. The family member admitted that same man had assaulted her. No one talked about those types of issues in the 1950s and 60s. No talking, no books, no guidance.

"Children experience challenges that adults—particularly parents—don't know about," the letter writer stated. "Children need help making it through these challenges. That's why books dealing with topics that upset adults—sex, gender, sexual assault, bullying, family issues, racism, and sexism—should not be banned or restricted." The letter writer went on to challenge banning or restricting books that provide valuable resources to help children understand there's a way to get help. She wished she'd had such guidance that might have not only helped her, but also helped prevent other assaults.

The Platteville School Board's decision sent the message to all freshmen students that they were not mature enough to handle a discussion about the sensitive themes in this book. The decision also undercut the professionalism of us teachers. It showed little confidence in our ability to choose appropriate educational materials and use care in approaching delicate subjects with our students. A few parents' opinions about what an entire class should or should not be reading took precedence over our education, training, and experience.

Literature is a catalyst for learning about ourselves. It often portrays and confronts societal issues that have existed among humans from the time people have been writing down their stories. Universal human experiences. "Teachers should just teach facts," some say. But rape and discrimination are just as real as the dates of battles in war or the properties of the atom.

Miss Clark helped us freshmen traverse mature themes in the twenty-four chapters of Nathaniel Hawthorne's *The Scarlet Letter*. Deciphering the language of mid-nineteenth century writers like Hawthorne was akin to wading through a quagmire. One paragraph could be one long sentence full of archaic vocabulary. I can't say I enjoyed the actual reading. But Miss Clark was an astute teacher. We made the journey as a class and learned valuable lessons in not only the evolution of language but also living among other humans.

For those unfamiliar with the story and for those in need of a refresher, Hester Prynne, a young, married Puritan woman of the 17th century, crosses the Atlantic Ocean to America with a group of British immigrants in pursuit of religious freedom. They settle in Boston, which was then a small colony. Hester's much older doctor husband sends her on the journey to the New World ahead of him so he can pursue scholarly ambitions in Europe before joining her. After the first year, it becomes apparent that Hester is with child. Uh-oh. A pregnant Puritan whose husband is nowhere in sight is not a good thing!

The Puritan community is livid. *How dare she commit adultery! Whose child is it? What should we do with her? Kill her? Stone her? Brand her?* Hester refuses to divulge the name of the baby daddy, and the usual punishment for her sin is death. However, because her husband has been away for two years and is suspected to be dead, the sin is one of fornication, not adultery. So, they end up sentencing her to three months in prison and three hours of public shame on the scaffold. They also make her wear the scarlet letter "A" for adultery on her bosom for the rest of her life. She is their scapegoat, a living, breathing pinnacle of sin.

As a naive freshman, I was bowled over when, half way through the novel, Hawthorne reveals that (SPOILER ALERT!!!) —the handsome young Puritan minister, the Reverend Arthur Dimmesdale, is the child's daddy. What the?? Come on. The minister? He's supposed to be holy and perfect. A minister wouldn't—couldn't—do something like this. Throughout my childhood and Catholic school experience, I had come to think of all priests and authority figures as faultless beings. Weren't ministers of the same ilk? Holy and respected?

I wasn't the only one in the class to be gobsmacked by this plot twist. This piece of literature taught a very important life lesson to my classmates and me: Just because someone is an adult in a leadership position does not mean that person is infallible— or trustworthy. Not long after that, John F. Kennedy's many extramarital affairs became common fare, as well as the sinful acts of others in leadership positions who preyed upon those in their midst. My Pollyanna world imploded. Untrustworthy people and institutions with bad intentions and policies do not like questions. Hence, I learned the importance of questioning.

For twenty-four out of twenty-seven years, *The Scarlet Letter* was a standard in my teaching repertoire for juniors. Its depth and forward-thinking themes of hypocrisy and feminism made for thought-provoking discussions. Most of the teens I taught were more canny than I was as a teen. Most suspected Reverend Dimmesdale's transgression with Hester long before it was revealed. However, it could be because my students were juniors, not freshmen, and despite my pleas, my former students often spilled the plotline to the upcoming classes.

It could also be they watched the blasphemous movie rendition with Demi Moore. That version takes much leeway with the original plot and modifies the ending into a mockery of Hawthorne's story. I'm sure when the film came out in 1995 the ground shook from him rolling over in his grave.

I decided it might be fun for students to act out a few of the scenes in class with me as their director. "Who wants to be Hester?" I asked, hoping they'd be game.

"I do. I do!" said Stella. Stella had flowing dark hair and was pretty, much like Hester was described in the novel.

"Okay, here is your 'A,' I said, handing her an elaborate red construction paper letter that someone from a previous year had made for a project about the book. "Now, tape it on your bosom and stand on this chair in front of the room."

"My what?"

"Your bosom. That's what people called a woman's chest in the 1600 and 1700s. Hawthorne used that word in the book. Remember?"

"Oh, that's what that meant," she said, grabbing a piece of tape from the dispenser.

"Now, the chair is the scaffold, okay? So, if you would please stand on the chair? Oh, and here's Pearl, your baby," I said, handing her a tissue box wrapped in a rag I used for wiping off the white board.

"Now, who wants to play Dimmesdale?" One hand went up. "All right, way to step up, Seth. Thank you!"

I explained and directed as the students ad-libbed the characters' lines using their own vocabulary. They enjoyed this so much that we did it on the days their reading was due. They told me it helped bring the plot and characters to life. Score! In this scene, the church magistrate grilled Hester about the identity of the father of her baby. But Hester refuses to divulge his name.

"Why do you think the women are so mean to Hester?" I asked. A couple of students acting as judgmental Puritan women had just called for her to be brutally punished, branded, or put to death.

"Maybe, because the father isn't known, they think the

baby's father might be their own husband," Stella said, looking down from her perch on the chair.

"Hawthorne describes Hester as being really beautiful," a classmate added. "Maybe the women are jealous."

"Yes, Hawthorne calls them termagants. You know, we have a word we use in today's language that means the same thing as termagant," I said, attempting to make the word relevant.

They chuckled. The "b-word" I was alluding to immediately popped into their minds. The next day Todd and Stella shared that they used the word termagant several times in conversation in the library. "Miss Jamison heard and didn't even yell at us," Stella said.

"Ignominy on you two for calling someone a termagant," I shook my finger at them, hoping they learned that knowledge is indeed power, if not, helpful and sometimes fun.

Another day students portrayed Hester and daughter Pearl walking through the streets of Boston. Pearl picks up rocks and throws them at the other children. Amy was Hester, and Stephanie volunteered to be Pearl. Stephanie graciously substituted wadded up paper for the rocks.

"Why is Pearl acting out like this?" I asked. "Is she a devil child like the townspeople are calling her?"

"Hey, I'd throw rocks too if other kids treated me like that," said Allen.

"Like what?" I asked.

"You know. Like they don't play with her—and they call her names," Allen said. "She's too young to understand what her mother did and why they're outcasts."

Finally, we got to the scene where Hawthorne reveals that Dimmesdale is indeed the father of Hester's baby. "Dimmesdale is a real wuss," I said, playing devil's advocate. "I can't find anything redeeming in the way he stands by and watches Hester and Pearl suffer. What do you think?"

240

"I agree," said John. "He should have owned up and helped raise the kid. His stupid pride got in the way."

"But the Puritans would have killed him," said Matt. "He couldn't tell."

"Well," Stella said, "when they talked about killing Hester—he just stands there like a jerk and doesn't say anything. He is a wuss—and worse!"

"Yeah. Telling the truth from the beginning would have been way better than lying," said Tessa. "Look at the misery Dimmesdale put himself through all those years just because he was too chicken to tell the truth."

After finishing the book, students named numerous people in high places who'd proven to be liars and suffered humiliation and other consequences because of it: Bill Clinton, Richard Nixon, Lance Armstrong, Michael Flynn, and Martha Stewart, just to name a few.

I was astounded, yet not so much, considering the *I Know Why the Caged Bird Sings* episode, to find out that, according to the online learning platform Study.com, parents in the United States have attempted to remove *The Scarlet Letter* from their children's high school curriculum many times through the years. Specifically, in 1961 and 1977 parents approached their school boards saying that the theme of adultery and the unflattering view of religion was not appropriate.

Banning books is not a new phenomenon. The Gutman Library site of the Harvard Graduate School of Education states that the first book banning in the United States took place in 1637. The Puritan government of the time was not happy that the book, *The New English Canaan,* critiqued Puritan customs and power structures. Over the last two hundred years, books that are now considered classics were also banned, like the Bible and the works of William Shakespeare.

Also concerning the control of curriculum, the state of Iowa proposed a bill that would require teachers to submit their lesson plans a year in advance so those plans could be scrutinized (*Teacher Related*, 3/30/22). In states such as Texas, the curriculum was so static that teachers were supposed to be on a specific page of the textbook on a specific day so it aligned with everyone else in the state. For those children who switch schools, districts, or even states, some modicum of continuity is important. But this over-standardization does not take into consideration the importance of individuality in education: the individual teacher, and, consequently, the individual student.

Wouldn't it make more sense to focus on the educational needs of the students in front of us? I thought so. Therefore, my first objective of a new school year was to get to know the individuals in my class. Then I could build on the knowledge, skills, and background they brought to their desks. Their personalities, their interests, their abilities could enhance how and what I taught them. With a set plan in place for units and lessons, I considered it a priority to monitor and adjust those plans in order to accommodate my students' needs.

Remember the guy on *The Ed Sullivan Show* who balanced all those plates spinning at the same time? He should have been a teacher.

As my teaching experience progressed, mandatory standardized testing, early release days, class meetings, assemblies and such, rained down from above and cut into the time I spent with my students. One of the tasks the principal assigned us teachers to complete on early release and work days was to analyze the students' most frequently missed questions on the standardized tests.

The only thing worse than taking standardized tests is spending hours analyzing their results.

This way we could design lessons to address the most frequently missed concepts in class. But, as this continued, it seemed that achievement scores, not achievement, became the priority. Better test scores made the district, the school, the principal, the teachers, and the students look good. How school districts looked seemed more important than the real substance and act of learning. Before we teachers could implement the findings from the last test, classroom instruction would be interrupted again with yet another test to evaluate.

No one ever runs their best race by focusing too much on the competition. Principals and administrators, communities and parents fretted over how other countries, other states, and other schools were doing on these tests. Everyone wanted to look good and earn a feather in their cap through exemplary standardized test scores.

On my Fulbright Memorial Fund-sponsored visit to Japanese schools, we teachers were surprised when Japanese high school teachers asked us, "How do you teach your students in America to be able to stand up and speak so well and comfortably in front of others?" We hadn't noticed our students to be particularly gifted in speaking. We had been focused on how much better Japanese students, and almost all other developed countries, were in math than our American students.

Apparently, Japanese administrators were pressuring their teachers to teach more like us. And, our administrators wanted our students to score as well as Japanese students on the standardized tests. I guess the students are always considered smarter on the other side of the ocean.

Standardized testing was not cheap. Companies who marketed the tests also marketed curriculum tools and practice tests to go along with the tests. According to an article written in 2005 by Barbara Miner, former managing editor of *Rethinking Schools*, "States are likely to spend $1.9 billion between 2002 and 2008 to implement No Child Left Behind mandated tests" (Government

Accounting Office, a nonpartisan entity, rethinkingschools.com)

I remember thinking, wouldn't better wages and better inservice training of local people, like the teachers and support staff that have direct contact with the students, be more effective than paying huge testing-for-profit companies? In her article, Miner also said, "As with any business, the testing companies are driven by the need to make profits, not to improve education. They will do what the market requires them to do—nothing more, nothing less."

Former lobbyist Bruce Hunter of the American Association of School Administrators noted a substantial rise in the presence of big testing companies in the political arena: "At every hearing, every discussion, the big test publishers are always present with at least one lobbyist, sometimes more." Another problem with standardized testing, according to Walt Haney, an education professor at Boston College, was that "there is more public oversight of the pet industry and the food we feed our dogs than there is for the quality of tests we make our kids take."

Time spent testing was time that was not spent learning in the classroom. Yes, occasional standardized test results can be useful to show teachers, parents, and students what skills need to be addressed. But testing too often can have a negative spiraling effect on learning. Testing does not teach or engage students; interesting lessons and interesting teachers do.

In some districts, administrator, teacher, and district compensation was tied to student test scores. Thankfully not in Platteville. Remember the Atlanta cheating scandal of 2009 when the district went to trial in 2014 for changing answers on students' tests because they feared their school would close and they would lose their jobs? I didn't at all condone what employees of that district did, but I understood the momentous pressure. Some years it seemed most of our instruction revolved around standardized tests and getting students prepared for them: MAPs

Tests (Measure of Academic Progress), Aspire Tests (pre-ACT), ACT, and Advanced Placement Language and Composition.

Yes, I was a reluctant rider on the mandatory standardized testing train. But, I had no choice. I knew that the more the students understood about the test, the better they would do on it. So, I coached students in getting familiar with the format, timing, and types of questions on a particular test. To provide motivation, our school offered students final exam exemptions for improved scores. And many students took the bait. But what did we gain? Precious class time and district money was forsaken for teaching to the test.

Good test scores was *one* indicator that could show teachers, parents, and themselves what they knew or didn't know in particular areas of study. Other important talents they possessed could never be assessed by standardized tests, like public speaking, interpersonal communication, collaboration, creating innovative art, or making something with their hands, just to name a few.

"Do the best you can and take the test seriously," I told them on the days leading up to the test, "but not so seriously that you start believing that your score is somehow connected with your overall intelligence or value." I could only hope they knew how sincere I really was.

As high school juniors, we were not required to take the ACT like Wisconsin students are today. In fact, I remember taking few standardized tests throughout my schooling. I signed up to take the ACT because it was recommended if we thought we might be going on to college.

On my assigned day in the spring of 1971, I entered the cavernous classroom in an engineering building on the University of Wisconsin Platteville campus. One hundred or so testers filled the long rows of desks. I took my alphabetically assigned seat, feeling unsophisticated and intimidated by my surroundings. My nerves were on high alert because I wanted to do the best I could. I sharpened my No. 2 pencil, placed my pink eraser on my desk, and waited until the ACT proctor said, "Begin!"

I opened the booklet, read the questions, and filled in the dots. My pulse raced as seconds ticked away. I looked around to see how others were coming along. When I saw time would expire before I finished on the math, science, and reading portions, I chose random answers, usually B or C, in hopes of statistically guessing a few correctly. It was over before I knew it, and I was spent!

I don't remember my score, but I guess I did okay. As long as students did okay and didn't totally bomb the test, scores were not a huge deal then. Not so twenty years later. Many of my students strived for stellar or perfect scores like they were the Holy Grail. Getting into the college of their choice depended on it. That had changed too. Most students who graduated with me went to state universities or vocational technical schools in Wisconsin. Now, it was fairly common for many of my students to travel with their families to college visits all over the Midwest and sometimes the United States.

In 2014-2015, whether they planned to attend a two or four-year college or none at all, every Wisconsin junior was required to take the ACT in an attempt to assess achievement of students in the state. The district-wide focus in my last few years teaching was on closing the "achievement gap" on those scores. This meant designing lessons in an attempt to close the academic divide among the disadvantaged, minorities, and whites.

In recent years, the middle of the score grid had waned. Just like our nation's economy where the middle class began to disappear, this phenomenom affected schools and learning as well. Some researchers proposed that this achievement gap was due to the tests being racially and economically biased. The results of a test are only as good as the test itself, and this topic of testing and test validity is an entire book unto itself.

How well and how fast one can read and comprehend is key in how well a student scores on all parts of the ACT and other standardized tests. After all, students have to read the questions, and the tests are timed. If a person had dyslexia or other learning disabilities, these tests posed "built-in" obstacles. Also, some students experienced test anxiety and found it difficult to perform, even though they were very capable, intelligent people.

My student Edward was a smart, confident, master test taker. In my Advanced Placement class he'd also proven himself to be a stellar reader, gifted writer, and avid thinker. Having studied the ACT testing format and taken numerous practice tests for years, Edward was a wolf tracking prey on test day.

As one of three proctors for the test, I noticed that his eyes didn't leave the booklet. His pencil formed every dot like a dart sticking the bullseye. His foot tapped rhythmically to the beat of his brain. If a horse had galloped through the room, I doubt he would have noticed. He aced the test with a perfect score of 36. Additionally, his PSAT scores earned him recognition as a National Merit Scholar, which helped fund his college studies.

When Edward revealed he'd be attending an Ivy League school, no one was surprised. His peers were thrilled for him. Edward had always been humble and personable while pursuing his various school activities beyond the classroom. He played an instrument in orchestra, competed at chess, and went out for basketball. He prioritized exploring varied interests and developing parts of himself that would have otherwise gone untapped. He took in everything that everyone had to offer.

The standardization trend directly affected us teachers, too, via our formal evaluations that took place every other year. The evaluation process is important for teachers. It gives them a chance to receive feedback and support from another experienced educator to help them become more effective in the classroom.

Before standardized evaluations, the principal or vice principal would randomly pop into my room a few times during the year to observe what I was doing and record their impressions. Along with this, a formal visit allowed me to meet with the evaluator to explain what I wanted to accomplish in my chosen lesson. After observing and taking notes about the lesson, we would meet and discuss how I thought it went and how the observer thought it went. The evaluator would complete the necessary form with comments, I would look it over, and we'd both sign it.

During the last few years of teaching, my evaluations were completed using a number rating system on a standard grid that was the same for teachers of all grade levels, all subjects, and all types of students. The principal would visit and observe a lesson, assigning a number to each grid as he or she recognized the various generic points described in each box. This data driven method was designed to remove any bias from the process.

However, this method felt robotic and created "Gotcha moments" where evaluators, instead of taking in the effectiveness of the lesson as a whole, tried to catch those elements the teacher missed. All lessons are not created equal or use every single element of the evaluation marketing design, nor should they. It also does not take into consideration the effectiveness of the methods used by that individual teacher. As with the standardized tests for the students, the standardized evaluation for teachers was *one* indicator of that teacher's effectiveness. I had to remind myself of that when the principal came into my room to check boxes, or not check them, as he observed me while I taught.

The merry-go-round of mixed messages from the state, administrators, and parents created echoes of cognitive dissonance: *Teach to the test. Teach to the child. Teach to the group. Teach this way. Teach that way. Teach this. Don't teach that.* Aaaaaaahhhhhhh! I had to hold on tight so I didn't lose my authentic self, which, as with every teacher, was my most valuable and reliable asset. There was no way I could satisfy everyone. All I could do was the best I could do and encourage my colleagues to do the same.

On January 30, 2023, research analyst Jacob Alabab-Moser evaluated the current state of Wisconsin teachers on the website *Wisconsin Watch*:

"The combined effect of Act 10's passage with long-term market trends including declining compensation and the loss of teachers' autonomy raised the percentage of teachers leaving the profession to 10.5 percent after the 2010-11 school year, compared to 6.4 percent pre-Act 10. The bulk of teachers who immediately exited were older and left to claim their retirement benefits, which were set to be cut under Act 10."

Then, with teachers burning out year after year, came COVID-19. The teacher/student connection became challenged, making attendance and collecting and grading work a problem. Some students didn't have any access, or reliable access, to the internet, and others were struggling with the pressures of home life with parents who lost jobs and were stressed. They missed the continuity and connections with teachers and peers.

As I said previously, I retired in 2019, just before the pandemic. Those teachers who hung in there and did the best they could preparing classroom lessons, video lessons, Zoom lessons, all while trying to keep their students and themselves healthy, deserve to be respected and rewarded now more than ever.

Working in the public school system for twenty-seven years bolstered my belief that society often blames its ills on public schools and its teachers. Schools are not the cause of society's problems, yet they are expected to fix them. The school itself embodies a microcosm of the society in which it exists, both the good, bad, and everything in between.

Dear School Board Members and Administrators,
Allow and encourage trained teachers to have the freedom
to choose the books and the curriculum they use in the classroom.
They know their students and what they need to teach.
Access to information, and learning to disseminate that information,
is what education is all about. If students cannot question
and evaluate all information out there,
how will they ever learn what is or isn't possible?
Sincerely,
Concerned Citizens for Public Education

Chapter 23 – All Good Things

There is no real ending. It's just the place where you stop the story.
Frank Herbert, author of the Dune book series

It was a warm evening in May. I was walking my dog, enjoying the stars and solitude. As I picked up dog doo with my plastic-covered hand, a male voice cried out at the top of his lungs, "Hi, Mrs. Kies!"

I looked up to see the torso of a person in a white tuxedo protruding from the moonroof of a limo, waving both arms like a jack-in-the-box. On Monday, Tyler one of my AP students, said, "I saw you walking your dog Saturday night. We were driving around town on our way to prom. Did you see me?"

Most were not as overt as Tyler, but all students wanted to be seen. Some sat in a corner in the back of the room—but they still wanted to be noticed. And, for some reason, they wanted to know me. In the middle of a lesson one day, Steven asked me where I got the shoes I was wearing. Eleanor wanted to know my middle name and my birthday. "What? Are you writing my biography or something?" I'd reply.

Platteville, as I said, is a small city, so most students knew where I lived. I'd be out weeding the flower beds in my overalls, covered in sweat and dirt, and kids would go by in cars and on scooters, arms waving, horns blaring, and voices chorusing, "Hey, Mrs. Kies!"

But I was a bit taken aback when, just after the bell rang one Monday morning, Jacob announced, "So, Mrs. Kies, I hear you were in the beer tent Saturday night at Dairy Days with some guy."

"Who says?" I asked.

"Sam's got a picture of you on his phone."

"A picture? Geez. What is he, the paparazzi? I am of age, you know. And that guy happens to be my husband." It's not good to get defensive with teens. If they sense they're getting to you, they pounce. Remember my mistake in telling the puppy story?

"Sam said you were totally smashed." There wasn't one ear in the room that wasn't tuned in to our exchange.

"You know that's not true, Jacob," I said, deciding upon sarcasm as the best method to ward him off. "You need to be careful about starting rumors. That's libel. The least you can do is get the facts straight, okay? If I had been drunk I would have fallen off that table I was dancing on, okay?"

Being a teacher in a small town has given the utmost compassion for Brad Pitt and—well—whoever Brad's with now.

My husband became accustomed to this notoriety. What choice did he have? One day while at the grocery store, I introduced him to Cyrus, one of my former students who worked there. Now, when he sees my husband and me, Cyrus says, "Hi, Mrs. Kies and Mr. Kies. How are you today?"

My children, on the other hand, abhorred the renown. One day my daughter and I were out for a stroll with our dogs. We were walking down the hill a few blocks from my home. All of a sudden, like a bird popping out from a cuckoo clock, Terry yelled from the drive-thru window of McDonald's where he was working, "Hi, Susan Kies! Have a good day!"

"How do you stand this?" my daughter asked. "You can't go anywhere unnoticed."

When our youngest three children attended PHS, each grade was large enough to warrant two English teachers. We thought it best if they had the alternate teacher instead of me, but in retrospect, I wish I'd have taught them. Whether the experience had been good or bad, we would have experienced a whole other level of knowing each other.

All the students at PHS knew my kids and kept me informed of their activities. And, vice versa, both good and bad. One of my students once said she saw my son downtown smoking a cigarette. "My son? No, that can't be. You must be mistaken," I told her. (Sometimes parents can be so naive.) Upon further investigation, she was not mistaken.

And, they would report to my children about my classes. "Tell your mom not to make us read that dumb book," or "Does your mom always correct your grammar at home, too?"

Even in retirement, I still run into former students. During the last years of my career, some students called teachers by their last names, dropping the Ms., Mrs., or Mr. This bothered a few teachers, but I didn't mind. Every so often, though, a few would push the envelope and call me "Sue" or "Susan." "Graduate first, then you may call me by my first name, okay?"

The other day I bumped into David at the coffee shop downtown, which is owned and operated by Hannah, a former student and her husband. David said, "Well, hi there, Susan," just like he tried to do in school. "It's legal. I can call you that now, right?"

A few weeks ago in front of the market on Main Street, I ran into Nathan. I hadn't seen him since he graduated. I congratulated myself because, not only did I recognize him, but I remembered his name. After having taught several thousand students, I am not always as adept at remembering names. I probably recalled him because I chaperoned prom the year he was a junior, and someone took our picture together. For a couple of years the picture sat on my desk.

"Nathan," I said, "how are you? It's so good to see you."

His face lit up. "Hi, I'm back in town to see some high school friends. You remember Jim, don't you?"

"Yes, of course. How are you, Jim?" We shook hands, and I asked how they were doing. Each had two little ones tagging along after them. They introduced me as their former teacher, and the kids looked at me in wonderment. I could see their brains processing this: *Wow, that was Dad's teacher?*

"So, how are things at the high school, uh—Ms. Schober—right?"

"No, Nathan. Mrs. Kies. I hope things are going well, but I'm not sure because I retired a few years ago."

"Uh, yeah. I'm so sorry. Sure—I remember—Mrs. Kies."

At least Ms. Schober was younger than I and not retired yet.

"I'm so embarrassed," Nathan continued. "I remember your class, though. I do. We did a debate unit, right?"

"Yes, yes, we did. Gee, you remember that?"

"The preparation you had us do was very influential in my life," Nathan said, scrambling to amend his faux pas. "My topic was abortion. You had us make lists of arguments on both sides of the issue. Today, I work as a lawyer and use similar research procedures when preparing for a case."

He and I reminisced how April was on the pro-choice side, while her dear friend was on the anti-abortion side. Their exchange during the debate became personal, and both young women began to cry. After a time out in the hall, they made peace with the idea that they could still remain friends and disagree about this emotional subject.

Nathan had redeemed himself. I reminded myself of the wise words Shakespeare assigned to Juliet, "What's in a name? That which we call a rose, by any other word would smell as sweet."

One day I shared details of an upcoming field trip with Mr. Trickel. If you remember, he had been my senior English teacher at PHS. He was also the principal who yelled at me in the hall after finding out students stole the mouse balls from the computer lab during one of my early teaching years.

"The funniest thing happened yesterday," I said. "Students

were working in groups, and one of them raised his hand to ask a question and called me 'Mom.' I've never had a student call me 'Mom' before."

He leaned back in his cushy chair and chuckled. The sides of his tweed sport coat fell away to reveal the paunch that had formed since his years as a teacher. "How was that? So, you're no longer the young teacher everyone had a crush on?"

Huh? My first thought was, *Students had a crush on me?* My second was, *Does this mean I'm officially a member the Old Teachers' Club or something?* I walked back to my classroom, pondering his interpretation of my anecdote. I shared it because I was surprised but flattered that a student had mistakenly called me "Mom." But, he saw it as a demotion due to age. Oh, my gosh. Was it?

This exchange led me to examine my relevance as an *experienced* teacher. As a high school student, I recalled the younger teachers, like Miss Brelig, who sat on her desk while teaching, her miniskirts garnering much attention, especially from the boys. Looking back, she was only a few years older than we were at the time.

After years in the classroom, I was now old enough to be my students' grandmother. How long could I remain relevant? Mr. Kabele, my older government teacher in high school, had much knowledge to impart on us as far as content goes, but his delivery was as interesting as an ancient rock formation. And his class management was lacking. As teachers aged, they seemed to either evolve and hone their craft, or burn out, becoming bitter or bored, or—the worst—irrelevant.

I promised myself I'd retire before that happened to me.

The UW-Whitewater Creative Writing Festival was in November, the Wednesday of the week before Thanksgiving. High school writers and their teachers from all over Wisconsin, as well as parts of Iowa and Illinois, attended. They entered their writing in different categories a month or so ahead of time, and on the day of the festival they hoped for a helpful critique or possibly an award from the judge in their genre. Over the years, some of my students won awards, and, better yet, became inspired to continue to create.

But on one occasion, the opposite happened. An ego-driven, overzealous judge pounced on something Shelly wrote that he perceived as a literary sin. In front of other attendees, he pointed this out, making a lesson out of her writing—and thus—out of her. He had lost touch with what it was like to be a teen, or a good teacher. How could he not realize how much it stung to pour one's heart out on paper and have someone squash it like a bug?

Unfortunately, I was not in the workshop where this happened to offer support. On the way home, Shelly was unusually quiet. When I asked her what she thought of the conference, tears welled in her eyes. "The judge didn't like my writing," she said. "He said it was immature and lacking in detail."

"I'm so sorry, Shelly. That judge was a jerk. Your writing has beauty and feeling in it. He had no business saying that."

"Yeah, I know—I believe you. But it still felt pretty rotten."

For her final exam, Shelly produced the most ingenious project I'd ever seen. She displayed her art work and writing in a video format, the words, pictures, and music flowing into a moving, original piece. I'd loved to have played that beautiful video in front of that judge's snarky face.

Coming home from the festival, we often stopped at a fast food place for snacks and a bathroom break. That year we stopped at a fast-food place in Monona on Madison's East side. As the nine students of various backgrounds, sizes, and complexions piled out of the school van and into the restaurant, Cassandra thought it would be hilarious for all of them to refer to me as "Mom."

"The customers will probably think that you adopted a bunch of kids from all over," Cassandra whispered and laughed. "Or that you were one *busy* lady."

The people in the restaurant *did* give us curious looks. But it was probably because of all the hysterical bursts of giggles every time one of them referred to me as "Mom." For the rest of the year, several in the group continued the private joke, requiring me to explain to students and colleagues that I was not really their mother.

One day I had coffee with Kaaren, a very good friend who was retired from teaching music to elementary kids. Still today, we often exchange "teacher stories," like the one I described above. One day the line of conversation turned a bit more introspective.

"Have you ever felt sometimes that when we were teachers we spent more time and patience with all those kids we taught than we did our own?" I asked. "You know, like the shoemaker's kids going without shoes?"

I hadn't expected tears to form in her eye. "Yes," she said. "But I don't know how we'd have done it any differently. How do you teach kids without caring about them?"

Like many moms and dads who are teachers, we'd both sacrificed precious physical and mental energy planning lessons, correcting papers and taking field trips on weekends and week nights with our own kids to ensure that other peoples' kids were well educated and cared for. Being a teacher, though, in many ways made me a better parent, like setting limits and sticking to them, understanding personality differences, and developing an endless amount of patience. I sometimes wish I'd taken the traditional route and been a teacher and then a mom, so I could have practiced on other people's kids first.

Being a teacher, though, in many ways made me a better parent.

257

* * *

As the twilight of my career approached, people began to ask, "So, is this the year?" or "How many more do you think you'll go?" I'm sure I'd asked those annoying questions of others too. I began to speculate. Were people hinting that I *should* retire? That I really *needed* to retire? Have I been slipping? I remembered my vow not to become one of those bored, burned out *irrelevant* teachers.

A couple of wise retirees told me, "Don't worry. You'll know when it's time." This seemed rather vague, but they turned out to be right. The year I turned sixty-five, I confidently submitted my letter to the district. Partly because I qualified for Medicare. (OMG, Medicare!) But mostly because I needed more than a summer's rest from all the responsibility involved in teaching.

Schools have taken on more and more in the rearing of our community's children. They not only educate students, but feed them breakfast and lunch, protect them both psychologically and physically, and compete with all the available media to gain their attention. Most frustrating was that parents were becoming more apt to blame schools for their children's behavior rather than expecting their children to be responsible.

The year I retired, the principal asked if I'd be the faculty speaker at the graduation ceremony in June. It seemed appropriate. It was like my second graduation from Platteville High School. As I looked out over those graduates who'd be leaving the building with me, I maintained hope. Hope for them and their futures, hope for me and my life beyond PHS, hope for the continued success of PHS, and hope for public schools in general.

Several former students carry on the teaching tradition at PHS. As teachers, we never know what impact we have had on our students. It's a long-term investment. When they came back to assume our jobs and carry the torch of education, it felt good. Like we did something right.

The future of education depends on the mentoring of future teachers. Over the years, I chose to advise forty to fifty observation students and student teachers. Veteran teachers knew that a good student teacher, one with initiative and desire, made our job easier and breathed new life into our own practices.

One of my most recent mentees, Elizabeth, came to Platteville from Goodnews Bay, Alaska. She told the students and me of the day when she had to call her high school to tell them she and her sister would be late that day. There was a grizzly bear on the porch, and she couldn't get out the door. After a neighbor fired a shotgun in the air, the bear left, allowing her and her sister to get to school. Derek, another student teacher, married a young woman who had been a senior when he was student teaching my sophomores and juniors. After announcing their engagement, he messaged me on Facebook: "Don't worry, Sue. Melissa and I weren't dating during the time I was teaching." That was good news but at that point, what was I going to do about it?

In one part of my speech to the class of 2019, I told graduates: "Don't do dumb stuff. If you have second thoughts and think something is dumb, it probably is. Trust your gut instinct and don't do it." Kylie, a student I'd had as a junior, said that her parents liked that advice. "Now, before I go out," she said, "they tell me, 'Remember, don't do any dumb stuff.'"

Celebrations ensued for the five of us staff members who were taking our final bows. One party was held in the auditorium for the student body, one at the end-of-year gathering of district staff at the Middle School, another with community members amid punch and cake in the School Board meeting room, and yet another in the PHS library among peers. The most meaningful of the festivities, however, went down at the Badger Bar among family, friends, and peers.

Through the years, I had congratulated many others as they left our ranks. Over time, we adjusted to their absence, welcomed the new hires, and found a new rhythm. This time around, the gifts, the cards, the farewells were for me. It had gone by so fast. When I was applying for teaching jobs, a Career Placement Specialist at UW-Platteville told me she used to teach high school Spanish but switched jobs because she became bored. "There are only so many ways to teach a language," she said. I had somehow managed not to get bored. And most of my students already spoke English.

After the students left for the summer in early June, I packed my personal books, plants, and pictures into boxes and carried them out to my car. On my last trip, I paused to take a selfie going out the door of my room and then the outer door of the school. My thoughts rewound to the time I exited that same door to attend the homecoming bonfire as a freshman and the time I twirled my fire baton for my senior speech out in the grass near the parking lot.

Years and times changed, as everything does. However, the all-important human aspect of education has not. Kids need other people to help them learn. They still need to feel accepted, valued, and safe. I laughed as I recalled the time Zane felt himself getting sick and ran to the front of my room to throw up in the wastebasket. He was so embarrassed. But his peers and I congratulated him on making it to the garbage instead of losing it all over the floor. And, the time Ryan and Colton wrote a song for me and sang it in front of the class, accompanying themselves on guitars. Or, when my colleague's construction class built me a chicken coop so I could tend layers in my backyard and have fresh eggs.

My mind was full and well satisfied. Content.

When someone asked Henry David Thoreau why he left his beloved life at Walden Pond, he said, "I left the woods for as good a reason as I went there. Perhaps it seemed to me that I had several more lives to live, and could not spare any more time for that one."

Like him, I'm not finished. I've still got more to do.

Dear PHS,

Thank you for allowing me the opportunity of an education as a student and to pass it on as a teacher.

Keep up the good work!

Fondly,

Sue Leamy Kies

Next Chapter

Going Back...Again

During the Fall of 2019, I returned to perform yet another role at Platteville High School: substitute teacher. Later that school year in 2020, COVID complicated school and teaching protocols across the nation, and I removed my name from the substitute list.

But, after three and a half years, I have returned! They just can't get rid of me.

Like Gatsby attempting to rekindle his youthful relationship with Daisy, this revisit to PHS reminded me that the past cannot be repeated. I no longer knew the students...and they no longer knew me. Many of the faculty and staff were unfamiliar, along with elements of the building. Names like Loyalty Lane, Motivation Avenue, and Success Street now designated each hallway, helping students and visitors find their way to classrooms. And just off the commons area, knocked-out walls covered with temporary lumber marked the first phase of a much-awaited facelift on the west side of the library.

At staff meetings we debated ad nauseam student dress and cell phone use as if the world would implode at the hands of sagging jeans, midriff tops, revealed thongs (not the kind on one's feet), texting during class, and all the other popular fads. Now, kids can wear hats and pretty much anything they want, as long as it isn't offensive or lewd. (See the Student Handbook on the PHS website for more specifics.) Every classroom had a large plastic pouch with individual pockets hanging by the door. Students put their cell phones in upon entering the room and retrieved them as they left. A simple solution for a once contentious problem.

I was glad that some things had not changed. When I handed students a copy of their test, each one said "thank you," something my own students used to do. Most kids got down to business without being told, even though their regular teacher was nowhere in sight. Sure, one student put his head down on his desk because he was tired. And another enjoyed lively conversation during a group project with classmates while others did the work. This brought back the challenges teachers face every day to engage students. If you're able to reel them into learning, and every teacher has a few of these success stories, these students live in your memory and your heart forever.

On my way down Empathy Boulevard to my assigned substitute duty, I passed the door to my room. That is, what used to be my room. My heartbeat sped. It wasn't the room I missed. It was what happened in that room. The exchange of ideas, the connectivity, the stimulation. Now, when I come across an intriguing book, story, film, poem, quote, or word, I miss not being able to incorporate it into a lesson or activity for my students.

My cousin who worked as a nurse for well over thirty years told me that when she retired she missed feeling like she "made a difference in the world." Ditto from me.

A few renowned people graduated from my alma mater, like Nobel Prize winner Herbert Spencer Gasser for Physiology and Medicine in 1944. And Coach Paul Chryst, UW-Madison's football coach from 2005 to 2022. PHS alum Robert Travis became a representative in the Wisconsin State Assembly from 1977 to 1987. But many of the truly important people are those who haven't received notoriety, like the teachers and staff who help students achieve their academic goals and encourage them to be contributing members of all branches of society.

These teachers provided foundations for young lives and their livelihoods, for graduates like Britt, an ag-futures specialist and Jake, a dairy farmer; Tony, Ashley, and Michael, firefighters;

263

Carley, Tessa, Brelyn, Corinna, Regan, and Charlie, skilled nurses; Nicole and Amber, beauty shop operators; Leah and Courtney, dedicated moms; Jason and Jeremiah, plumbers; Meghan, an engineer; Natalie and Connor, part of the skilled and friendly Culver's crew; Steph and Jacob, braving the political realm; Jeff, a policeman; Melanie and Nick, communications specialists; Sarah, Connor, and Cayla, taking on social work; Trevor, Joe, and Molly, lawyers all; doctors Alyson, Julia, Bri, and Christine; Daniel and Daniel, both professional musicians; Ally who became a pharmacist, Sam an optometrist, and Tricia and John physical therapists; Cooper, a restaurant manager; and Liz, an insurance professional. Katherine and Chris, serving in our military; and, of course, Karina, Travis, Anna, Maria, Mary Ann, Ashley, Isaiah, Jake, Emily, Ryan, Max, Brandon, and others, who, I hope remain teachers for a good, long time.

These names are drops in the deep bucket of talent that PHS launched. I wish I could mention every single one. This book is my anthem to all the teachers, staff, and students that show up at public schools everywhere in the name of learning. Thank you.

Dear Parents,

If you want your child to go to a good school,

help make it a good school by partnering with

teachers and staff. When choosing a school for your

child or children, visit the school rather than relying

only on published data or others' opinions.

Go meet the teachers and staff, watch what is going

on, and see for yourself.

Sincerely,

A Parent, Grandparent, and Retired Teacher

Acknowledgements

First and foremost, thank you to my students one and all! You allowed me into your world, taught me how to teach, and gave me hope for the future. Also, kudos to the hard-working, caring teachers and librarians at PHS and everywhere. Stand tall. Be proud of what you do and what you've done. You are my people!

A heartfelt thank you to administrators and school board members. Though they took a few jabs in this book, I know they desire the best for our kids. They have a whole other dimension to their jobs in education that I have not experienced. The Platteville District had, and continues to have, some truly great leaders.

The publication of this book would not have been possible without my smart and supportive editor Lisa Lickel, as well as the staff of the Wisconsin Writers Association. I am honored that, right from the start, she had faith in this project and in me. She believed that the teachers of our Wisconsin Public School System deserved a voice, and I appreciate being able to bring these stories from the trenches to light. I hope that my memoir encourages those who want to teach, supports those who do, thanks those who did, educates those who haven't, and entertains anyone who reads it.

Thanks, also, to Marja Mills, an inspirational teacher and author of *The Mockingbird Next Door*. My book took shape in her valuable memoir writing class through the Wisconsin Academy of Sciences, Arts, and Letters. It was here that I met my current writing family: Lauranne Bailey, Joan Liegel, Sheila Thomson, Monica Urbanik, and Joan Westley. You women rock the page with your voices! Thank you for your candid comments and encouraging words no matter how many times you heard a passage. Wednesday evenings are special because of you.

Sue Leamy Kies

Many thanks to my friend Kaaren Risic, a retired music teacher. Over the years we've exchanged numerous teaching successes, and otherwise, over coffee. More than thirty years ago Kay Young, my retired college librarian friend, asked if I wanted to be in a writing group. She and other members helped me write regularly. I still hear their voices when editing.

And then there are my high school teaching colleagues who continue to meet on Friday afternoons at the Badger Bar. This socialization, something we didn't always have time for while teaching, helped me find my voice. Thanks to the Regulars: John, Mike, Travis, and Matt...and all the others who come when they can.

My two book clubs provide a wealth of writing inspiration, one for over twenty years. Thank you, ladies, for the insightful and invigorating hours of talking about books and authors.

And how could I not thank my teachers? In third grade Mrs. Orth explained similes, and in college Franco Pagnucci taught about avoiding cliches. Also valuable were the writing workshops and conferences with instructors through the University of Wisconsin Madison like Laurie Scheer and the late Marshall Cook.

Author Michael Perry (*Population 485*) read a few of my stories at a workshop at Shake Rag Alley in Mineral Point. He said, "People want to know about this, so tell them." Patricia McNair (*And These are the Good Times*) and Gary Jones (*Ridge Stories*) also provided me with sage tips at the Alley. Thank you to all these teachers and every one I've ever had! Much appreciation to friend, photographer, and PHS grad Ric Genthe for taking my picture for the cover. Also to Karina Zidon, another PHS alum, for her expert help in planning my book launch.

And, finally, thank you to my family and my husband Dave. I'm sure he would rather not be mentioned. But, that's the way I roll.

Just so everyone knows: The PHS Class of '72 still rules!

266

About the Author

Sue Leamy Kies, a retired high school English teacher, lives in Platteville, Wisconsin with her husband Dave, border collie mix Jojo, and her backyard chickens. She enjoys spending time with family and friends, growing flowers, kayaking and walking in nature, cooking and eating good food, listening to music and reading and writing books. Before teaching, Sue and her husband ran a dairy and hog farm and had five children.

She has published poetry, essays, movie reviews, and short stories for regional magazines and newspapers, including *The Illinois English Bulletin*, *The Voice of the River Valley*, and *The Wisconsin Academy Review*. Also, in 2021 CADA (Center for Applied Drama and Autism) chose her play *Back* about a disabled veteran to be performed for their One-Act Play Festival.

Sue has written two children's books. The Platteville Library Foundation published *Saving Sadie* about a bookworm that lives in the library in 2017. *Sassy's Vacation* about a turtle who lives at the arboretum was published by the Platteville Community Arboretum in 2022 to promote literacy and nature education on the Rountree Branch Trail.

Visit www.plattevillearboretum.org/

Find more about Sue and her work at www.sueleamykies.com Sue would love to visit your group or bookclub. Check her contact information and the discussion guide questions on her website.

Wisconsin Writers Association

www.wiwrite.org

Founded in 1948, the Wisconsin Writers Association, Inc.
is a creative community dedicated to the support of writers and
authors. WWA sponsors and hosts year-round workshops
and events throughout Wisconsin, offering discounts
and exclusive resources. WWA aims to share experiences
and knowledge while encouraging members in their pursuit of
this most noble art.

Develop your craft.
Discover resources.
Expand your network.
Build your audience.

WWA Membership

Membership in WWA is open to anyone with an active interest
in developing their writing craft. WWA welcomes aspiring and
also published writers, librarians, educators, artists, students,
dramatists, musicians, filmmakers, translators and others.

A passion for the written word is the #1 WWA criterion.

Join now at wiwrite.org/about-wwa-2/join
Facebook www.facebook.com/WIWrite/
Linked In www.linkedin.com/company/wiswritersassoc/
E-mail: hello@wiwrite.org

Wisconsin Writers Association Press

We are looking for manuscripts that feature Wisconsin
in setting, culture and theme, whether historical,
contemporary, or futuristic.

Submission guidelines, contact information, and pertinent
FAQs can be found on the WWA website page:
www.wiwrite.org/WWA-Press

Wisconsin Writers Association is a 501(c)3 not-for-profit organization.

Milton Keynes UK
Ingram Content Group UK Ltd.
UKHW020513240524
443175UK00007B/104/J